"Blast from the past!
There are archeological cross-sections . . . real time-travelling magic.
It's enough to make anyone misty with nostalgia."
TV Guide

"Every decade expresses its kooky collective unconscious on the tube,
celebrated affectionately at Billy Ingram's TVparty. Ingram provides
a hilarious glimpse into the American pop psyche."
Yahoo Internet Life magazine

"For a walk on the wild side . . . take it from us:
TVparty is the ultimate . . . for anyone who has ever picked up
a remote control." (Grade A+)
Brian Hartigan, *TV Guide* (Canadian edition)

"There's too much to mention here . . . has to be seen to be believed.
TV lovers shouldn't miss it." (4 Stars)
Access magazine

"Take a trip down memory lane . . . TV not required!"
St. Petersburg Times

"*TVparty* is like a huge mall stocked with everything
you never knew you needed!"
Wild Web TV show

"The main attraction is simply the volume of detail
on each show—and the humorous tone in which it is presented."
TV Guide Online

"*TVparty* has features that pull no punches."
Houston Chronicle

TELEVISION'S UNTOLD TALES

Billy Ingram

bonus books
Chicago and Los Angeles

PLAY

FIRST EDITION

Book designed by James Counts
with Billy Ingram

Library of Congress Control Number: 2002111596
International Standard Book Number: 1-56625-184-2

PUBLISHED BY BONUS BOOKS

SP 0:01

Welcome to your TVparty!

The story of this book is the story of *Winky Dink*.

Winky Dink, in case you don't know, was a children's show from the '50s that encouraged kids to draw on their television set with the help of a "magic screen" and "magic crayons." If you're not familiar with *Winky*, neither was I until almost a decade ago, when I overheard a couple of friends talking at a party one night.

This was one of those less-than-zero-crowd LA parties, and when one of the guys mentioned *Winky Dink* my friend's eyes exploded and they carried on the most animated conversation I'd ever witnessed over something I'd never heard of.

A few years later I decided to put together a Web site devoted to popular culture and the first article I wrote was about *Winky Dink*. For some reason the name had stuck with me, so I did some research but there wasn't much out there. I posted what little I had and responses began pouring in like crazy. A write-up appeared in the *LA Times* a few weeks later referencing the Web site, and TVparty started getting national recognition almost immediately.

I went out in search of other TV memories that captured people's imaginations. Memories that are forged mostly during childhood, because that's when a connection develops between person and appliance. Over the next eight years, hundreds of thousands of people have written exuberant e-mails to TVparty detailing their emotional connection to *Winky Dink* and dozens of other lost television artifacts we've been able to recover from the cathode mists.

This book represents TVparty's best and most requested, but I didn't write the whole thing myself. Like any good party, this one comes with contributions from a wide range of interesting people. An amazing new writer, Ben Glenn, II, contributes two extraordinary essays on subjects I've never seen explored before; Julian West explains why there are no more local kid show hosts; Rick Goldschmidt paints a portrait of a true television original; Ed Golick takes us back to 1950s Detroit; Bob French offers a glimpse of a star lost in history; and TVpartyers from all over the world offer their points of view. It's a real mix-up!

If you're still up for it, there's an Afterparty at the back of the book, so you can get more information about the shows and stars you'll experience here.

Please feel free to contact me at *billy@tvparty.com* if you have any requests for future TVparty volumes, because after all, *it's your TVparty!*

Your pal, Billy Ingram

03

(As I was writing this, a brand new *Winky Dink* kit just arrived in the mail from out of the blue. I believe coincidences are the signposts of life . . .)

This book is dedicated to **Frances Adele Rives Ingram**
The best mom in the world and the best grandmother, too.

CONTENTS

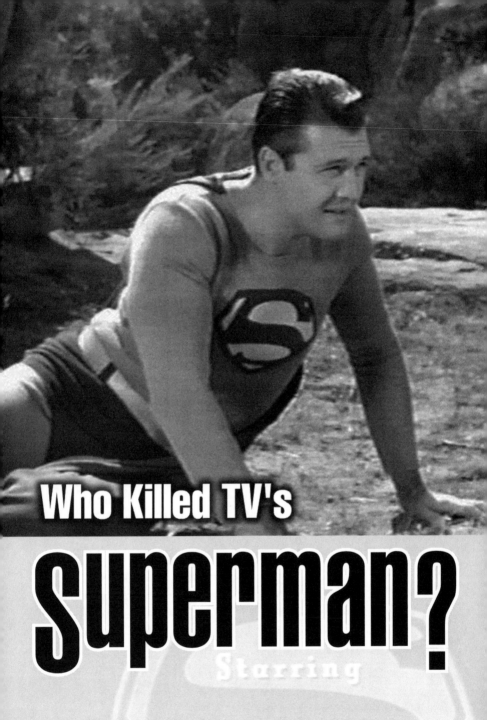

Who Killed TV's

Superman?

Starring

GEORGE REEVES

Almost every kid who grew up in the '60s heard a story of how George Reeves died. Depending on which version you heard, TV's Superman, thinking he was the character he portrayed (or despondent over being typecast), jumped off a building to see if he really could fly (or put a gun to his head and shot himself).

The coroner's report officially ruled the death a suicide, stating that the star was killed by a single gunshot to the head in the early morning hours of June 16, 1959. Truth is, we may never know the whole story; intrigue and confusion cloud the issue to this day. Many people who have taken a hard look at the case agree that murder, not suicide, was a much more likely scenario.

George Reeves was a moderately successful film actor in 1951 when he accepted the role of Superman in the feature film *Superman and the Mole Men*. A television series underwritten by Kellogg's for first-run syndication was put into production with the same cast just a few days after filming on the feature concluded.

When *The Adventures of Superman* debuted in late 1952, it was a big hit, by far the most imaginative and exciting adventure series the medium had ever seen. Even though there were no color televisions available to the public, in 1954 *The Adventures of Superman* became only the second TV series to be filmed in color (*Cisco Kid* was the first). This was a prescient move undertaken to make the show more commercially viable in the future.

When the series ceased production after six successful seasons, George Reeves found himself typecast as the Man of Steel and good roles became scarce. Despite a couple of lean years, things began to turn around in 1959. The producers of *The Adventures of Superman* decided to film another season's worth of shows in 1960 and Reeves agreed to return, signing on with a hefty raise. He was scheduled to shoot a film in Spain, and was to be married to his fiancée Lenore Lemmon on June 19, 1959—just three days after his supposed suicide.

There was another side to George Reeves that went unreported in the press—this was a guy who liked to party. Late night booze fests were common at his home on Benedict Canyon. Reeves enjoyed the LA nightlife as well, and he ran into some shady characters along the way. He engaged in a seven-year affair with Toni Mannix, the wife of Eddie Mannix, an extremely well-known, powerful MGM executive with reported mob ties. Mannix was in poor

Superman first appeared in comic books in 1938.

health at the time and was aware of their relationship. People who knew the couple assumed that George and Toni would marry after Eddie was no longer around.

Toni Mannix was devastated when their relationship came to a halt in 1958. Reeves' new love, Lenore Lemmon, stated that the jilted lover was calling Reeves repeatedly at all hours of the day and night, harassing the actor for months before his death. So much so that Reeves retained an attorney to try to convince the disturbed woman to stop the calls that were coming up to twenty times a day, calls that were sometimes nothing more than annoying hangups. The attorney wasn't persuasive, according to Lemmon, and the harassment continued unabated.

On the night of June 15, 1959, Lemmon, Reeves, and two guests were partying at the actor's home. At about 1:15 the next morning, George Reeves went upstairs to bed. He had been drinking heavily and was under the influence of painkillers prescribed for injuries he sustained in a car accident.

Moments later, a shot rang out upstairs and the actor was found dead, sprawled out on his bed, naked, with a bullet hole in his right temple. When police arrived, the death was treated as a suicide since all of the houseguests agreed there could be no other explanation. There was no sign of forced entry and the high alcohol content in the actor's blood, in combination with narcotics, made suicide a strong possibility.

Was there another explanation? Police at the scene wondered about two fresh bullet holes found in the bedroom walls. Lenore Lemmon explained that she had accidentally fired the gun earlier when she was just fooling around with it.

There were no powder marks from the gun's discharge on the actor's wound, so the weapon would have to have been held several inches from the head before firing, most unusual in a suicide. There were reportedly no fingerprints on the pistol and the actor's hands were not tested for gunpowder residue.

Many who knew Reeves at the time agreed that the actor was happier than he had been in years, looking forward to his upcoming marriage, and eager to begin another season of his still-popular television series. Money wasn't a problem either—he wasn't super-rich, but the actor was still being paid residuals every time *Superman* was rerun in major markets.

Still in mourning over her fiancée's death, Lenore Lemmon suffered another indignity when the will was read—Reeves' entire estate was willed to Toni Mannix, who said the actor must have meant the money and the house on Benedict Canyon to help the charities that they both worked with. "Toni got a house for charity and I got a broken heart," was Lemmon's dramatic statement to the press.

Leading the charge for more concrete answers about what happened that fateful night was George Reeves' mother, who held up cremation of the body for three years

All of the actors in the *Superman* series were left hopelessly typecast, a shame since they were all so talented.

while noted Hollywood investigator Jerry Geisler looked into unanswered questions surrounding the highly suspicious death. Coincidentally, both Geisler and Reeves' mother died of natural causes before they could prove foul play was involved.

Had someone entered the house, someone with a gun and a ruthless reputation, murdered the television star and warned everyone in the home to stay silent about what happened? *Superman* producer Tommy Carr thought so, and said so for years in interviews. Co-stars Noel Neill (Lois Lane) and Jack Larson (Jimmy Olsen) generated publicity for the case in the late '80s, maintaining in press and TV interviews that foul play was indeed the cause of death. After thirty years, they were trying to keep the case alive by asking for a more thorough inquiry into the troubling circumstances surrounding the "suicide" of their old friend.

Oddly, in a 1998 edition of *USA Today*, Larson reversed himself and stated emphatically that he believed Reeves did commit suicide and that Larson's longtime friend Toni Mannix (recently deceased) definitely had nothing to do with it. He didn't want her memory sullied by unfounded accusations.

Another theory has it that Reeves and Lemmon argued that night and Lemmon shot her lover in the heat of the moment. But why would her guests—witnesses to a crime—risk their reputations and freedom to cover for her? Perhaps someone will provide new clues to this puzzling mystery—but with the passage of time, that becomes more and more unlikely.

Because the facts here are so murky, I asked George Reeves expert Jim Nolt what his thoughts on the case were.

Phyllis Coates was the first actor to play Lois Lane on TV.

Jim was an on-camera consultant when the television show *Unsolved Mysteries* did a segment on this baffling story.

Here are his comments:

Almost from the moment the fatal shot was fired, friends of George Reeves have been questioning what happened in the early morning hours of June 16, 1959. Lenore Lemmon said George killed himself because he could find no work after Superman, but many who knew George remain skeptical to this day. No one is even sure who was in the house that night, and we have only Lenore Lemmon's word for the happenings. According to Lemmon, the only people in the house that night, in addition to George and herself, were Carol Von Ronkle, William Bliss, and writer Robert Condon.

Lemmon says George Reeves committed suicide. However, no fingerprints were found on the gun, no powder burns were on George's head wound. No powder burns were found on his hands. The spent shell was found underneath his body . . . the gun on the floor between his feet . . . the bullet in the ceiling. Other bullet holes were found in the bedroom floor, and the bullets were recovered from the living room below. Were all the shots fired at the same time, or were the other bullets fired days . . . perhaps weeks earlier?

We do know Lenore Lemmon and the other guests had been drinking. Indeed, Reeves' blood alcohol level was .27, well above the point of being intoxicated. The police were not called for about thirty to forty-five minutes after Reeves' death, but Lemmon never explained why she waited so long to notify the authorities.

There is no doubt Lenore Lemmon and George Reeves had a volatile relationship. They were seen arguing in public earlier in the evening. Could that argument have continued back at 1579 Benedict Canyon Drive? I believe it's quite likely and that George's death was the result of that argument. If Lenore did shoot George, it would have simply been

easier for her to say it was suicide. It would save much time and energy on her part explaining how it all happened. None of the other guests ever gave public testimony regarding the events of that night, and Lenore left California the next day . . . never to return.

We also heard from expert Michael J. Hayde on the subject, also an on-camera consultant for the *Unsolved Mysteries* segment on Reeves' death.

Superman was created by Joe Shuster and Jerry Seigel.

There is so much more to the story than can be told here, and even the book *Hollywood Kryptonite* didn't do as thorough a job as it should have (spending more time on a sensationalized and exaggerated account of Reeves' night life and attitude toward Superman).

Even to say that the police botched the investigation is simplistic. The day after the autopsy, when Chief Parker announced that he "was satisfied with the verdict" of suicide, there were two LAPD detectives in Reeves' bedroom pulling up a carpet to discover the other bullet holes. Why, if the case had just been closed? By then, Lemmon had left town for good, and there was no evidence to link Eddie Mannix or his wife to the crime. Without witnesses or a credible confession, there was just an overwhelming amount of circumstantial evidence, which implicated no one.

I can't help but think about the final two lines of dialogue from the last episode of *The Adventures of Superman* broadcast in 1958. Jimmy Olsen fawns, "Golly, Mr. Kent, you'll never know how wonderful it is to be like Superman." George Reeves (as Clark Kent) replies, "No, Jimmy, I guess I never will," gives a wink to the camera, and fades into electronic oblivion.

Odd that television's Superman should have trouble with a woman named Lenore Lemmon. In the Superman comics, the Man of Steel was always being plagued by women with double-L initials—girlfriends Lois Lane, Lana Lang, and Lori Lemeris were just some examples.

THE END

a short history of the laugh track

by Ben Glenn, II

What would TV history be without the laugh track? While much maligned by television critics, the laugh track is, in fact, any true TVPartyer's best friend. Over the years, having watched rerun after rerun, we all have come to know and love those nameless laughers whose voices we recognize, and who can always be counted on to assure our amusement.

Such classics as *The Beverly Hillbillies*, *The Munsters*, or even *Bewitched*, wouldn't be nearly as fun—and indeed, would be almost inconceivable—without the laugh track. Case in point: Cartoon Network's newly remastered versions of *The Flintstones* omit the 1960s laugh track, and the jokes largely fall flat with a thud.

But where did all of this merriment come from? Strangely, while everyone recognizes the presence of laugh tracks, very few industry sound engineers will discuss their work or even acknowledge this aspect of post-production. So here's the "unauthorized" history of the laugh track that I've been able to compile thus far.

While most associate the laugh track with television, this innovation was actually used in radio during the later 1940s. While many radio shows were done before a studio audience, as the medium's popularity waned late in the decade, recorded laughter was used from time to time. After all, who would know?

The television laugh track was introduced to viewing audiences in 1950 on NBC's *The Hank McCune Show*. The program itself appears to have been rather run-of-the-mill, but in its review *Variety* noted the innovation: "There are chuckles and yocks dubbed in. Whether this induces a jovial mood in home viewers is still to be determined, but the practice may have unlimited possibilities if it's spread to include canned peals of hilarity, thunderous ovations, and gasps of sympathy."

Invented by engineer Charley Douglass, the laugh track went on to become a television staple throughout the 1950s, whether providing the entire response track (as in *Topper* and *Car 54, Where Are You?*) or as a "sweetener" for shows recorded before an audience but in need of enhanced audience response.

Early uses of the laugh track are quaint by today's standards: *The Adventures of Ozzie and Harriet* used only one laugh throughout its half-hour running time, and *The Abbott and Costello Show* used an uproarious laugh track which ran continuously, regardless of the action on screen. Even *I Love Lucy*'s sound engineer regularly peppered many of the episodes with a handful of easy-to-recognize laughs.

As the 1960s approached, most sitcoms increasingly relied on the laugh track. More and more motion picture studios (particularly Columbia) began producing television shows, and their soundstages simply were not equipped with studio-audience facilities. Also, the sitcom trend began to border on "fantasy" subjects whose special effects could not be achieved before a studio audience. Thus, the "golden age" of the laugh track entered full swing.

Glen Glenn Sound had refined the process, and their tracks and engineers dominated the industry—which is why the very same laugh tracks can be heard on nearly every sitcom of the era, regardless of production studio or network. While still somewhat of an industry secret, here's how the process worked.

First, of course, reactions were culled from studio audiences. Industry legend has it that *The Lucy Show* and *The Red Skelton Show* were used most often—*Lucy* for its uproarious sight-gag reactions, and *Red Skelton* because the weekly pantomime sequences contained no dialogue.

Engineers looked for reactions of all types which ended very cleanly and which were dominated by one or two audience members; this made the process of patching them together easier. Later in the decade, editing processes were refined so that a distinctive laugh within a crowd could be brought to the surface and even isolated over silence.

In addition, distinctive whistling and sped-up applause tracks were recorded in the mid- to later 1960s and used on nearly every 1970s variety show discussed here in *TVparty*. All of these tracks were then installed into a device known as, appropriately enough, a laugh machine.

This twenty-eight-inch-high apparatus resembles an organ, having ten horizontal and four vertical keys and a foot pedal. The engineer "orchestrates" the laugh track by using the keyboard to select the type, sex, and age of the laugh, while playing the foot pedal to determine each reaction's length.

Every few years, the tracks were slightly changed and updated—new laughs added, others banished forever, still others put "on hiatus" for a few years and revived later. Thus, many sitcoms can be dated by listening to the laugh track—just listen to the tracks on *Mister Ed* (early 1960s) vs. those on *Bewitched* (mid-'60s) vs. those on *The Partridge Family* (early 1970s).

Interestingly, a few all-time classic tracks recorded in the late 1950s and early 1960s were never retired, and can still be heard on *Frasier!* Today, these classic laugh tracks most likely reside in the tape vaults of Todd-AO in Hollywood.

By the late 1970s, the post-production industry apparently tired of the standard laugh track, with its easy-to-recognize laughs heard throughout the 1960s and early '70s. More and more shows were returning to having a studio audience (thus the familiar announcement over the credits: "*All in the Family* was taped before a studio audience!"), which made the laugh track sound more artificial than ever.

So, engineers devised an entirely new track comprised of "looser," more relaxed group laughs; these tracks can best be heard on *The Love Boat* and *Eight Is Enough*. This trend in laugh tracks still prevails today.

The laugh machine remains in use, but few "laugh men" (as they are known in the post-production industry) have come forward to acknowledge or discuss their work. Some of the legendary "laugh men" work at Sound One, a leading post-production house in Los Angeles. And, with modern digital sound techniques, the patching in of the laugh track is becoming harder to detect—but it's still there.

Meanwhile, syndication of classic sitcoms perpetuates the familiar laughs we've come to love as part of American television history.

In 1950, less than one out of ten homes had a TV set.

TELEVISION'S FIRST STAR
Broken and Discarded.

As early as the 1920s, RCA engineers in New York were trying to develop a watchable television signal. In 1926, they beamed the blurry picture of a rotating ceramic Felix the Cat statue to the far reaches of Kansas. People viewing primitive two-inch, sixty-lines-per-screen TV receiving sets picked up the moving image with the same enthusiasm that you probably felt when you discovered the Internet for the first time.

Felix didn't reign as television's biggest (and only) star for long. As the months wore on, he fell off his rotating pedestal one too many times and was replaced by a papier-mache Mickey Mouse.

"Of course, you didn't tell the real reason that Felix was replaced by the Mickey Mouse statue, and who can blame you? We've all heard the sordid stories of Felix and his drinking; the arguments with the RCA engineers; his inability to remain on the rotating platform. These are the stuff of tabloids, and the press of the 1920s had a field day with Felix's problems at the RCA test studios. Hopefully, though, a new generation will come to love and respect Felix's

W*inky D*ink!

"Dear TVparty;

"My memories of Winky Dink *over the years had grown understandably vague. All I remembered was the magic screen and the rescue premise. I experienced blank stares from fellow baby boomers when the revered one was mentioned. My husband and I recently relocated to upper Michigan, and while we were building a house had occasion to rent a home from a delightful local farmer and his wife.*

"One day while chatting about childhood memories, the farmer mentioned a show he used to watch as a child, that no one ever acknowledged remembering to which I responded without hesitation at all—Winky Dink.

"He was astounded that of all the possibilities, I would pick the exact one, and an instant friendship was sealed." —Greyharein

Winky Dink and You was a favorite of children everywhere, originally seen at 10 AM on Saturday mornings from October 10, 1953, until April 27, 1957, on the CBS network. Broadcast in glorious black and white, this half-hour kiddie show centered around the adventures of a star-headed cartoon lad named Winky Dink and his dog Woofer, interspersed with the in-studio antics of host Jack Barry.

Joining them was Dayton Allen (from *Howdy-Doody*, later the voice of Fearless Fly) as Mr. Bungle, the assistant that never got anything right. The voice of Winky Dink was Mae Questel, who also voiced Betty Boop after Helen Kane. A veteran of many films, radio and television shows, Questel is probably best known as "Miss Blue Bell" in those '70s paper towel commercials and as the grandmother in *National Lampoon's Christmas Vacation*. She passed away in 1998.

At key points in the show, Jack Barry would prompt the boys and girls at home to help Winky Dink out of a jam by drawing whatever Winky needed (rope, ladder, bridge, etc.) on the TV screen. This was done with the aid of a Winky Dink kit which was sold by

Mr. Bungle was the name of a very popular alternative band of the '90s.

mail for fifty cents. "We sold millions of those kits," the show's host bragged, "It was well thought out."

The child would place the clear, green sheet of plastic that came with the kit over the television screen and draw what the host indicated with his finger. By doing this, kids could help Winky Dink cross to safety or move to the next level, then trace letters at the bottom of the screen to read a secret messages broadcast at the conclusion of the show. This gave Winky Dink the distinction of being the world's first interactive video game.

Because of this highly personal interactivity, the show is still fondly remembered by many. Steve P. writes us, "There was one episode where the secret message was 'sabotage' and I went around to every adult trying to get an answer as to what it meant that was satisfactory to a six-year-old! Some difference from today's world of terrorism, eh?!?!"

Another TVparty viewer explains her special connection to the show: "Every Saturday morning as a six-year-old in 1953 I would wander up the back porch steps from my parents' flat in Chicago to my grandparents' flat. They had a TV! My grandmother would tune into WBBM and my favorite show as a child would appear . . . *Winky Dink!* My grandmother would spoil me by taking me to local dime stores on every shopping trip and buy me a toy. I knew I would not have a problem asking for

INTERACTIVE TV (SPACE) PIONEER

CAPTAIN MIDNITE
1954–1956

Ovaltine sponsored this long-running radio program that became a popular movie serial, then was transplanted to television for a two-year run starting in 1954.

To create an interactive experience, viewers could send away for a Captain Midnight Secret Decoder that could help them decipher scrambled messages displayed at the end of the show.

When the series was syndicated without the Ovaltine sponsorship, the show was retitled and crudely redubbed *Jet Jackson*.

and getting my Winky Dink screen. I will always cherish the time I was able to spend with my grandparents (now deceased) and in 'saving' Winky Dink from his perils."

Of course, it goes without saying that scores of children without kits drew on the television screen itself, ruining many a family's first television set. "I remember that my mother didn't want to buy me a Winky Dink screen," Charlie Jamison recalls. "That was not going to stop me from helping my old pal Winky Dink; I just used a permanent marker! The very next week, I had a Winky Dink screen."

Another viewer tells us: "I used to watch *Winky Dink* on WBBM in Chicago when I was a kid in the '50s. I had the kit, but I would intentionally draw the wrong things. When Winky needed a ladder to get out of a hole, I would draw a cover on the hole. When he needed a parachute, I would draw an anvil to pull him down, etc. I would tease my younger sister and tell her that I was making Winky die! Whenever she left the room crying, I would laugh and laugh. Winky was cool."

Alan Rosen recalls that "the green screen that stuck to the TV had a little Winky Dink logo on the bottom center that now (forty years later) looks something like the transparent logos that the networks are using during shows. The Dinkster *was* ahead of his time!"

There were actually *two* Winky Dink kits. One for fifty cents that you could order from the television or the deluxe Winky Dink kit with extra crayons that was sold in toy stores for the then hefty price of $2.95. No matter what the cost, the Winky Dink kit was a prized item.

"One day I had a dentist's appointment that I definitely did not want to go to," Mike Monahan writes, "And my behavior made that point perfectly clear to my parents as I defiantly told them that I was not, under any circumstances, going to go. Then, the mailman came and I saw the envelope from Winky Dink. Well, I almost had a heart attack when my mother told me that I could not open it until I went to the dentist 'and you'd better behave yourself!' I don't remember the dentist visit, but I sure do remember drawing on that plastic screen the following Saturday morning!"

George Pirkle held onto his kit; "Winky Dink had a couple of friends named Merton the Mouse and Poo the Indian Boy. I confess, the only reason I remember them is that I have one of those fabled deluxe Winky Dink kits. I have heard rumors that a pristine kit will bring several thousand dollars in the marketplace. Sorry, mine is anything but pristine. A couple of the crayons and some of the little plastic geometric shapes are missing, and the box shows some wear, but it's priceless to me, and it's a small miracle that it's lasted all these years."

By 1949, networks and TV stations around the country were losing over twenty-five million dollars a year.

Winky Dink and You was Jack Barry's second successful kid's show. *Juvenile Jury* was the first, running from 1948–1955 on both NBC and CBS. On that program, a panel of kids dispensed advice to other children with problems relevant to life in the '50s—questions like, "What to do when Mom says clean up your room?" (Answer: you do it.)

THE CREATORS

On every *Winky Dink and You* program and every toy tie-in you will find the names of the two creators of the first interactive television program. One is Harry Pritchett, Sr., who, sadly, died in 2000. Mr. Pritchett contacted TVparty shortly before his death, saying in part, "Bless you for remembering Winky and all those who have responded to your site." He was amazed that Winky Dink was not forgotten after all these years.

The other creator is Edwin Brit Wyckoff, who thankfully is alive and well in New York City. He tells us how it was all done: "Creating *Winky Dink* and the participation technique now called 'interactivity' was pure joy for both of us. Making it work was explosive excitement from which we never recovered. Jack Barry and Dan Enright produced the 1953–57 show with us on CBS. It ran 'live' on about 175 stations on Saturday for a year. Then CBS added a Sunday lineup of stations because kids wanted to play with Winky day after day.

"Watch a kid playing with the kit and videocassette today and you'll see them explode with the same excitement Harry and I experienced when a kid's drawing turns from cannonball to car wheel to tennis ball to wrecking ball . . . and saves Winky from the bad guys. The magic screen is not cellophane. It is pure magic and no one yet has guessed why that tinted green plastic stuck to the screen. I know and I ain't telling.

"That marvellous musical theme came from John Gart. Norman Mazin, who is my partner in a video production company here in New York, drew all the original stories. Harry Prichett, Sr., drew the original character of Winky, who didn't appear in those stories because his blinking-winking head was too big to let the other characters be seen."

Ed Wyckoff handled the limited animation with a pair of tweezers and a bunch of interchangeable Winky heads, bodies, eyes and arms. "We used a 16mm Animatic filmstrip projector which was faster than the eye and damn good in terms of budget. The Winky Dink screen was magic. The crayons were magic; ordinary crayons didn't work. The show was pure magic.

"For those *Winky Dink and You* fans in the baby-boomer generation who feel left out . . . you're not alone. Check with Bill Gates, who loves the show and had it included in a book on interactive TV he sponsored. And try Rosie O'Donnell, who said it was her favorite kid show and will sing the theme song if you ask her nicely. She probably can handle all the songs, including 'Winko Blinko' and my favorite, 'Magic Crayons Make Magic Pictures on a Magic Window.'"

CANCELLATION AND REVIVAL

With multiple daytime successes under his belt, *Winky Dink* host Jack Barry turned his attention to prime-time and inadvertently changed the course of television forever. In 1956, he began hosting and co-producing a wildly popular prime-time game show called *Twenty-One*. As a result, *Winky Dink and You* ceased production the next year.

Barry lamented the loss but was quoted, saying, "It strictly didn't rate that well. *Winky Dink* was on for almost four-and-a-half years, but it never got the kind of audience the straight cartoon shows started pulling." *Twenty-One*, on the other hand, was riding a wave of massive popularity that game shows in general were enjoying on network prime-time schedules. *Twenty-One* was as popular in 1957 as *Who Wants to Be a Millionaire* would be forty years later.

In the fall of 1958, almost every network game show was driven off the air when it was revealed that *Twenty-One*'s big $129,000 winner, Charles Van Doren, was provided with some of the answers in advance. (The story was well told in the 1994 movie *Quiz Show*.) The stakes were high—$129,000 would be worth well over a million in today's dollars. Jack Barry, as host and producer of the show that broke the industry-wide practice of prompting some contestants, took the brunt of the bad publicity. His career went into free-fall.

Because of the immense scandal and moral outrage that ensued when people found out their favorite TV quiz shows were rigged (the end of innocence in America, it might be argued, if such a thing ever existed), it was another ten years before Jack Barry was seen on American television again. Instead, he worked in Canada, hosting a children's game show called *The Little People*.

In 1969, *Winky Dink* was revived (without Barry and Enright), this time as a stand-alone five-minute cartoon feature, complete with a new Winky Dink kit for kids to send away for. The character was redesigned with rounder lines to appeal to a more modern audience. Consumer groups argued that kids shouldn't be playing with their eyes so close to the television sets, and the character was hastily withdrawn.

Jack Barry got back into the business as the host of the long-running CBS daytime and syndicated game *The Joker's Wild* from 1972 until his death in 1984. Barry also hosted a syndicated children's version of *The Joker's Wild* called *Joker! Joker! Joker!* from 1979 until 1981, bringing his career full circle.

In a surprise development, as I was preparing this book, I got word that the Winkster was about to undergo another revival.

"Kids have never needed *Winky Dink* more than today." That's what renowned media psychiatrist Dr. Carole Lieberman thinks, and

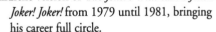
By 1960, nine out of ten homes had a TV set.

she's spent the past decade working to bring Winky back. "I believe that *Winky Dink* is the best TV show ever produced, because of its unique ability to empower children. Each time a child creates something that helps Winky and Woofer solve a problem, they get that 'I can do it!' feeling which builds self-esteem." Produced by Adam Snyder of Rembrandt Films, the new *Winky Dink and You* kit comes in an adorable clear plastic suitcase and includes the requisite magic screen, magic crayons, cloth eraser and a video with nine *Winky Dink* episodes. The new character design hearkens back to the 1969 version, but the packaging also has a small picture of the original Winky, a tribute to the character's long, and, until recently, largely forgotten history.

COMPARING THE '50s AND '60s VERSIONS:

I was about twelve when the second *Winky Dink* series appeared in syndication (in LA on KCOP Channel 13). I considered myself too old to really partake of the whole drawing exercise, but I was very into animation and liked the graphics. I was also completely taken in by the novelty of the cartoon's interactive nature (not to mention that catchy theme song).

Recently, I visited the Museum of TV and Radio Broadcasting and saw the mid '50s version for the very first time. So, let me assure those who are nostalgic, the late '60s show was a definite improvement.

The earlier *Winky Dink* series was a live action telecast with Jack Barry as the host who talked to Winky Dink (who appeared on a nearby television screen—sort of like *Captain Kangaroo's* "Fred on Channel 1").

The main focus of the show was two approximately ten-minute episodes using *extremely* limited animation and featuring a variety of characters (all voiced by Mae Questel) in ongoing storylines. Barry narrated the story and prompted the kids when to draw. Between cartoon segments, the host would also banter with live action actors (one was Dayton Allen, who was cast as the beleaguered director on the "Lucy's Hollywood Movie" episode of *I Love Lucy*).

In contrast, the late-60's version of Winky Dink completely eliminated the concept of a live host (so integral to any daytime kid show during the 1950s) and instead concentrated on Winky Dink himself, featuring Winky in every cartoon as well as having him prompt the kids to draw. Standard TV commercials were the only thing that separated the episodes. Apparently, however, Jack Barry was still connected with this show.

In this day of interactive computers and videos, it would nice to see some of the old shows recycled to at least give Jack Barry his due. —*Bob Cruz*

Bette Davis

ON TELEVISION

"I'm the nicest goddamn dame that ever lived." —Bette Davis

Bette Davis was one of the greatest motion picture actresses of all time and a huge box office draw in the 1940s. As demanding as she was talented, one critic described her as a "force of nature that could find no ordinary outlet."

When Bette Davis courageously ended her relationship with Warner Bros and struck out on her own in 1950, one of her first film vehicles was *All about Eve*, a smashing success on all levels. In the movie, Davis played Margo Channing, a glamorous, aging Broadway star who discovers her ambitious young protégé Eve (Anne Baxter) is stealing all her best roles—on and off stage.

Bette's character in *All about Eve* hit close to home in many ways. Davis was quoted as saying, "Margo Channing was not a bitch. She was an actress who was getting older and was not too happy about it. And why should she? Anyone who says that life begins at forty is full of it. As people get older their bodies begin to decay. They get sick. They forget things. What's good about that?"

With four years of money-losing duds behind her, *All about Eve* was the hit Davis needed. Years of battling the studio for better scripts and more reasonable working conditions left her with a grand movie-star lifestyle and a reputation for being difficult to work with.

Unfortunately, the features that followed *Eve* were withering flops. In 1952, with no movie offers forthcoming, Bette appeared on television for the first time as a special guest on a live Jimmy Durante variety program that had her doing sketch comedy and delivering a Pet Milk commercial. The new medium was desperate for major names like Davis, but it was an inauspicious debut leaving critics largely unimpressed. "I was scared to death," the film star declared. "That I got through it at all was a source of great wonderment to me!"

Bette turned to the musical theater next. In what should have been a great triumph, *Two's Company* turned into a high-profile Broadway disaster as she thrashed around onstage, venting

All about Eve, 1950

her frustrations by maliciously fighting with producers, cast, and crew—when she wasn't refusing to show up at all.

By the mid-'50s, an abusive marriage, health problems, bad career choices, poor investments, and a general reluctance to get along with her employers and coworkers left the actress with virtually no money and few options. Her career in ruins, it was with great reluctance that Bette turned again to television, considered the last refuge for a scoundrel among those in the film community.

Despite her initial hesitation, she embraced the medium wholeheartedly thanks to the quick cash it offered for a week or two of work. She was seen in 1957 on the Edward R. Murrow show *Person to Person*. "I'm terrified," she told the press before the live interview program, echoing her earlier TV-induced anxiety. "It's much harder to be yourself than play a part." To ease some of that uncertainty, Miss Davis gave a dramatic reading of Robert Frost's poem "Fire and Ice."

Roles on *GE Theatre* (hosted by Ronald Reagan) and *Schlitz Playhouse of Stars* followed in March of 1957, but she abruptly bowed out of a live *Playhouse 90* telecast just a few weeks later because of exhaustion and was replaced by Anne Baxter, of all people. After portraying Dolly Madison on *Ford Theater* (broadcast April 24, 1957), Bette brought to life a teacher trapped in a blizzard who must guide her students to safety in "Stranded," on the anthology program *Telephone Time*. Proving she could play lighter material, Bette was a guest on the musical-comedy *Dinah Shore Chevy Show* soon after.

Another dramatic part on *GE Theater* came in early 1958, a teleplay called "The Cold Touch" that featured plenty of foreign intrigue and a pistol-packing Bette. *Alfred Hitchcock Presents* and *Suspicion* followed that same year. The *Suspicion* tale, entitled "A Fraction of a Second," was an unintentionally hysterical tour-de-force that displayed a pop-eyed Bette being hauled off to a sanitarium, then ignominiously flattened by a load of lumber. Reviews for the production were crushing as well: "They call this a suspense series," *Daily Variety* scratched, "but the only note of suspense arising here is why they ever made the picture." Fortunately, Davis was cast in more effective half-hour dramas like "A Little Talk," concerning an aspiring writer who exacts her twisted revenge after being humiliated at a writer's conference.

A charming comedy/drama pilot was lensed in 1958, the first of many TV series tryouts Bette Davis would star in over the next twenty-five years. *Paula,* co-starring her contentious husband Gary Merrill, was an idealized tale of married New York theatrical agents ("When she's through being an agent for 10 percent every day, she comes home and then she's 100 percent wife"). Television was gruelling work compared to the leisurely pace of major motion pictures, so *Paula* was structured in a way that Davis and Merrill could switch off playing the lead on different weeks. The initial outing focused

Scenes from *Paula* and *A Little Talk*.

on Bette's efforts to get a troubled actor (Michael York) back on the stage after opening to devastating reviews. Using Times Square as a backdrop, this engaging half-hour was a pleasant pastiche of great-white-way cliches leading to *All about Eve*–style confrontations as Paula gets over on everybody with that patented Bette Davis haughty—staccato—manner.

One thing all her pilots would have in common was an open-ended premise that allowed guest-performers to push the stories along, like an anthology program with Bette cast as the mother hen, always hovering somewhere nearby, ready to jump in with the best lines. *Paula* was an ill-fated venture all around. The couple was almost killed in a fire at LA's Chateau Marmont Hotel the night before filming, and the stress shows in their faces. Bette and her husband, known for their violent, drunken rows, split soon after.

The June Allyson Show followed in 1959, with Bette playing an educator that befriends an eleven-year-old girl accused of murder. Later that season, she threw her energy behind another pilot, this time for a western series to be called *Madame's Palace*. Broadcast as an episode of *Wagon Train*, Bette starred as Madame Elizabeth McQueeny, a flamboyant western hotelier. Again the show's concept would allow for the guests to take center stage while Bette cavorted around and collected a check. The networks passed.

Undaunted, Bette chatted on *The Jack Paar Show* in 1960 and filmed two subsequent appearances on *Wagon Train* (which starred her old friend Robert Horton) in 1960 and 1961.

This was a particularly turbulent period for the actress as she prepared for the Broadway premiere of Tennessee Williams' *Night of the Iguana*. "I'm returning to the stage, to refine my craft. That's what Hollywood actors always say. But that's a bunch of BS. No one leaves movies for the stage unless they can't get work; and I'm no exception." In spite of this deferential confidence, she abruptly left the produc-

Scenes from *Paula*, 1958

"She has a cult. I have fans. There's a big difference." —*Joan Crawford on Bette Davis*

29

tion just a few weeks into the run after viciously terrorizing the cast, director, and author non-stop for months. Bette's simple philosophy summed it up: "Until you're known in my profession as a monster, you're not a star."

In 1962, desperate for any opportunity to re-ignite before the public, Bette did the unthinkable, agreeing to co-star in a film with her bitter enemy Joan Crawford. Davis once said of Crawford, "I wouldn't piss on her if she was on fire." (Now you know where that came from!) *Whatever Happened to Baby Jane* raked in millions at the box office. Thanks to a brilliant performance, an Oscar nomination, and a healthy percentage of the box office, Bette Davis was sure the film would put her back on firm footing.

On *The Andy Williams Show* in December 1962, Miss Davis came on to a fanfare so highly dramatic you'd think they were carving a new head on Mt. Rushmore. This preceded Bette singing "Turn Me Loose on Broadway," ironic since she had just walked out on the Broadway role of a lifetime. Of course, there had to be some scripted back-and-forth between host and guest and Davis handled the nonsensical patter with a fair ease:

ANDY: "I think everybody agrees that *Whatever Happened to Baby Jane* is probably your greatest triumph." (Audience applauds.)

BETTE: "Andy. You know something? You've got a head like Santa's bag. Filled with goodies!"

ANDY: "I saw the picture *Whatever Happened to Baby Jane* just a couple of weeks ago and I still have the goosebumps. I think it's one of the most shocking and suspenseful pictures I've ever seen in my life."

BETTE: "Andy? Have you really seen the picture?"

ANDY: "No, but I'm going to say I did . . . No, I have and it's just wonderful."

BETTE: "Well, I brought you a Christmas present. Yes, I did. A Baby Jane doll. For you! Yes, I did."

Bette presented her host with a grotesque life-size prop from the movie, then launched into a thoroughly wretched rock-and-roll novelty song called, inappropriately enough, "Whatever Happened to Baby Jane." The tune was released as a single but deservedly went nowhere. Davis was not known for her singing ability, and this performance would have been a complete embarrassment to any other star, but Bette Davis, by this point, masked her insecurities with indomitable bravado.

Ever wonder where Aunt Bee worked before Andy and Opie?
I'll bet Mayberry looked awfully good after working for Bette Davis!

1962 brought a return visit to *The Jack Paar Show* and a role on *The Virginian* playing a blackmailing bank teller. When surgery forced Raymond Burr to miss filming three episodes of his top-rated *Perry Mason* series in 1963, Bette eagerly stepped in to solve "The Case of Constant Doyle" as the star of one of those fill-ins.

Madam Sin, 1972

Once again choice movie roles passed her by and Bette's early-'60s screen comeback proved short-lived. Bitter and frustrated, the actress left Hollywood to live in Connecticut and tried again in earnest to launch a TV series. She needed steady work to support her family now that she was single once more. Many ideas were pitched back and forth; *The Decorator*, about an interior designer who lives briefly with her clients, actually made it to film. The pilot was produced in 1964 by a young Aaron Spelling, but there were no takers.

The Disappearance of Aimee, 1976

By 1965, the once-proud actress was reduced to doing a low-budget Hammer horror film, *The Nanny.* To promote the film, she appeared on *What's My Line* in October 1965, but with that highly distinctive voice she was easily recognized by the blindfolded panelists. Maybe she *wanted* to be recognized?

Bette found herself on the variety show circuit, singing and doing a comedy sketch with Bert Lahr as host of *The Hollywood Palace* in 1965 and serving as co-host for a week on *The Mike Douglas Show* in 1966, where her birthday was celebrated in front of a studio audience. That same year Bette appeared in a memorable episode of *Gunsmoke* as a vengeful matriarch who captures Matt Dillon to hang him in retaliation for her outlaw husband's death. A few weeks later, she was seen doing silly sketches on *The Milton Berle Show. It Takes A Thief* with friend Robert Wagner was next; she played a retired safecracker with arthritis. In her final variety show bookings, Davis appeared on *The Dean Martin Show* in 1967 and on *The Smothers Brothers Comedy*

Strangers, 1979

Right of Way, 1983

Hour in 1967 and 1969. After fifteen years of experience on every conceivable television program, she was more at ease than ever riffing on her aloof image:

TOMMY SMOTHERS: "Bette was one of our first guests last year and I just was wondering if you noticed any difference in the shows from then until now?"

BETTE: "No, I think it still has that special . . . *Smothers* quality."

TOM: "What do you mean by that?"

BETTE: "It's a dumb show."

Her film output during this period consisted solely of schlockmeister Hammer's *The Anniversary*, where she appeared in a most unflattering eyepatch wielding an axe. With one awful exception (*Bunny O'Hare* in 1971), she didn't make another major motion picture in the U.S. for the next eight years.

Turning to commercial endorsements for money, Bette hawked Awake powdered orange juice on TV in 1969 and posed, drink in hand, for Jim Beam print ads in 1972 beside pal Robert Wagner. Bette filmed another pilot in 1971 (from the producers of *The Rockford Files*) called *The Judge and Jake Wyler*, about a crusading retired jurist (Davis) and her ex-con partner. The hour-long drama wasn't picked up, so the studio padded it with new scenes and released it as a TV movie in 1972. "By the time Universal added enough scenes to make it run for two hours," Miss Davis explained, "there was no similarity to the pilot film we shot. You can't win!" A Johnny Carson prime-time special followed in 1972, with the actress singing "Just Like a Man" from *Two's Company*.

Since none of this kind of pickup work was especially lucrative, Bette was fortunate to embark on a new career starring in TV movies beginning in 1972 with *Madame Sin*, another unsold pilot, this time with Robert Wagner ("Even the diabolical Dr. No would have to say yes to Madam Sin"). Another dark teleplay followed in 1973, *Scream, Peggy, Scream,* putting Davis in danger of becoming eternally typecast in the cheesy horror genre. While some of her TV films contain excellent performances (or several fine scenes, anyway), she was tired and only worked because she had to. In private, she lamented that making movies was no longer fun.

Another sitcom pilot, *Hello, Mother, Goodbye,* was produced at MGM in 1973 (airing in 1974) but again the networks passed. In the fall of 1973, she turned up on *The Dean Martin Show*, being "roasted" by stars like Henry Fonda, Howard Cosell, and Nipsey Russell. Looking around the dais she topped everyone: "What a dump!" quoting a line from her 1949 film, *Beyond the Forest.*

Bette sat down for ninety minutes of funny and frank discussion with Dick Cavett in prime-time on September 19, 1974. Following a final disastrous Broadway attempt in 1975 (*Miss Moffat*), Davis found her success in the TV movie realm gave her a much needed boost in the film industry, leading to theatrical releases like *Burnt Offerings,*

Patrick Kelly designed the outfits that Bette wore on later talk shows.

Return to Witch Mountain, the star-laden Death on the Nile, and another suspense movie, Watcher in the Woods, all opening between 1976 and 1980. In addition, Davis kept up her TV output with The Disappearance of Aimee (playing the mother of evangelist Aimee Semple McPherson) in 1976 and the Dark Secret of Harvest Home mini-series in 1978.

The AFI Lifetime Achievement Award was presented to Bette Davis in 1976 in a glittering, star-studded televised ceremony, and she won an Emmy Award for the telefilm Strangers: The Story of a Mother and Daughter in 1979. Unknown to anyone, Davis had just had a facelift, and when she spoke with Mike Wallace on 60 Minutes in January 1980, he innocently broached the subject. The embarrassed actress stopped the filming. She had always maintained publicly that she would never go under the knife, but privately explained to Wallace that she felt it was necessary for her to secure film roles.

She may have been right, since a string of quality TV movies followed—Skyward (directed by Ron Howard) and White Mama in 1980, Family Reunion in 1981, A Piano for Mrs. Cimino and Little Gloria: Happy at Last in 1982, and HBO's Right of Way with Jimmy Stewart in 1983 all garnered respectable reviews and healthy audience numbers. Bette Davis was, personally and professionally, at her strongest point in years.

In 1983, at age seventy-five, Bette Davis finally got a weekly series picked up—Hotel, from the producer of Dynasty. In the pilot film, Davis starred as Laura Trent, owner of San Francisco's luxurious St. Gregory Hotel, a kind of land-locked Love Boat with James Brolin, Connie Selleca, and Shari Belafonte greeting the guests. Once again the format offered an opportunity for Miss Davis to barge in and out of people's lives—only now, with a looser morality in effect on television,

AFI tribute show, 1977

Interview, 1980s

Entertainment Tonight, 1988

Last press conference, 1988

Bette suggested they rename Hotel more honestly: Brothel.

she could butt into their sex lives as well. The telecast did well in the ratings. Nighttime soaps were incredibly popular in 1983 and Bette Davis's bitchy persona was a natural for the genre. After all, wasn't Joan Collins doing her best Bette Davis imitation on *Dynasty?*

Bette fell ill and was hospitalized just after the first regular episode was filmed but was expected to return to *Hotel* after recovering from her unexpected radical mastectomy. Nine days after the operation she suffered a stroke that left an arm, a leg, and her face partially paralyzed. Producer Aaron Spelling did everything he could to accommodate the ailing legend, but she ultimately dropped out before ever returning to the production, ungratefully trashing the series as vulgar in the press. Believe it or not, Anne Baxter swooped in and took over the role as Victoria Cabot, Mrs. Trent's sister-in-law.

Even with paralysis severely affecting her face and voice, Bette Davis continued to make TV films—*Murder with Mirrors* in 1985 and *As Summers Die* in 1986. In 1987, she made her best motion picture in decades, *The Whales of August* with Lillian Gish.

Bette Davis turned in a brilliant *Tonight Show with Johnny Carson* performance to promote *Whales*. There she happily took the opportunity to insult her former co-star from *The Disappearance of Aimee*. With Crawford long dead, one wonders if Bette felt she needed to go after the actor who portrayed Joan in *Mommy Dearest*:

CARSON: "Who is one of the worst people you know in Hollywood?"

DAVIS: "That I worked with?"

CARSON: "That you wouldn't want to work with again. You don't have to comment on that . . ."

DAVIS: "Faye Dunaway. Everybody you can put in this chair will tell you exactly the same thing."

CARSON: "What is it about Miss Dunaway that makes your . . ."

DAVIS: "Well, she's just totally impossible. I don't think we have the time to go into *all* the reasons . . ."

In a prime example of the kettle talking, she went on to complain about Dunaway keeping the cast, crew, and extras waiting one day:

DAVIS: "She's very unprofessional, a difficult woman."

CARSON: "You had a reputation at certain times as being kind of tough yourself."

DAVIS: "Oh no, I never had a reputation of that kind of thing. No, no, no, never. I have never behaved in an unprofessional manner. Ever. No. That includes keeping actors waiting, keeping crews waiting, all those things. No. Never, never, never."

CARSON: "You are a true professional. That's for sure."

DAVIS: "Yes, and that is really what *she* isn't."

In 1988, Bette was a presenter on both the Golden Globes and the 59th Annual Academy Awards telecast. At the Academy Award dais, she appeared to be disoriented and in trouble—but recovered beautifully, despite the director cutting away unexpectedly from her and Robert Wise, who was accepting the award. Bette was bitter about the affront; after all, she was a past president of the Academy: "Someone kept saying to me, 'Name the winner! Name the winner!' Then before I could say 'Mr. Paul Newman cannot be here tonight,' they shoved someone onstage to replace me."

Her description isn't entirely accurate. She read the list of nominees, announced the winner and, before she could be hustled offstage, delivered a rousing tribute to Mr. Wise, one of the industry's most respected directors. When she finished her accolades, the program cut away quickly to hosts Chevy Chase and Goldie Hawn, who seemed flustered, commenting; "Are you guys through over there?"

Bette Davis taped a *Barbara Walters Special* that aired the same night as the Academy Awards ceremony. In her last in-depth TV interview, she talked about life, love, and regrets:

BARBARA: "You say, what you always hoped to have, from the song title— "Someone to Watch over Me." You never found it."

BETTE: "And then I say, it's no wonder. Nobody ever thought I needed it. I was always competent, earned my own way, and nobody would have ever thought I needed someone to watch over me. And I never did find it."

One of Bette Davis' last public appearances was on NBC's *Late Night with David Letterman* in 1989, where she began by repeating her famous line from *All About Eve*: "Fasten your seat belts—it's going to be a bumpy night!" She died just a few months later, on October 6, 1989.

I think Bette Davis's finest TV work—and the greatest work in the last two decades of her career, is *Strangers*.

This 1979 telefilm teams Davis with another great actress, Gena Rowlands. They play an emotionally estranged mother and daughter who have been out of touch for many years. Rowlands abruptly shows up on Davis's doorstep one day. They argue and fight but slowly over time, Davis's heart begins once more to open to her daughter. Then we learn why Rowlands has returned home.

The two actresses are extraordinary together and much of the film is so real and emotionally agonizing, it is at times difficult to watch.

Also of some note is *Skyward*, which Ron Howard directed, and *A Piano for Mrs. Cimino*, which co-starred Keenan Wynn. George Schaefer, a TV filmmaker of some taste and sensitivity, directed *Piano* in 1982. The following year he made *Right of Way*, a telefilm for HBO starring Davis and James Stewart.

This was an unusual, disturbing, and rather controversial film about euthanasia and suicide. Davis' character learns that she has only a short while left to live. Stewart, her loving husband of many years, can't bear the thought of her suffering further and can't imagine living without her. Accordingly, they decide to end their lives.

No one, not even David Lynch, has ever filmed a more matter-of-fact/creepy scene than the sequence here in which Jimmy Stewart visits a hardware store to purchase materials for the couple's planned double suicide. This would have understandably been a rather short movie if the couple hadn't confided their plans to daughter Melinda Dillon, whose strong objections result in legal action and increasing loss of dignity and privacy for Davis and Stewart.

Two endings were filmed for this movie and I've seen both of them. Each is troubling, with one much more satisfying than the other, given the almost unsolvable ethical situation. After airings on HBO in '83 and '84, the movie was in syndication; there has never been a video release to my knowledge.

It was Stewart's final starring performance, not counting the curious religious TV special *Mr. Kruger's Christmas*, and it was his first leading role in any project since the cancellation of his TV show *Hawkins*, as well as his first and only appearance opposite Davis. Jimmy, always a gentleman, took second billing to Bette.

After *Right of Way*, director Schaefer went on to make the Lucille Ball dramatic telefilm curio *Stone Pillow* and three TV films starring Katharine Hepburn.

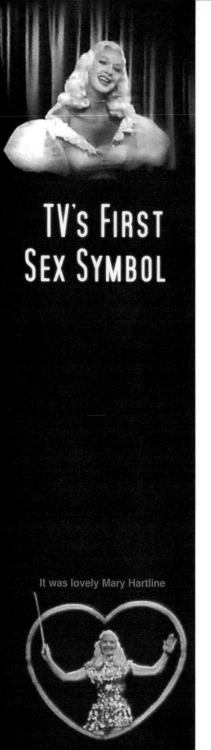

It was lovely Mary Hartline

TV's First
Sex Symbol

Wholesomely sexy Mary Hartline was a breakout star in the days when there were very few TV stations on the air nationwide. A successful model, she entered Chicago's burgeoning broadcast industry in 1946, appearing on the ABC radio program *Junior Junction* (later known as *Teen Town*), about a city inhabited solely by teenagers. The producer of the show was her husband Harold Stokes. They had met the year before and were married in 1947 (Stokes was forty-two and Mary twenty-one).

Mary Hartline left *Teen Town* in 1949 to join *Super Circus*, a weekly live kid's program also produced by her husband. *Super Circus* began life as a Chicago radio contest program in the 1940s starring former real-life circus barker turned commercial announcer Claude Kirchner.

Starting on TV as a Chicago local in 1948, *Super Circus* was presented live on Sunday afternoons beginning in 1949 (from the Civic Theater in Chicago) over the ABC network. In addition to lovely Mary Hartline, regulars included Cliffy, Scampy, and Nicky the clowns, and Mike Wallace (yes *that* Mike Wallace) as the show's commercial pitchman. With an authentic circus feel and Mary's sparkling, low-cut outfits, the program became an instant national sensation and Mary was catapulted to fame as one of TV's first bright shining lights, with both kid and adult appeal.

Mary would open every show with a rousing number fronting the ultra-brassy Super Circus Band. Her rhythmic moves and smooth baton twirling were a real live manifestation of every '50s girl's dream—to be the lead majorette, as pretty as a china doll. Platinum blond, statuesque, and perfectly formed, Mary was wildly popular with the little girls—and their daddies—inspiring an entire line of dolls and other toys.

Mary Hartline was so popular she appeared in a weekday

children's TV show of her own, a fifteen minute live afternoon program where one lucky viewer got a call from Mary herself, along with a chance to win prizes like a Mary Hartline Doll from Ideal Toys. *The Mary Hartline Show* ran from February to June of 1951.

Mary remained on *Super Circus* until 1955, when the show was revamped and production moved to New York. Jerry Cologna was made host with Sandy Wirth taking the baton. Still a top-rated show, *Super Circus* ended in 1956 because of sponsorship difficulties.

Mary Hartline married well—and often. She divorced her first husband in 1951. Mary hitched up with her tax lawyer until 1960, when she married Chicago contractor George Carlson. Carlson died soon after their nuptials.

A short time thereafter, she married Woolworth dime-store heir Woolworth Donahue. Together they entertained the rich and famous in Palm Beach, where they owned three magnificent homes (with another in Southampton). Donahue died in 1972. A yachting enthusiast, Mary remains a local fixture of the Palm Beach old-money set.

Mary Hartline Doll

"Dad (Claude Kirchner) passed away in March of 1993 from lymphoma. A brief blurb in the *NY Post* mentioned his illness just before he died. I saved every single letter (over five hundred) and have them in albums.

"I still can't get over the response and emotions shared concerning those who watched *Terrytoon Circus* every night. I guess it was a ritual, but some kids were watching to escape unbelievable abuses and found comfort from the show. If anyone reading this was one of the correspondents, thank you sooooo much! What memories we all have from those good old TV days!

"A couple of shows dad had that some of you might recall: *Marx Magic Midway* (mid '60s on Channel 4, I think). Did you know that he was the voice-over artist for all of those Marx commercials for a long time?

"We had a closet full of Marx toys, but, for some reason, my brother and I were not allowed to touch them! I guess they were to give away. The other show was *Super Adventure Theater*; I think it played old science fiction movies.

"I have tons of stuff of dad's including his original boots and ringmaster costume. He wore it late in life for a show called *Remember When . . .* hosted by a reporter named John Johnson. Dad and Mary Hartline both still fit in their costumes from the '40s! I videotaped it, but our son accidentally recorded over it.

"I also have many of the *Super Circus* shows with all those live commercials. Oh yeah, I also have Clownie!" —Lynn

TV's first married couple to share a bed!

As a motion picture actor in the '40s, Ida Lupino was known as "Queen of the Bs" and "the poor man's Bette Davis," but she was much more than that. Intensely creative, she wanted control to shape her own film projects at a time when only a couple of women had ever directed a motion picture at all and few women were taken seriously in the business.

While continuing to play the sultry roles the studios offered her, Lupino began writing, producing, directing, and starring in films for her own production company in 1948. Tackling issues that Hollywood wouldn't (like unwed mothers, bigamy, and rape) these noir films are well-regarded today.

In 1951, Ida Lupino married her co-star (from 1949's *Woman in Hiding*) Howard Duff. The next year she embarked on a career in the fledgling television industry, first as an actor on dramatic anthology programs, by 1955 graduating to directing series episodes.

In 1957, Lupino stopped making movies and teamed with her husband to star in a novel sitcom, *Mr. Adams and Eve*, the everyday story of a famous movie star couple

"[Television is] the triumph of machine over people. " —*Fred Allen*

living in Beverly Hills. The show was loosely based on their real-life circumstances (exaggerated for comic effect), as Lupino wanted the show to have a ring of truth to it. The result was a hilarious and stylish program, a wonderful send-up of Hollywood in the '50s, that golden time when women were dolled up with no place to go.

The show followed the awkward attempts of sheltered celebrities "Howard Adams" and his wife "Eve Drake" to relate to real life as they encountered it—dealing with agents, farcical production details, demanding directors, and clueless studio heads. The stellar supporting cast featured Hayden Rorke (*I Dream Of Jeannie*) as their manager, Alan Reed (Fred Flintstone) as the studio head, and Olive Carey as the couple's sassy live-in maid Elsie.

Despite a brilliant cast, stylish art direction and clever scripts (many by *Bewitched*'s Sol Saks), *Mr. Adams and Eve* made it through only two seasons on CBS. Maybe the show was too "inside" for '50s audiences. A little-known fact: this was the first series to show a married couple that slept in the same bed—and the last until *The Munsters* in 1964.

After the series' cancellation, Lupino directed dozens of classic TV programs over the next fifteen years, shows like *Alfred Hitchcock Presents, The Donna Reed*

However, the first couple to ever share a bed in a TV series was . . .

So This Is Hollywood
January 1, 1955–August 19, 1955

From producer Richard Bare (*Beverly Hillbillies*) comes the story of two struggling actresses (Virginia Gibson, Mitzi Green) making a go of it in LA. Some of that struggling takes place under the sheets, apparently, as these thrifty gals are content to share a bed together.

Network censors had no problem with this arrangement in spite of the fact that Ricky and Lucy were a real-life married couple playing a married couple on TV but *they* weren't allowed to be seen sleeping in the same bed.

With rare exceptions like *Mr. Adams and Eve* in the '50s and *The Munsters* in the '60s (Herman and Lillie were often seen in bed), a twin set of single beds remained the norm for television couples until the '70s.

Mitzi Green never did another TV series but Virginia Gibson did have a nine-year run hosting ABC's daytime children's series *Discovery* (1962–1971).

Ronald Wesley Hyatt writes: "*So This is Hollywood* may also hold the record as being the first to show an opener of upcoming scenes from that night's show before the first commercial, as well as a preview of a scene from next week's episode."

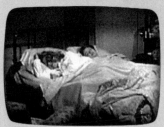

Executive producer of this show, Collier Young, was a former husband of Lupino.

39

Show, Gilligan's Island, The Ghost and Mrs. Muir, The Twilight Zone, The Untouchables, and *The Fugitive.*

As an actor, Ida Lupino made memorable guest appearances on a wide variety of programs, including *Alias Smith and Jones, Batman,* and *The Wild, Wild West.* She also returned to making motion pictures in 1966, retiring twelve years later at the age of sixty. She died due to a stroke on August 3, 1995.

Howard Duff went on to become a regular on a number of TV series, including three years on *Felony Squad* in the 1960s, and one-year stints on *Flamingo Road, Knots Landing,* and *Dallas* in the 1980s. He died in 1990.

FILM HISTORIAN JEFF VILENCIA ADDS:

One day I got a phone call from the office of Fredrick DeCordova (producer at the time of the Carson *Tonight Show*). A few weeks earlier I had sent him a VHS copy of *Mr. Adams and Eve* (he produced the series). He wanted to thank me and to talk about that show. He said the two season negatives are in legal problems in somebody's estate, which is why the show has not been seen for years in syndication. He also sent me an 8x10 autographed photo, which was cool.

The other video copy of that film is with the Museum of Broadcasting in NYC. I made them a video master in 1986; UCLA now has the original reel of film, which I gave them.

One day DeCordova's office calls me and asks if I would be so kind, to phone the American Cinemathéque; they were doing a special tribute to Ida Lupino.

Cool, I call them—they want to use the episode along with the one *Twilight Zone* episode that Ida Lupino was in. They had contacted CBS and the network told them they couldn't locate a copy of *Mr Adams and Eve*, so I shipped them a copy.

They have the tribute, and a week later the CBS legal department calls and asks if I was the one who "licensed" the show for them to use? Having worked in this stupid biz, I was keen on wordings. I said, "No, I let them use my private copy. I don't own the rights to the show. There was no money etc, etc, etc." They asked how I got a copy of the show. I told them, back in the '70's when I was in high school, I knew people who worked in television film exchange and the print was a discard. They asked me if I had the rest of the two seasons and I said no, just that one episode.

As it turns out, they couldn't even find the 35mm film negatives to the series! I don't know to this day if they ever found them. Just like *The Goldbergs*, nobody knows what happened to the 35mm film negatives. So the history of Hollywood television seems to have gone the same way as the old movies in the 1920s— lost, thrown away, misplaced.

On *Mr. Adams and Eve* even the maid is seen in bed!

Gertrude Berg as Molly

The Goldbergs was one of the most successful entertainment ventures ever, a radio and television show that reached across every medium. It all hinged on one woman—Gertrude Berg, a true multimedia pioneer. Beginning on network radio in 1930, *The Goldbergs* had a phenomenal seventeen-year run, second only to *Amos and Andy* as the longest-running program of radio's golden years. A Broadway play and daily comic strip were also spun off from the show.

The Goldbergs followed the adventures of Molly Goldberg, her husband Jake, and their family as they meandered through life's everyday challenges. Producer Gertrude Berg both wrote the scripts and portrayed Molly in the radio sitcom.

What a remarkable woman Gertrude Berg must have been, one of the few of her gender with any power in an industry growing more competitive each year. From 1930 until 1955, *The Goldbergs* was broadcast live. It's hard to imagine anyone writing and performing a live, top-rated network series for over twenty years, especially

The Goldbergs lived at 1038 East Tremont Ave. in the Bronx. In real life, Gertrude Berg lived next door to Tallulah Bankhead.

when you consider there were very few changes made in all that time. *Life* magazine said: "For millions of Americans, listening to *The Goldbergs*, a warm-hearted radio serial about a Jewish family, has been a happy ritual akin to slipping on a pair of comfortable old shoes that never seem to wear out."

The series was so resistant to change that when the actor who played Molly's husband Jake for fifteen years died in 1945, he wasn't replaced for another two years. Molly simply referred to her spouse and spoke to him without giving the character any lines. *The Goldbergs* ended on radio in 1947, after earning Gertrude Berg national acclaim and millions of dollars. Berg took a stage version of her show called *The Goldbergs, Molly and Me* to Broadway in 1948 before deciding to tackle the latest technology.

The move to television in 1949 was (at first) an easy one for *The Goldbergs*. This was the original "show about nothing," just the ordinary daily frustrations of life as seen through the eyes of patient, wise, resourceful Molly. For the first TV season on CBS, the show was the third most popular program on the air. The production was very successful in illuminating for the eyes what the radio show presented so well for the mind's eye. That was no easy task, only a small number of radio sitcoms successfully transitioned to the small screen—and they all tried.

Not even a woman with as much determination as Gertrude Berg could stop what was going on in Washington, DC, in 1950. The Senate investigation into communists infiltrating our daily lives was in full swing, reaching deep into Hollywood. Writers and actors with left-leaning tendencies were labelled "controversial" and blacklisted—refused work by the networks and studios and even fired from existing contracts.

Such was the fate of Phillip Loeb, the actor who played Molly's husband Jake on television. Labelled a communist by the Senate committee (Loeb insisted he wasn't), *The Goldbergs* sponsor General Foods demanded the actor be fired. Gertrude Berg refused to do so and the series ceased production in 1951 with ratings in a free-fall over the adverse publicity.

When it became apparent that neither network nor sponsor would budge, Berg reluctantly replaced Phillip Loeb (but kept him on the payroll at full salary) with

Gertrude Berg won the very first Emmy for "Best Actress in a Continuing Performance."

actor Harold J. Stone when *The Goldbergs* returned to the air in February 1952 on another network, NBC. The part changed hands again when Robert H. Harris took over the role in 1953. Phillip Loeb, the struggling performer who finally achieved the success he worked so hard for, then lost it all so harshly, committed suicide in 1955.

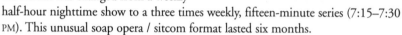

When *The Goldbergs* moved to NBC, the format was changed from a weekly half-hour nighttime show to a three times weekly, fifteen-minute series (7:15–7:30 PM). This unusual soap opera / sitcom format lasted six months.

The Goldbergs was brought back for a few weeks in the summer of 1953, this time as a half-hour on NBC. The struggling Dumont network picked up the show in April of 1954, but this run only lasted a few months. In 1955, Gertrude Berg shook things up a bit, syndicating the show to individual stations in a new format called *Molly.*

This time the Goldberg family had "moved on up" to the suburbs (Haverville, NY), but the situations remained basically the same. Still written by Gertrude Berg (with her son Cherny), the production refreshingly updated the characters without disturbing the careful chemistry of the easygoing scripts. Possibly out of step with the times, *Molly* was cancelled after only one year.

Gertrude Berg triumphed on Broadway in a two-year run with *A Majority of One*, winning the Tony Award for Best Actress in 1959. She also turned up as a guest on a number of variety shows and dramatic productions before returning to CBS in 1961 with *Mrs. G. Goes to College.* Surrounded by an all-star cast that included Sir Cedric Hardwicke, Leo Penn, Marion Ross, and Mary Wickes, this sitcom about a widow (the same basic Molly Goldberg character) who returns to university life received tepid ratings. The series was renamed *The Gertrude Berg Show* mid-season but was ultimately expelled after a freshman year marked with bad reviews.

Gertrude Berg died on September 14, 1966 while preparing for another Broadway run.

Film archivist Jeff Vilencia writes:
Talk about lost shows, get this—when Guild Films in NY went bankrupt, the negatives to those *Goldberg* shows (along with others like *The Joe Palooka Story*), were placed in a bank vault.

Time passed and now all of the 35mm negatives are lost. The only copies of the last season of *The Goldbergs* are with UCLA, Cherny Berg had a complete set in 16mm, and I had about eighteen shows in 16mm.

The first six years of the show was live and the network contract stipulated that they destroy the kinescope recordings after 90 days. So there are only a handful of "live" *Goldbergs*!

A kinescope is the process of literally filming from a television monitor.

But Whatever Happened to

Joe DiMaggio's First Wife?

by Bob French

Her 'screen credit' name was Dorothy Arnold.

She was a blooming starlet at Universal when she met Joe and was swept, with little forethought, into a marriage which she soon regretted. The first prerequisite was that she depart "show biz" and become totally subservient to her new husband. She acceded and became pregnant almost immediately, although Joe wasn't particularly pleased. Their son was born and Dorothy was required to leave him with "Grandma" DiMaggio while she had to follow Joe hither and yon . . . even to training camp, because he wouldn't let her out of his sight.

Came the divorce . . . an anathema to Italian Roman-Catholic grandma, who defacto disowned both Dorothy and Joe, retaining control of Joe, Jr. Seldom was Dorothy allowed to see him until he reached an age when he could make periodic sneak visits to see his mother. But the years took their toll and a real mother-son relationship never materialized. Joe Jr. never mentioned his father to Dorothy, so what sort of quasi-relationship existed there was unknown to her. But (and Dorothy arranged it, because Joe constantly harassed her) Monroe entered the picture and Joe Jr. became quite close to his glamorous stepmother while the short-lived marriage lasted.

Bob French in Charcoal Charlie's

I met Dorothy when I moved to the Palm Springs area in 1970. She and her (third, I think) husband, Ralph Peck, owned and operated a little steak-and-booze club called Charcoal Charlie's on the outskirts of Cathedral City (adjacent to Palm Springs). I worked for them from time to time as their lounge entertainer, and I *loved* it when Dorothy had enough under her belt to get up and sing to an adoring crowd. Her trademark drink was Boodles' Gin Gibsons, and I can still see and hear her strutting around the room singing "I'm Going Back" from *Bells are Ringing*. She really tore the place to pieces with that one!

Dorothy got a few spasmodic screen jobs during the years after I met her. The last being in MGM's *Lizzie* (a precursor to *Three Faces of Eve*) wherein she played Eleanor Parker's mother. I think I counted three or four lines in that one. And even though she was playing a drunk, she was still gorgeous!

Those were glorious days for me, but they got even better. In following years, after Charlie's was razed due to a city "upgrade," our friendship became strictly personal and *very* close . . . like family, literally. Talk about "golden years!"

Dorothy retained her beauty (a true peaches-and-cream complexion) up until the time of her demise from pancreatic cancer and those sapphire-blue eyes never lost their luster!

And the *stories* she could tell! Tales of Walter Winchell, Bogart, Methot and Bacall, Kilgallen (who detested Dorothy because she suspected her husband, Dick Kollmar, of having the "hots" for her, although everyone knew Kollmar was, indeed, a closet queen), Elsa Maxwell, Adela Rogers St. John, Anita Loos, and lots of others I would have to search my memory to recall.

The last time I saw Dorothy was just before she fled to a clinic in Mexico. She had accepted her mortality and had to get away from Ralph, with his constant whining and boo-hooing. She needed solitude and privacy to prepare for a positive departure and Ralph's negativity was detrimental, to say the least.

We received word that Dorothy had left us only days later. And we are confident she had a direct flight to her own paradise. And, trite as it may sound, she is still alive in our hearts.

Joe DiMaggio's son John is the voice of Bender on *Futurama*.

TALLULAH!

If you've ever been in the presence of a flamboyant, bitter drag queen, you're looking at Tallulah Bankhead's residual energy on this planet. This uninhibited woman said and did shocking things simply to get a rise out of the public, much like Madonna might today, but that kind of activity didn't get you as far in the '40s and '50s as it does in modern times.

Tallulah Bankhead was the only silent film star who successfully made the transition to talkies, then went on to conquer publishing, radio, and television. One of the most important dramatic actors of the theater and screen, by 1941 she was looking back at a decade of disappointments in both arenas.

Trouble was, this lady liked to drink. A lot. Unrestrained public displays and far-too-frank interviews alienated her from the mainstream public. In spite of her excesses, Tallulah was such a consummate professional that even heavy boozing rarely adversely affected her stage performances. And, if it did, there was always tomorrow night. In a near-constant state of fuckedupedness, she was outrageous and outspoken on stage and off. "Cocaine isn't habit-forming," the actor was famously quoted as saying. "I should know—I've been using it for years." When her performance was criticized during a radio program she pointedly told the host, on the air, "In the play I'm Tallulah and only Tallulah. Why should I be ashamed of that? Now please fuck off and have a sandwich!"

She had a habit of calling everyone daaahling, "because all my life I've been terrible at remembering people's names. I once introduced a friend of mine as Martini. Her name was actually Olive."

With few film roles coming her way, Miss Bankhead turned in the '40s to guest-starring on popular radio programs like *The Charlie McCarthy Show* and *Duffy's Tavern,* where she would parody her over-the-top, campy persona for grand comic effect. One particular skit on *The Fred Allen Show,* a satire of cheerful morning programs, was such a hit it was repeated five times, almost unheard of in those days.

Radio audiences weren't particularly sophisticated in bygone days, so any slurring of speech due to intoxication easily blended with Tallulah's naturally husky, lurching vocal affectation. That raspy voice was a byproduct of a lifetime of overindulgence—at one time she would consume a kaleidoscope of pills including Benzedrine, Dexedrine, Demerol, Dexamyl, Morphine, and Tuinals (nine at a time), not to mention drinking two bottles of bourbon, and smoking up to 150 Craven A cigarettes a day. Whenever she felt her voice was giving out from the assault, she merely sprayed her tonsils with a self-blended cocaine-based concoction.

This was a woman who couldn't stop partying under any circumstances—insisting on entertaining even while she was on the toilet or in the bath. A friend once remarked, "Tallulah can not only talk 'till the cows come home, but while they're being milked, given hay, put to bed in their stalls, and until they wake up the next morning."

Thanks to the national coverage radio offered, Tallu was once again big box office on the legit stage and on the road. "Tallulah's name on a contract is $250,000 in the bank," one of her theatrical producers was quoted as saying in 1950. Multiply that sum fifteen

"I'm as pure as the driven slush." —*Tallulah Bankhead*

times for today's dollars and you'll understand why Bankhead's peculiar eccentricities were indulged.

After triumphantly touring the country for several years in Noel Coward's *Private Lives*, Tallulah embarked on one of her greatest successes in 1950, hosting NBC Radio's *The Big Show*. This was a Sunday night, ninety-minute parade-of-stars spectacular with Tallulah front and center as mistress of ceremonies.

Weeks after signing for the series, Tallulah flew into a panic, convinced the show was going to be a career-ending debacle and that she would be constantly upstaged by the stellar guests. And if there's one thing Miss Bankhead could not countenance, it was being upstaged. She wrote in her unusually candid autobiography, "When I realized—the day before we went on the air—that I could be my old, dry caustic self, introducing my fellow stars, I decided to employ whatever wit was within me to cement the proceedings together."

The clever digs and often improvised dialogue between the acerbic host and her guests became the highlight of each broadcast:

MARLENE DIETRICH: "Tallulah, I wouldn't admit this to anyone else but one day last week I had lunch alone."

TALLULAH: "Nooooo! Well, if you think that's something, as long as you've opened up to me, I'll tell you something. One day, about a month ago, I had breakfast alone!"

Groucho Marx, Bob Hope, Judy Holliday, Jimmy Durante, Ethel Merman, Beatrice Lillie (to whom Tallulah sniped, "Your face looks like four yards of corduroy"), Clifton Webb, Louis Armstrong—practically every star in the universe went before the *Big Show* microphone. Tallulah (and the program) was a hit, managing the nearly impossible task of drawing an audience away from their brand-new TV sets. For her troubles, the star was pulling a cool salary of ten thousand dollars a week (20 percent of the show's entire budget).

In 1951, riding the crest of a new wave of popularity, Tallulah made the mistake of a lifetime by suing her former housekeeper for embezzlement. The trial turned into a '50s-style media circus with shocking allegations coming to light. "She was never sober, or rarely so," the housekeeper told the court, "She spent a fortune, enough to send your kids to college . . . on cocaine, marijuana, booze, and scotch, and champagne." She also testified that she had to roll Miss Bankhead's joints by the hundreds. Good help was *so* hard to find!

The housekeeper seized the opportunity to reveal as many lurid details of the actor's private life as possible and the tabloid movie mags had a field day. Never one to be outdone, Tallulah didn't hold back with reporters, saying at a press conference: "I'm glad to see there's a man here from the *New York Times* because if I say 'goddammit,' they will print it 'good heavens' or 'good gracious.'" When asked, "What is your opinion of love, Miss Bankhead?" she replied, "Love? Do you mean fucking?"

In his memoirs, film director Robert Lewis stated that, besides liquor and pot, Tallulah often partied with "some witch's brew concocted of Coca Cola and spirits of ammonia. For an additional high, she popped and sniffed some odd capsules that her sister Eugenia insisted were used to revive horses that slipped and fell on the winter ice."

"It's the good girls who keep diaries; the bad girls never have the time." —*Tallulah Bankhead*

As you might expect, her sex life was equally scandalous—at one time employing a full-time black gigolo (Tallulah was raised in segregationist Alabama) and bedding a cornucopia of Hollywood legends including Yul Brenner, John Barrymore, Greta Garbo, Billie Holliday, and Hattie McDaniel, who played the maid in *Gone With The Wind*. Her longest-lasting relationship was with fellow actor Estelle Winwood.

In the end, the lure of television proved too great. Radio was dying by 1952 when *The Big Show* was cancelled. Tallulah, however, had no trouble changing with the times and threw herself into ambitious new projects. NBC brought the *Big Show* concept to television with the *All-Star Revue* in 1952, featuring a rotating slate of hosts. Tallulah hosted five episodes during the second and last season. Soon after, she appeared on *The U.S. Steel Hour* in a rare dramatic production of Ibsen's *Hedda Gabler*. She was also seen at the Sands Hotel in Las Vegas in a musical revue and in several Broadway plays.

Tallulah Bankhead made a flurry of guest shots on television variety shows and comedy specials, generally spoofing her "Daaaahhling" image all throughout the '50s. Typical was a turn on *The Milton Berle Show*, where she demonstrated her ability to deliver catty comments like no one else:

BERLE: "Tallulah and I are great friends."

TALLULAH: "Of course we are, but not each other's." (Audience breaks up.)

BERLE: "Tallulah and I have come a long way . . ."

TALLULAH: "Yes, and you are to be particularly commended, Milton, because you started from so much further back!"

In 1957 alone, Tallulah appeared on more than a half-dozen different TV programs, from *Shower of the Stars* to *The Steve Allen Show* but it was her guest appearance that year on the second episode of the *Lucy-Desi Comedy Hour* that remains a TV classic to this day.

Bob Schiller, the writer of the episode, recounted in later years that Tallulah was drunk for the entire two-week rehearsal period, removing her panties for no reason and calling Vivian Vance "cunty." Still,

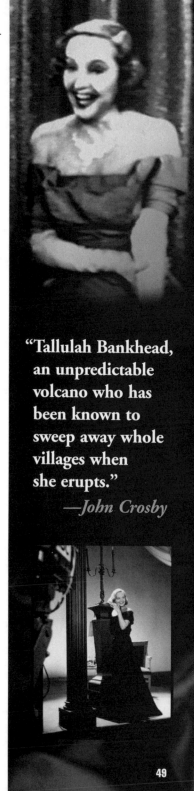

"Tallulah Bankhead, an unpredictable volcano who has been known to sweep away whole villages when she erupts."

—*John Crosby*

she delivered a flawless performance during filming, when it counted. Tallulah defended her behavior to the press: "They had this plot. They were living in Connecticut, or somewhere, and rehearsing a play for the PTA, whatever that is. I did have pneumonia at the time." The performers fought viciously all through rehearsals, but in true old-Hollywood fashion, Ms. Bankhead said this about working with Lucy: "She's divine to work with! And Desi! He's brilliant! He has a temper, however. But that's because he's fat. It worries him." (Insert cat noises here.)

In 1959, Tallulah appeared on the first episode of *The Big Party*, a flop CBS ninety-minute live variety show that alternated with *Playhouse 90*. That same year she signed a deal to do ten appearances on *The Ed Sullivan Show* for one hundred thousand dollars but quit after only one episode, steadfastly refusing to return the money that had been paid up front.

Tallulah concentrated mostly on theatrical productions in the early '60s, but by mid-decade failing health and severe alcoholism forced her to cut back on performing. As was the trend, she did a cheesy Hammer horror film for theatrical release in 1965. Following that were TV assignments on *The Andy Williams Show*, *What's My Line*, and *The Mike Douglas Show* in 1966, and *The Smothers Brothers Comedy Hour* and two episodes of *Batman* (as the murderous Black Widow) in 1967. Her very last appearance was on *The Tonight Show* in May 1968.

On *The Andy Williams Show*, looking older and more frail than previously, Tallulah was clearly in her cups. She had trouble lip-syncing the opening musical number and was a bit unsteady coming down the stairway for her grand entrance. Fortunately, as the dialogue unfurled between her and the host, Tallulah gained control. Her persona was so extreme, who could tell if she was messed up anyway?

TALLULAH: "I gave this party in honor of my friend, the Duchess of Marne; we're very good friends. Well, as a matter of fact, we're not very good friends, we just know too much about each other."

ANDY: "I danced with her earlier. She's wearing the largest diamond ring I've ever seen in my life."

TALLULAH: "She has to wear the largest diamond rings; look at those revolting knuckles!"

She was also seen on *The Merv Griffin Show* three times between 1966 and 1968. Griffin described one of Tallulah's appearances this way: "She was on the show with Margaret Truman, who at one point started discussing the reluctance of American women to reveal their age. 'I don't think we should make such a big thing about it,' she said, 'I'm quite willing to say that I'm forty-three years old.' Tallulah gasped, 'Oh please, dahling,' and pointed to the camera. 'People are eating!'"

Pneumonia, influenza, and emphysema killed Tallulah Bankhead in December 1968. The last words she mumbled were reported to be, ". . . codeine . . . bourbon."

"When I get hold of [Bette Davis], I'll tear every hair out of her mustache!" —*Tallulah Bankhead*

LIST*O*MANIA!

by Lypsinka

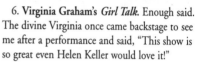

What is it about lists? There's the 100 greatest American films list. Then there's Modern Library's 100 greatest modern novels. And let's not forget Monica Lewinsky's unheeded laundry list.

Perhaps, here at the beginning of the millennium, lists represent a subconscious desire to sum up, to reflect on our cultural past. So, who am I to not join in? After all, I, the Fabulous Lypsinka, am the (Self-Anointed) Official Celebrity of the New Millennium!

Therefore, at TVparty's thoughtful request here is my extremely biased list of the twentieth century's ten greatest television moments.

Maybe some of you will agree.

1. **Vivian Vance's rendition of "I'm Lily of the Valley,"** complete with red-hot-mama coda, in the operetta episode of *I Love Lucy*—never fails to put a smile on my face.

2. **Tallulah Bankhead as the villainous Black Widow** on the mid-1960s *Batman*, garbling her lines and dragging her mink coat on the ground, cannot be topped.

3. **The "Models Amalgamated" scenes in the May 1995 Martin Short special**, parodying *Models, Inc.* Airing in the *Saturday Night Live* slot, it contained the most satisfying sketch comedy performances ever. Short appears as two characters: Lettie Hale (patterned after Bette Davis) and a vapid male model; and the brilliant Jan Hooks pops up in three roles—including Faye Dunaway and an insipid '90s bimbo who utters the immortal line, "Brittany, don't go there!"

4. *Pee-wee's Playhouse:* the most subversive, smartest show of the '80s.

5. *The Carol Burnett Show:* the Joan Crawford parody "Torchy Song," Harvey Korman as the Jewish yenta from next door on "As the Stomach Turns," and Carol, Lena Horne, and Marilyn Horne sing Sondheim's "You Could Drive a Person Crazy." (Did I dream that last one?!)

6. **Virginia Graham's** *Girl Talk.* Enough said. The divine Virginia once came backstage to see me after a performance and said, "This show is so great even Helen Keller would love it!"

7. **Anything Lily Tomlin has ever done.** Personal fave: Bobbi Jeannene, the airport lounge organist.

8. **Jacqueline Susann on** *Hollywood Squares.* I don't remember this appearance, but I'm thrilled to know it happened!

9. **Leslie Uggams's desperate, messy attempt** to cover up the fact she doesn't know the lyrics to "June Is Busting Out All Over," on a recent, lousy major network fourth of July spectacular, is always a party pleaser.

10. **The 1968 Academy Awards telecast**, the year *Oliver!* won for Best Picture, prompted an enormous show-biz endorphins high from which I've never recovered.

Honorable mention: Karen Morrow's rendition of "I Had a Ball" on *The Ed Sullivan Show*, Dolores Gray and Kay Thompson together on *The Milton Berle Buick Show*, Mitzi Gaynor dancing to "Turkey Lurkey Time" on one of her silly specials, Lucy as Mad Margo the interior decorator on *The Lucy Show*, Judy Garland's Christmas show (Liza's "beau!"), Pernell Roberts on *Bonanza* (meow!), and all the girls on *Laugh-In* dressed as Tiny Tim, complete with ukulele, singing "What's the News Across the Nation?"

Groucho
ON TELEVISION

"Hollywood is a place where people from Iowa mistake each other for stars. —*Fred Allen*

Halsman

From 1950 until 1961, legendary film comedian Groucho Marx ruled on NBC-TV Thursday nights with, of all things, a game show.

Broadcast on radio beginning in 1947, *You Bet Your Life* moved to television initially as a radio program with cameras. People tuned in to experience Groucho grilling the contestants; the game itself was almost inconsequential. In that era of big-money quiz shows (with many programs giving away hundreds of thousands in today's dollars), *You Bet Your Life* rarely gave away more than a few hundred bucks—and that was for a pair of contestants to split.

Groucho's TV show was almost cancelled before it began. The sponsor assumed when they signed the comic that he would appear in his familiar black frock coat and painted-on mustache, resembling the Quackenbush character from his films. When he refused to dress the part, DeSoto automobiles tried to pull the plug but discovered that there was no clause in the comedian's contract requiring him to wear a costume. "If I can't be funny on television without funny clothes and makeup, to hell with it" was Groucho's attitude.

The focus of *You Bet Your Life* was on the comedic banter between Groucho and the carefully selected and rehearsed contestants. Serving as referee and comic foil was commercial spokesperson George Fenneman. Often one of the contestants was a semi-famous person, an actor, writer, or sports personality, and all players had the opportunity to "Say the secret word and win a hundred dollars," at which point a papier-maché duck would drop down with the loot.

Groucho's quick wit and surefire delivery made for some of the funniest moments in television history, with much of the humor coming from the leering comments Groucho directed at the many gorgeous, well-endowed women who frequented the show.

GROUCHO: "Does your husband like his work?"

CONTESTANT: "Yes he likes it very much; he works nights and you'd be amazed what you can do when your husband works nights."

GROUCHO: "You might be amazed but I wouldn't!"

The series was a top-twenty smash right away, with Groucho Marx winning an Emmy in 1951 (the third year of the ceremonies) as "Most Outstanding Personality." Ratings rose over the next few years, fuelled by the enormous popularity of prime-time game shows in general. Groucho was cavalier about it all, remarking to a contestant during the program: "I don't care about the story you're going to tell, but I have no alternative but to sit here and listen to you. You see, I happen to be glued to the seat. I'm what they call the oldest stool pigeon in show business."

You Bet Your Life may have been a simple show to produce but it was expensive. Twenty-seven dollars towards the purchase price of every DeSoto car went to sup-

The Hollywood Palace was taped at the El Capitan Theatre in Los Angeles.

port the television show. Prize money increased over time to keep up with the competition, and other sponsors signed on as the seasons passed.

While fellow Marx brothers Chico and Harpo found employment hard to come by, a long-running TV series provided Groucho with the financial security and Hollywood power base his brothers lacked. Groucho made supporting appearances on many other television shows and landed starring roles in several movies and special productions (such as his version of *The Mikado*), and even published a few books and magazine articles under his byline during the '50s and early '60s.

You Bet Your Life was the fourth most popular TV show in the nation from 1953 to 1956 and a solid top-ten hit in 1958 when a massive quiz show scandal rocked the nation, casting aspersions over any and all game formats. Although Groucho's show was really more of a chat show disguised as a game, the scandal and a move to a later timeslot caused ratings to drop precipitously.

In the fall of 1960, the series was revamped and re-titled *The Groucho Show*, a move meant to further distance it from the sensational headlines generated by the rampant cheating uncovered on top TV games *The $64,000 Question*, *Twenty-One*, *Dotto*, and others. Changes instituted on *The Groucho Show* were mostly cosmetic. For instance, whenever a contestant uttered the secret word, lovely Marylin Burtis was lowered down on a swing with cash in hand. On one episode, Harpo Marx descended from the swing to the delight of the studio audience. Despite stunts and special guests, NBC cancelled the series in 1961.

Giving in to public demand, NBC reversed their decision in January 1962 and returned Groucho to Thursday nights in a familiar format, a game called *Tell It to Groucho*. To avoid even the appearance of impropriety, the top prize was a mere five hundred dollars, which a contestant won by recognizing a celebrity photo puzzle at the end of the match.

Groucho explained the concept this way: "I am doing a new show which is precisely the same as the old show except that we have traded Mr. Fenneman for a sprightly young doll with oversized knockers who leaps around the stage with all the abandon of a young doe being pursued by an elderly banker." The emphasis here was even more on Groucho's charm but, after much fanfare, *Tell It To Groucho* was gone by summer. Quiz shows in any form had fallen completely out of favor with the disillusioned viewing public.

After his series was cancelled, the comic guest-hosted *The Tonight Show* after Jack Paar left the program and just before Johnny Carson began his decades-long run. Groucho was being considered for a permanent hosting role, but this was deemed impractical since he was already seventy-two years old at the time. Still, Groucho introduced Johnny on his first outing and was Carson's first *Tonight Show* guest.

Groucho could be seen on a number of musical comedy broadcasts in the mid-'60s, including *The Perry Como Show*, *The Jackie Gleason Show*, and *Kraft Music Hall*. One memorable *Hollywood Palace* episode in 1965 had Groucho hosting with Margaret Dumont as one of his special guests. Dumont played the stuffy dowager in several Marx Brothers movies and together they recreated one of their classic scenes. This was a rare TV appearance for Dumont and her very last—she died before it aired, just a few days after the program was filmed.

"Go to your nearest DeSoto Dealer and tell him Groucho sent you."

Preferring variety and talk programs where he could improvise and didn't have to learn lines, Marx's only sitcom appearances were on single episodes of *I Dream of Jeannie* in 1967 and *Julia* (as Doctor Hackenbush) in 1969.

By this point, Groucho was becoming somewhat feeble and more difficult to deal with. One of his last, best appearances came on *The Dick Cavett Show* in the summer of 1969. Groucho suffered a series of small strokes that summer, but, because the show was taped earlier, viewers tuning in the Cavett show saw Marx in fine form, telling funny stories, dropping sharp non sequiturs, and singing "Hello, I Must Be Going," "Father's Day," and "Lydia the Tattooed Lady," a particularly strenuous song-and-dance number.

The comedian reminisced about his childhood in New York and his motion picture days, telling Cavett: "We made eighteen, nineteen pictures. I don't mean that's the year we made them, 1819 . . . You know they used to have men put the body makeup on the women? And then the unions got on to that and stopped it. Somebody stopped it, I think it was the vice squad."

He also told stories he later used in his live performances: "I had a priest stop me up in Montreal some years ago, and he comes up to me and says, 'Aren't you Groucho Marx?' and I said, 'yes' and he says, 'May I shake your hand?' and I said 'fine' and I shook hands with him and he says, 'I want to thank you for all the joy you put in the world' and I said, 'And I want to thank you for all the joy you've taken out of it!'"

Originally filmed for a thirty-minute slot, the response to the airing was so great that Cavett presented the unedited film a few weeks later, filling an entire hour. Groucho also put in an appearance on ABC's *The Music Scene* later that summer.

After a failed Broadway show based on his childhood (written by his son Arthur in 1970) and some outrageous public comments in 1971 (joking that Nixon should be assassinated, for example), many in Hollywood were convinced that eighty-year-old Groucho Marx was unemployable.

A comeback of sorts came to Groucho in the form of a mini concert tour that began with a rousing sold-out show at Carnegie Hall in 1972. An LP recording of the performance (*Groucho at Carnegie Hall*) was released; it preserves a remarkable evening with the comedian reprising his greatest hits and bits. At the same time, Groucho was becoming an underground icon on college campuses, with Marx Brothers movies being rediscovered on television and at on-campus screenings, in addition to Groucho's face staring down from posters on dorm-room walls all over the country.

Suddenly Groucho was a hot property again, thanks to his much younger and oh-so-ambitious manager/companion Erin Fleming. Introduced by the producer of TV's *The Odd Couple* in 1970, the unemployed actor and the doddering old superstar bonded immediately. Before long, Fleming moved into Groucho's home and took over all of his personal and business affairs, using her newfound proximity to stardom to push for greater visibility for her client—and promote herself.

You Bet Your Life was one of the few game shows to be filmed.

55

Sadly, Groucho's health was failing just as his popularity was rising, and the concerts amounted to little more than the old guy standing at a podium reading breathlessly from cue cards while pianist Marvin Hamlisch did his best to prod and cover for him. Groucho suffered another stroke just weeks after completing all but one of his live commitments, but bounced back with a funny guest shot on *The New Bill Cosby Show* in 1972. TVpartyer Ernie A. Mehaffey remembers that special episode: "At the top of the show, Bill came out to announce he had a very special guest star, Groucho Marx. Then he did a monologue about going to the movies when he was a kid which he ended by putting on a fake mustache and eyebrows and walking around the stage doing some of Groucho's best known lines. At the end of this routine, the real Groucho joined him and sang 'Hello, I Must Be Going.'

"At one point, Groucho looks at Bill and says 'You smoke cigars, I see.' Bill replies that he really became interested in cigars because of Groucho. Groucho replies, 'They're a handy thing to have for a comedian—assuming, of course, you are a comedian!'"

Not so successful was a concert in December of that year at the Dorothy Chandler Pavilion in Los Angeles. The performance was filmed for a television special, but the excruciating footage was deemed unusable. The stroke he suffered months earlier left Groucho hazy and incoherent much of the time onstage, but the packed audience cheered him on enthusiastically anyway.

At eighty-five, Groucho was awarded a special Oscar in 1974 but he was growing noticeably weaker. Accepting the coveted gold statue and a standing ovation from his peers, he publicly thanked Erin Fleming, saying it was she who "makes my life worth living and who understands my jokes." That year, reruns of *You Bet Your Life* entered syndication and a flurry of books were printed about the comedian. Fleming began to give lavish parties and small get-togethers in Groucho's home where Hollywood's biggest celebrities, writers, and producers would drop by and pay homage to the sometimes barely conscious comic—and hear a pitch from Fleming about her suitability for their latest project.

There was a sad glimpse of a befuddled Groucho when he turned up as a presenter on the 1975 Emmy Awards telecast with a wigged-out Lucille Ball (who had just been sadistically told backstage that her son was dead). His appearance on a star-studded Bob Hope special appearing alongside George Burns and a *Merv Griffin Show* in 1976 were his last on television. On the Hope show, writers had to have Billy Barty in a Groucho get-up hovering around so that the audience would remember who this feeble man was. Groucho could barely breathe his lines, the funniest being: "Am I having fun yet?" Was he?

That same year, a walk-on part was prepared for Groucho on *Welcome Back Kotter*, but he backed out of the filming at the last minute, instead putting in an awkward appearance on the set to have his picture taken with the Sweathogs. Groucho was so

Groucho's son Arthur wrote *My Life with Groucho* in 1988.

fragile that the studio audience didn't recognize him when he was helped onstage to sit in Mr. Kotter's chair for the cast photo. The pictures were never released. The sight of the shrunken, pitiful legend being led around by Erin Fleming that day greatly disturbed several of the cast members, especially Robert Hegyes, whose character Epstein often imitated Groucho on the hit series. "How can I go out and make people laugh after seeing that?" was his stunned reaction. There was another aborted guest-shot when Erin and Groucho walked out during the middle of a *Donny and Marie* taping in September 1976, leaving home viewers wondering why they caught a brief glimpse of Groucho Marx in the show's finale. Or was that his ghost?

While many people felt Erin Fleming was too aggressive in pushing Groucho to perform, she undoubtedly helped him reach a whole new audience by putting his face before the public. Even if that face was barely recognizable and the voice a scarce whisper.

Did she go too far? Groucho's son Arthur sued to have Fleming removed as his father's caretaker in 1976, believing he was being unfairly manipulated by an opportunistic, failed actor. Groucho dispelled these accusations in the press and in court, but Arthur Marx felt the comic was being forced to perform against his will while being physically threatened and abused. A trial was held to determine a conservator over the fading, now bedridden comedian. Ex-employees and household staff testified about Fleming's violent temper and psychologically abusive manner. Narcotics and used syringes found on the grounds of Groucho's estate led to tabloid headlines and talk of Fleming's supposed drug use, along with opening up the possibility that she was drugging her charge.

Fleming lost the case and control over Groucho during the last few months of his life. Groucho Marx died in August 1977 from complications due to pneumonia.

Lawsuits tied up the money Erin Fleming claimed was due to her for managing Groucho's career. In 1983, a motion was filed alleging that Fleming abused her client and therefore was not entitled to monies already paid to her—and besides, she wasn't a licensed talent manager. Celebrities including George Burns, Carroll O'Connor, Bud Cort, and George Fenneman, along with Groucho's family and household staff, paraded before Judge Weiss to testify about the last time they saw Groucho. Some had nice things to say about Fleming and her treatment of the comedian; most didn't. Because of her theatrical courtroom demeanor (like angrily telling the judge, "There is nothing wrong with me. YOU might have a few problems!") and in spite of being represented by superstar attorney Melvin Belli, Erin Fleming lost and was ordered to pay over two hundred thousand dollars in damages to the Marx estate—money she didn't have.

Erin Fleming resurfaced in 1990 when she was arrested with a .357 Magnum in a bizarre incident that took place in the West Hollywood Police Station. By mid-decade she was reportedly in and out of mental institutions and seen living like a street person, bumming spare change from her former show business friends in Hollywood and accepting handouts from area restaurants.

Erin Fleming had a small role in Woody Allen's *Everything You Ever Wanted to Know About Sex (But Were Afraid to Ask)*.

PLAYBOY

Playboy magazine, which began publishing in 1953, was enjoying robust sales in the '80s. To expand the empire, founder Hugh Hefner launched a subscription-based cable component, the Playboy Channel. It quickly became one of the first subscription cable TV success stories.

Not as well-known is the fact that there were two earlier attempts by Hefner to create a television spinoff of his famous magazine. While neither caught on in a big way, both were critical and audience hits with unique formats that presented timeless performances by some of the greatest comedians, jazz, soul, and be-bop artists of all time.

Hefner's first nationally televised series, *Playboy's Penthouse*, premiered on October 24, 1959. Produced in the studios of WBKB-TV in Chicago, the program was syndicated to a loose network of stations across the country that specifically signed up for the show. The format was modelled on a hip, swinging bachelor party, the kind of bash where cool people could lounge in their cocktail clothes and exchange ideas. Beat poets, writers, comics, and musical immortals like Ella Fitzgerald, Cy Coleman (composer of the *Playboy* theme song), Nat "King" Cole, Sarah Vaughn, the Limelighters, and Harry Belafonte mingled in an impromptu fashion with Hef and his assembled party-goers.

There hadn't really been anything like *Playboy's Penthouse* on television. From a historical perspective, this may be the first national program where whites and blacks sat down and partied as equals.

Hef's first "Penthouse Party" (as the show was also known early on) featured raucous comedian Lenny Bruce, a controversial choice. It was rare for any TV production to book the up-and-coming nightclub comic because of his rambling delivery and outspoken views on race, religion and politics. Hugh Hefner was making a point on his very first outing; these were subjects *never* touched upon in '50s television culture. *Playboy* helped bring Lenny Bruce from the small clubs to the mass marketplace with this TV segment and through publishing Bruce's autobiography *How to Talk Dirty and Influence People* after serializing it in the magazine beginning in 1964. Hefner and Lenny Bruce discussed the format of *Playboy's Penthouse* on that first program:

BRUCE: "This is a kind of a . . . an interesting party. You know, I first figured it would be like, sort of a TV, you know, a typical fake party. But

The first three issues of *Playboy* were produced in Hugh Hefner's Hyde Park apartment.

AFTER DARK

it's got a good party feeling to it, with some pretty chicks, which is a good composite."

HEFNER: "Well, [we have] the girls and we serve real liquor . . . it does the trick."

BRUCE: "You think you'll get any objection to drinking on the show? I don't think I've ever seen that on a show."

HEFNER: "Well, we'll find out. We hope not."

BRUCE: "That's what grooved me about the show. That it's an honest . . . it's actually a party. So whatever happens at a party, within, you know, limitations . . ."

HEFNER: "Well, (laughs) we're trying to build the personality of the show out of the magazine itself and make the thing a sort of a sophisticated weekly get-together of the people that we dig and the people who dig us."

This telecast provided an opportunity for a larger audience to see and hear what Lenny Bruce had to say for himself, rather than read what other people were saying about him in the newspapers (especially after a series of obscenity and drug busts that began in 1961).

The musicians that dropped by usually engaged in conversation with Hef to start out, peppering their talk with musical asides; then an intimate and lengthy concert segment would follow. For instance, folk singer Pete Seeger talked extensively about the roots of popular music in the United States, singing some early and quaint examples of the art. Throughout his expansive musical discourse, Seeger took pot-shots at corruption in Congress and the ubiquity of brand names.

Hefner was not your typical slick TV host; he had a nervous, disarming quality that worked to the benefit of the proceedings. He was smart enough not to hire a professional to headline, revealing in a 1959 interview, "If we did the thing our-selves, and the viewers could meet me as a human being every week, then hopefully they would begin to discover, those people who did not read *Playboy*, well, son of a gun, this guy isn't a dirty old man."

Playboy's Penthouse ran for two seasons (re-syndicated in 1963) and helped extend the magazine's image as a source of sophisticated, diverse entertainment. Shortly after filming the premier season's episodes, Hefner opened the first Playboy Club in Chicago and moved into the first Playboy Mansion.

Skip ahead to January of 1969. With magazine sales topping 5.5 million a month, Hefner (then forty-two) again entered the television arena with *Playboy after Dark*, a 26-week color version of his earlier series. Once again the party format was carried forward, with an elaborate thirty-five-thousand-dollar bachelor pad set built for the series on a CBS Hollywood soundstage, complete with a den, sunken living room, and curvaceous bar. Twenty girls and nineteen guys (guess who gets *two* girls) pro-vided the atmosphere and mingled with the exceptional guest stars.

Film producer Allan Carr (*Grease*) was the Talent Coordinator for *Playboy's Penthouse*.

Playboy after Dark again had Cy Coleman's jazzy theme and once again viewers were given a chance to hear discussions on a wide variety of subjects that were taboo on other talk/variety shows, and to see entertainers shunned (or outright blacklisted) on the tube. The program also provided a way for Hefner to get some face time with the magazine's growing audience. "Fame is as meaningful to me as fortune" was his revealing quote to the press in 1969.

Guest stars on *Playboy after Dark* (surrounded by the ubiquitous Playboy Bunnies) included Marvin Gaye, The Checkmates, improv group the Committee, Janis Ian, the Byrds, Buddy Greco, Shari Lewis (in her post-Lambchop, adult comic days), Pat Henry, and others.

Lenny Bruce's eccentric mother, former stripper Sally Marr, appeared on the opening episode as part of a tribute to her son (who had died three years earlier). Included were clips of Lenny from the first episode of *Playboy's Penthouse* a decade earlier, almost as if to say, "The party's still on—welcome back!"

Ratings were high overall for *Playboy after Dark*, but the show was cleared for broadcast in only twenty-three cities, not enough to ultimately warrant continuation. It was successful in attracting new magazine readers, however—sales of *Playboy* peaked at over seven million copies a month by 1971.

Ironically, while the *Playboy* name translated into viewers in the cities that ran the show, it made it difficult to get airplay in the Midwest and South. Many stations couldn't carry the show because the brand name meant smut to older, more conservative audiences.

This television production provided an opportunity for Hef to get out of his Chicago digs and shake things up in Los Angeles. He liked it so much, he decided to make LA his base of operations in 1971, purchasing the now-famous Playboy Mansion West in the Holmby Hills. Like Batman changing Batcaves, Hefner became an LA party-scene fixture from that point on.

Hugh Hefner, ever modest, had this to say in 1969 about *Playboy after Dark*: "It's better than the Johnny Carson show or the Joey Bishop show and I do a better job hosting than Ed Sullivan does."

Perhaps Hef can do us all a favor and revive the show again!

Pete Seeger (above) was virtually banned from network television for his unpopular views.

KIDS, TV & GUNS

Some modern-day experts contend that violent video games encourage savage behavior in our young people, while others say that's just another example of the latest entertainment medium becoming society's scapegoat *du jour*. Keep in mind, the same breed of expert said the exact same thing about comic books in the 1950s—and look at how great the baby boomers turned out.

Long before technology gave us realistic video games that allowed kids to simulate predatory gun fighting electronically, America's children took to backyards and playgrounds with toy cap guns to battle it out in the neighborhood. Playing army or cowboys and indians in the dirt was how many American kids spent their playtime in decades past.

When did this behavior start? Perhaps at the beginning of recorded history, in the 1950s. Cowboys like Roy Rogers, Gene Autry, Hopalong Cassidy, and the Lone Ranger ruled the daytime TV airwaves, attracting a legion of kids who wanted to play shoot-em-up at home. Not a problem, since all of the television cowboys and detectives had their own line of realistic-looking toy firearms for sale at the nearest dime store. And best of all—no pesky background checks!

The most popular western cap gun sets of the '50s were Mattel's Fanner 50 realistic Winchester rifle, Buc'N Bronco, and the Hubley pistols.

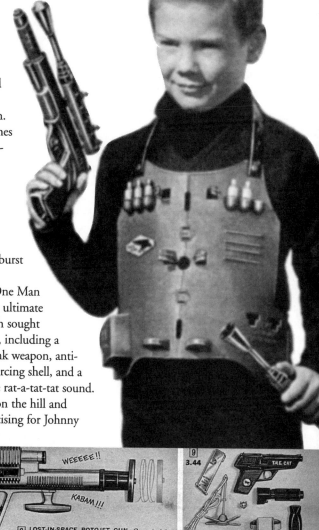

When cowboys and pistol-waving detectives started to lose favor in the early-'60s, toy gun lines lost their key salespersons and innovative products had to be created from scratch. Products with catchy names like the TommyBurst sub-machine gun, Remco's Monkey Division (for "jungle warfare" with two-way wrist radios), Secret Sam, and the Fan-O-matic (with Greenie Stick-M caps for ammo) burst onto the market.

Johnny Seven OMA (One Man Army) by Topper was the ultimate killing machine and much sought after—with seven actions, including a grenade launcher, anti-tank weapon, anti-bunker missile, armor-piercing shell, and a detachable pistol with the rat-a-tat-tat sound.

"Just position yourself on the hill and attack!" invited the advertising for Johnny

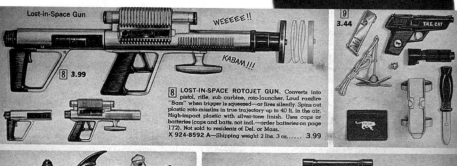

Lost-in-Space Gun

WEEEEE!!

KABAM!!!

8 3.99

8 LOST-IN-SPACE ROTOJET GUN. Converts into pistol, rifle, sub carbine, roto-launcher. Loud ramfire "Bam" when trigger is squeezed—or fires silently. Spins out plastic roto-missiles in true trajectory up to 40 ft. in the air. High-impact plastic with silver-tone finish. Uses caps or batteries (caps and batts. not incl.—order batteries on page 172). Not sold to residents of Del. or Mass.
X 924-8592 A—Shipping weight 2 lbs. 3 oz..... 3.99

9 3.44   T.H.E. CAT

10 4.44

11 2.44

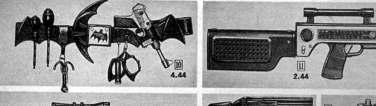

12 10.88

13 3.88

14 2.99

Eagle, another of Topper's most popular toy gun lines from the mid-'60s. The brand included the Red River, Mugambo, and Lieutenant lines. The ad campaigns flashed iconographic images of kids with their weapons drawn, firing down from the hill against a catchy jingle set to the tune of "When Johnny Comes Marching Home." These handsome rifle and pistol sets could be wall mounted on their own simulation wood-grained plaques.

Another highly effective toy campaign was for an all-purpose weapon called Zero-M from Mattel. Who wouldn't want a portable radio or camera that turns into a rapid-firing weapon? Sure comes in handy in music class. Back then you didn't expect the electronics to actually work (and they didn't) as long as the gun fired.

In the Zero-M TV commercials, a boy, portrayed by a young Kurt Russell, is summoned by a secret society hidden in his bedroom closet. The old guys in the closet, led by Alfred from the *Batman* series, instruct Kurt to go out into the community armed to the teeth to do their bidding (see also: *Escape From New York*). Needless to say, modern

attel's new M-16 Marauder
..u think this gun looks great, wait'll you hear it!

BRAAP
BRRA-A-A-AP
BRAP
BRAP

WOW! Here's the most authentic-looking and sounding rifle you've ever seen!

Just pull back the cocking lever and this amazing gun is ready to fire. Brap! You can squeeze off single shots. Brra-a-a-ap! Or short bursts.

And listen to this! Keep cocking the fantastic M-16 Marauder and you can cut loose with a solid blast almost a whole minute long! Over 50 rounds! And all with the loud, realistic sound of the actual M-16 rifle!

And another neat thing about Mattel's new M-16 — it doesn't need any caps! No batteries either! You never reload!

So get on target. Get Mattel's new M-16 rifle. It's the greatest!

See and hear Mattel's M-16 Marauder at your nearest toy store today.

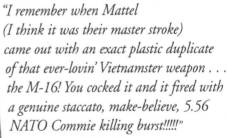

"I remember when Mattel (I think it was their master stroke) came out with an exact plastic duplicate of that ever-lovin' Vietnamster weapon . . . the M-16! You cocked it and it fired with a genuine staccato, make-believe, 5.56 NATO Commie killing burst!!!!!"

—J. Michael Elliott

kids would never fall for a setup like that. They don't listen to adults.

When you talk about fearsome weapons of mass destruction, red-blooded American boys could easily obtain the mother of all artillery weapons—Big Bertha. Easy to find because it was sold exclusively in grocery stores (the next frontier for retail handgun sales, I predict). During the Vietnam era, war toys like these were very popular, getting kids used to the inevitability of being drafted after they finished school. You'll notice they're popular again.

Realistic toy guns were pulled off the market in the '70s due to parent group protests and the fact that children were being tragically gunned down by police who thought they were armed with real weapons. Guns started to become very politically incorrect in the media as well, with the Vietnam War being over and us losing and all.

Dads (fresh from the killing fields) were only too happy to share their knowledge of guns with their children. I mean, if you were a carpenter, wouldn't you show your kid how a hammer works? If parents feel that their children deserve to play Army man just like they did as kids, why shouldn't they give them real automatic weapons if the toy guns are no longer available?

Was this a turning point for American kids? Considering the recent wave of misanthropic but well-armed kids shooting up the hallowed halls of our high schools, is it possible that, by taking away the realistic toy guns, we've encouraged our children to pick up the real thing for fun and games? Consider this fact: there are millions of guns in the United States but almost no episodes of *Romper Room* in existence. (That's called juxtaposing two unrelated facts to create an illusion of profundity—politicians do it all the time . . .)

Alfalfa, 'Our Gang' Star, is Killed In Fight With Friend Over $50 De...

"Are you a Little Rascals *fan? I'm a huge fan of Carl 'Alfalfa' Switzer and recently I have been doing research on him in regards to his murder.*

"I have in my possession some newspaper articles from the time that clearly show that Alfalfa may have been unarmed at the time of his murder—contrary to the popular belief that he pulled a knife on the accused murderer.

"I'm on a mission to show other Alfalfa fans that he may have been murdered in cold blood and possibly a smoke screen and cover-up were created to hide the truth as to the real reason why he was murdered. There seems to be a growing number of Alfalfa fans who agree with me."

—LAscandals

Ask someone how Alfalfa died and he'll probably tell you that he was shot to death in a bar over a drug deal—that's the story heard most often.

HOW WAS CARL "ALFALFA" SWITZER KILLED?

Several generations grew up with the *Our Gang* kids, the stars of dozens of short subjects produced in the '30s by the Hal Roach Studios. These black-and-white films enjoyed a whole new life on television from the '50s until the late '70s. Stations used them to fill holes in their early morning and Sunday schedules and on their locally hosted children's programs.

Watching the *Our Gang* comedies today, you might be struck by how decrepit and dingy everything was in the '30s. These Little Rascals were kids of the depression playing in their natural environment—and life was not pretty back then!

Spanky, Darla, Buckwheat, Alfalfa, and the gang were part of the very first wave of juvenile stars the entertainment industry ever produced, and they faced some of the same problems their television counterparts would encounter decades later.

In that context, I was intrigued when I received a package of newspaper clippings from someone calling herself "LAscandals." This collection of material told the story of a desperate North Hollywood resident who died an ignominious death in 1959.

Here's the part of the story that no one disputes—M.S. (Bud) Stiltz shot Carl "Alfalfa" Switzer to death in the Mission Hills home of famous cowboy star "Crash" Corrigan's ex-wife. The details of what really happened that night depend on who you ask.

THE STORY BUD STILTZ TOLD

Stiltz told the UPI that Alfalfa came to his ranch-style LA Valley home on January 23, 1959, with friend Jack Piott and started beating angrily on the door. Stiltz opened the door and Alfalfa raged, "I want the fifty bucks you owe me and I mean now!" A violent argument ensued; Switzer grabbed a glass-domed clock and smashed it on Stiltz's head.

According to Stiltz, Mrs. Corrigan had her three children in the house and they all ran to a neighbor's house at this point. Stiltz grabbed a gun from the dresser. When Alfalfa went for it, the gun went off. Switzer briefly gained possession of the gun but Stiltz wrestled it back. At that point, Carl "Alfalfa" Switzer drew a knife and screamed, "I'm going to kill you!"

Stiltz told a UPI reporter, "I took the gun away from Alfalfa and he threw the knife at me, that's when I shot him." A knife was found beside the body.

WHAT DID THE OTHER WITNESSES SAY?

That's what the killer had to say, but what did other witnesses to the altercation report that night? Remember, Switzer arrived at the home with a friend, still photographer Jack Piott. Piott stated in the papers that the two went over to Stiltz' home to collect a debt, but that Carl Switzer was unarmed at the time. He had no knife with him, according to Piott.

Odd, because Stiltz told a strange story about that knife—one that stretched credibility (but covered his ass more completely) when he testified before the coroner's jury on January 26. Stiltz stated: "Alfie charged me with a jackknife. I was forced to shoot, and he closed the knife as he fell to the floor." A convenient explanation as to why the knife was found under Switzer's body—with no blade exposed. Was it placed there to support a self-defense plea?

The coroner's jury ruled the death "justifiable homicide." LAscandals thinks drugs were involved: "There are a few reasons why I believe that Carl Switzer was into the drug scene. First, a drive-by shooting the year before when Switzer suffered a flesh wound by an unknown assailant in front of the Wolf's Den in Studio City. His physical deterioration was evident between 1957 and 1958. Carl actually looks like a strung-out junkie in some scenes from his final movie, *The Defiant Ones.* Third, I'm clairvoyant and I've had psychic contact with Carl Switzer's spirit (I'm not bullshitting you). Fourth, Alfie's father swore at the coroner's inquest that Stiltz had threatened Alfie with death before he went over to collect the money. The real question may be, how much methamphetamines could fifty dollars buy someone back in 1959?"

A reference in Kenneth Anger's epic *Hollywood Babylon* states that Alfalfa was killed in a dope burn. Did Anger know something that police (or the press) didn't know? Very likely, when you consider that the book was written in 1959, and Anger was a Hollywood insider.

"You are free to do whatever you like. You need only face the consequences." —Sheldon Kopp

If drugs were a key factor, that begs other questions. Was Carl's death really the result of that struggle or cold blooded murder? Did the police do a thorough investigation?

The true story about anything concerning almost any star would have been difficult to ascertain in those days. The LAPD was more than willing to bow to pressure from the city's biggest employer, the entertainment industry. LAscandals also points out that Interstate Television Distribution was making millions on the syndication rights to the *Little Rascals*, and a "Drugs and Murder" headline would have seriously degraded that property's value just when the films were becoming massively popular on television.

WHAT WAS "ALFALFA" LIKE?

One thing's for sure: Alfie was no angel. Children's TV historian Kevin S. Butler tells TVparty: "Alfalfa abused a lot of people during the filming of the *Our Gang* and *Little Rascals* comedies at Hal Roach Studios and later at MGM. Before they died, "Spanky" McFarland and Darla Hood told me of the cruel pranks Alfalfa used to play on them.

"Alfie once put sharp fish hooks in Spanky's back pants pockets and poor Spanky had to have stitches placed on his tush. Alfie put an open switchblade knife in his pocket and tricked Darla into putting her hand into his pocket on the pretense that he had a ring for her from a Crackerjack box. She almost lost her fingers.

"According to a story on the E! Entertainment TV series *Mysteries and Scandals*, some of the surviving *L.R.* kids, Rev. Waldo Kaye, Jerry Tucker, Tommy 'Butch' Bond, and Sidney 'Woim' Kibrick stated that Alfie would not pay attention to his school lessons in Mrs. Fern Carter's class. He'd be kept after school often and kept everyone waiting on the set of the films.

"Spanky told me of Alfie's worst and most stupidly dangerous stunt. When they were filming a scene for *The Big Premiere* at MGM, the staging called for the kids to show their own movie on a process screen. The rear projection system and the lights (with a thousand watts per bulb) were taking a long time to set up, so Alfie decided to use his time by going behind the screen and peeing on the bulbs. This is extremely hazardous, for even spitting on those bulbs is tantamount to setting off series of bombs. The lights exploded and filled the studio with a hideous stench. Everyone had to be taken off of the set as the crew and director fixed the bulbs and cleaned up the mess that Alfalfa created that day.

"Because of his obnoxious behavior, maybe the authorities and the press decided not to dig further into Alfalfa's death even though he may have died tragically. In a sense, I don't feel too sorry for Alfalfa because of the way he abused people. Who could have become his friend during his lifetime?"

Life after stardom was rough for Carl Switzer, and roles were hard to come by. Darla Hood described producer's reactions whenever he would audition for a part; "They used to say to him 'Hey, Alfalfa, sing off key for us.' It used to drive him crazy."

A life of alcohol abuse and minor brushes with the law followed. Carl Switzer was convicted of stealing trees from the Sequoia National Forest and selling them for Christmas trees in 1958. He was given a suspended thirty-day sentence, fined $225 and put on probation for a year—but Alfie would be lying in the morgue just a few weeks later.

40 YEARS LATER, A WITNESS SPEAKS

In 2000, a new witness came forward to finally clear up the facts in this case—Tom Corrigan, Bud Stiltz's stepson. Remember, he was there in the living room that deadly night. Four decades later he decided to talk about what he saw.

Tom, son of cowboy star Ray "Crash" Corrigan, was only fourteen years old on January 21, 1959, when the violent confrontation between his stepfather and Carl Switzer broke out. Tom was friends with Alfie, they had known each other for years, and his story differs greatly from Stiltz's self-serving alibi. Tom Corrigan said it looked like just plain murder to him. "He didn't have to kill him."

According to Tom, Alfalfa was drunk when his mother, Rita Corrigan, opened the door, but Stiltz was waving the .38-caliber revolver when Alfalfa first entered the living room. During a struggle, the gun went off and Tom was grazed by a plaster fragment or bullet. The fighting stopped when everyone realized the kid was hurt.

Young Tom Corrigan stepped outside and things got quiet. He didn't see the exact moment of impact but heard the unexpected shot, turning just in time to witness Alfie with a shocked look on his face, sliding down the wall. It was then that Corrigan saw the small penknife, which he assumed fell to the floor, closed, out of Switzer's pocket.

Only by begging for his life was Alfie's companion Jack Piott not killed also (he had cracked the glass dome over Stiltz's head in the initial struggle, not Switzer, Corrigan claims).

Why didn't Tom come forward sooner? A statement detailing this chain of events was taken from the teenager in 1959. Though fearful of his abusive stepfather, the youngster agreed to testify truthfully but was never called. Stiltz was easily exonerated.

The kicker to Tom's story: every Christmas (until his death in 1984) Bud Stiltz received a holiday card signed "Alfie."

And that's how every Hollywood mystery should end—with another mystery.

There is a picture of a hunting dog on Alfalfa's grave that someone defaced to look like Petey, the mutt from *The Little Rascals*.

Memorable Kid Shows of the '50s & '60s

*These daily excursions
into the subconscious were the
original electronic babysitters
for the first generation
raised on television.*

"PLUNK YOUR MAGIC TWANGER, FROGGY!"

"I dearly remember what must have been the lowest budget network kid show, *Andy's Gang*! Yep, that's Andy Devine, doing his endearing, big-hearted best with a bleacher full of kids, a table, some smoke bombs, hand puppets, and live animals dressed up and jerked around with wires!

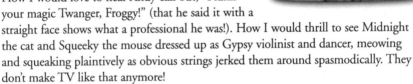

"Maybe somewhere there are some kinescopes? How I would love to hear Andy call out, "Plunk your magic Twanger, Froggy!" (that he said it with a straight face shows what a professional he was!). How I would thrill to see Midnight the cat and Squeeky the mouse dressed up as Gypsy violinist and dancer, meowing and squeaking plaintively as obvious strings jerked them around spasmodically. They don't make TV like that anymore!

"Even some history would be interesting. How did Andy get stuck doing the show? How many Squeekys did they run through? DID Andy keep a straight face? Does anyone but me remember this? Was it as bizarre as I remember? Did it really exist? After all, I was really young when I saw it. And then I did the '60s, and, well, you know . . . And NO ONE I have ever mentioned it to remembers it!"

—*Jerry*

"Thank you, thank you for proving that I'm NOT nuts! I've been telling my husband and kids for years about this 'horror' called Froggy. My husband, who has a superb memory of everything TV, couldn't recall the show when he was a kid so he thought I was making it up or was having some sort of weird '50s hallucination. My kids just thought it was too bizarre to be real!

"Yes! It was as weird as we all imagined. The Froggy voice has been the subject of my kiddy nightmares. It was an absolutely frightening and disconcerting show for children to watch. Was it an early attempt at brainwashing? Was it a cult? All I know is that it was so weird and frightening to me that I must have blocked it out.

"And for that matter, what is a 'Magic Twanger' anyway? Sounds obscene to me!"

—C Martin

"I'm baaack! See 'ya in your dreams, Mrs. Martin!"

"There I was walking down the isle of an antique mall when I passed a creature that lured me back to the locked display case. I gazed into the case and almost hidden in the corner was Froggy. It must have been a subliminal message sent out by the frog who can only be remembered by someone whose birthday is in the '40s. I walked away saying, "Plunk that magic twanger, Froggy!" . . . and the next thing that occurred was a flood of suppressed memories poured out of being captivated by the old frog with Andy Devine.

"I walked away a mature man not letting that frog lure me back. I checked out the rest of the displays and was drawn back to Mr. Froggy's temporary home. No way was that frog going to tell me what to do and, being an empty nester, I had no intentions whatsoever to take the responsibility of bringing home another pet. I survived the United States Marine Corps, thirty years as a police detective, and no friggin' way was this frog coming back into my life . . . I am now the proud owner of a rubber Froggy who, by the way is looking over my shoulder as I write this confession . . ."

—Ed Duvall

"I am looking for a newspaper editorial—it could've also been in a magazine— written in the late '60s about the kid's TV show *Andy's Gang* in which the writer blames Froggy for causing the protest movement of the '60s. He said Froggy's disrespectful behavior towards adults, which he demonstrated every show, influenced the kids who were watching him and those kids grew up to become the protesting college students of the '60s who likewise showed disrespect towards their elders."

—Jeff Ohiowa89

"I didn't see where anyone mentioned Froggy's line when he materialized from the puff of smoke: "Hiya, kids, hiya, hiya!" (This was delivered in a low, raspy voice.)

"Froggy was the original agent provocateur who would thoroughly confuse and befuddle the 'experts' who were supposed to teach us how to do something. If the chef was to bake a cake, Froggy would start out with helpful suggestions which the chef would follow. Finally Froggy would turn mean and have to tell the chef to dump the batter on his head. The chef would proceed to do this and then turn on Froggy, who would promptly disappear.

"It's a considerable stretch to correlate the behavior of the first baby-boom wave and our opposition to the war in Vietnam as one letter suggests, but, if it were true, I believe Froggy would be proud."

—Al Evans

MILKY THE CLOWN

by Ed Golick

What's the magic word? If your answer is "Twin Pines," you've probably spent count-less Saturday afternoons in front of the family TV enjoying the mystifying magic of Milky the Clown. Milky is one of the legends of Detroit TV. Clare Cummings was the man behind the legend.

Clarence R. Cummings, Jr., was born in Chicago, Illinois, on February 4, 1912. In 1917 Clarence Sr. moved the family to Birmingham, Michigan. At an early age Clare became fascinated with performing, often entertaining the neighborhood children with Punch and Judy shows. At age twelve he received a $1.25 magic set for Christmas. Cummings soon mastered all of the tricks, performing them for friends and classmates. Looking to expand his repertoire, he devoured every magic volume in the local library. Noting his son's fascination with magic, Clare's father would take him to see Houdini, Thurston, and other popular magicians of the day. In a 1960 *Detroit News* article, Cummings said, "When Thurston found I was neglecting my studies for my magic, he slapped my face and told me to get busy with my books and forget my magic."

Cummings' first professional show was in 1929 at Birmingham's Baldwin Library. While still in high school Cummings performed at school assemblies, birthday parties, and banquets in and around town. 1933 found Cummings working with Danny Thomas, then known as Amos Jacobs, on Chuck Stanley's *Happy Hour Club* radio show. They received no pay for their radio appearances, but were paid three dollars each for outside jobs. In 1941 Cummings got a job at the E.I. DuPont company as an automo-tive paint salesman. He would sell paint during the week, and perform his magic on weekends. During World War II, he served as a sergeant in the U.S. Army's Finance

Division in Florida, while entertaining the troops in the Army's Special Services Division. While in Florida, he sent for and married his hometown sweetheart, Peg Haldane. In 1944 their daughter Peggy was born. After the war, Cummings returned to his DuPont job in Detroit and resumed his magic career. He was now performing in places like the Grosse Pointe Yacht Club and Detroit Athletic Club as "Clare Cummings, Delineator of Deceptive Dexterity."

In 1950, while Cummings was working a part-time job at the Hall Magic Company in Detroit, a WJBK television producer spotted him. Charmed by his magic skills, gap-toothed smile, and gentle manner, the producer thought that Cummings would be the perfect host for a new children's show he had planned. The show was *Peter, Clare and Oscar*, a program much like the popular *Kukla, Fran and Ollie*. Peter was a live rabbit, Clare was the straight man who could understand Peter, and Oscar was a marionette, operated by Detroit policeman Herb German. The fifteen-minute show lasted for thirteen weeks. Later that year, the Twin Pines Dairy wanted to sponsor a children's show, which would feature cartoons, movies, and a magic clown. The advertising agency handling the Twin Pines account contacted WJBK, who contacted Cummings. Milky the Clown was born. Cummings himself created the distinctive Milky makeup. His wife Margaret created the costume, which was patterned after the clown in the opera *Pagliacci*.

Milky's Movie Party premiered on December 16, 1950. The two-hour show featured cartoons, Westerns, and Milky's magic tricks. In the beginning there was no live audience, only Milky, the Twin Pines Milkman, and the weekly winner of the "Sunshine Smile" photo contest. Peggy Tibbits, Cummings's daughter and an occasional visitor to her father's set, recalls, "One time the child who was chosen got sick and I was his replacement. I got to help with the tricks, say the magic words, drink lots of milk and juice during the commercials, pet the kittens and puppies that were up for adoption, and generally feel pretty important." Milky was also assisted by Creamy the white rabbit, a hand puppet who taught the boys and girls traffic safety.

In 1952, a marionette show created by Ed Johnson called "Willie-Do-It" became a part of the *Movie Party*. Willie was a mischievous boy who had amazing adventures with his pal Gee Whizzer, a bizarre-looking gremlin with a whizzer on his tail so he could fly. Applesauce the dragon was also a part of the gang. Sonny Eliot, another Detroit TV legend, was the voice of Willie-Do-It.

In 1955, *Milky's Movie Party* moved to WXYZ, home of *Soupy Sales, Ricky the Clown*, and *Wixie Wonderland*. The show stayed the same, except for the addition of *Little Rascals* shorts. The show moved to WWJ in February 1958 with a new format and a new name.

Milky's Party Time featured a live studio audience, the serial *The Adventures of Sir Lancelot*, *Bozo* and *Felix the Cat* cartoons, magic, games, prizes, and the "Stars of the Future" contest hosted by perky Mary Lou. Pierre the Frenchman, who really was French-Canadian, assisted with the games. The games were a team effort, usually the boys versus the girls. In the early days at WWJ, the winning team would get to grab two fistfuls of pennies from the big goldfish bowl. The losing team would get one. Peggy Tibbits recalls that the first goldfish bowl had a larger opening in the top. The studio bigwigs thought that the kids were grabbing too many pennies, so they found a goldfish bowl with a smaller opening. That way the kids would scrape their knuckles and drop most of their treasure. In later years, when the show's budget was bigger, kids would get to pick prizes from the "Twin Pines Toy House."

Early in the show's history, Cummings suggested that an announcer, dressed as a Twin Pines milkman, should pitch the commercials. The dairy's famous phone number, Texas-four-one-one-oh-oh, was repeated by four different spokesmen.

Earl Hayes, the first milkman, died of lung cancer in 1953. Dale Young, a staff photographer at WJBK, replaced Hayes. The third milkman, Bob Leslie, was also Santa Claus in the J.L. Hudson Thanksgiving Parade. Leslie was killed in a tragic home furnace explosion. Bob Allison, a staff announcer at WWJ, was the last person to don the uniform. Allison is now celebrating the fortieth anniversary of his *Ask Your Neighbor* radio show, which started on WWJ-AM. It can now be heard on WNZK. Allison also hosted the popular *Bowling For Dollars* show on WWJ in the '70s and '80s.

Milky's Party Time was so popular that there was a two-year wait for tickets. Twin Pines executives loved the show, too. The dairy's delivery routes had more than tripled, as Detroit area moms wanted "worry-free home delivery." Cummings would do more than 130 school assemblies a year. Detroit mayor Louis C. Miriani declared December 16, 1960, "Milky the Clown Day," and presented Cummings with a key to the city.

Party Time ended for Cummings in 1964, when he needed to devote more time to his job as a full-time paint salesman at DuPont. Karrell Fox, a talented local magician and emcee, donned the familiar pointed hat and white makeup until the show was cancelled in 1967. Cummings retired from DuPont in 1971, though he still made occasional personal appearances. Cummings's farewell performance as Milky was in 1992 at the Oakland Mall.

Clare Cummings died on October 31, 1994, of congestive heart failure, on the anniversary of Houdini's death. He donated most of his magic tricks and one of his costumes to the American Museum of Magic in Marshall, Michigan, where they are on permanent display.

Milky may be gone, but his memory lives on. Milky collectibles sell for amazing prices at flea markets and antique shops. A promotional Milky the Clown clock recently brought over five hundred dollars on an Internet auction. 8x10 photographs usually sell in the forty-dollar range. Even old Twin Pines milk bottles bring hefty prices. Perhaps people are trying to buy back a small piece of their childhood, a time when "Twin Pines" was the magic word and Milky the Clown's face was on the side of the milk carton, rather than the face of a missing child.

THE MERRY MAILMAN

"I was still pronouncing my 'R's like 'W's when Ray Heatherton asked me on camera:

"'What's your name?'

"'Wicky,' I replied.

"'Oh, Wicky?' the Merry Mailman cracks wise.

"'NO —WICKY!!!' I protested, hopelessly unable to modify my articulation. Apparently all the parents were doubled over laughing.

"I am fifty-years-old and have still not lived this incident down in my family (my brother still addresses birthday cards to Wicky)."

—R Lieberman

CAPTAIN KANGAROO

From 1955 until 1984, the wonderful *Captain Kangaroo* could be seen for an hour, weekday mornings on CBS. Hugh "Lumpy" Brannum played sidekick Mr. Green Jeans, joined by Cosmo Allegretti's handpuppets Mr. Moose and Bunny Rabbit in the Captain's Treasure House.

Before Bob Keeshan was a captain he was a clown, probably the most famous clown of the 1950s—Clarabell from the *Howdy Doody Show* starring Buffalo Bob. *Howdy Doody* first aired on December 27, 1947, and is credited for selling more people on the future of television than any other single event. Millions of children tuned in to the daily live kid's show and, though he never spoke a word, Clarabell the clown was an important part of the Doodyville ensemble, selling millions of Poll Parrot shoes, assorted toys, dolls, and packaged cereals for the show's delighted sponsors.

Unfortunately, Buffalo Bob and Bob Keeshan didn't much care for each other. Keeshan was fired in 1950 and replaced by another performer as Clarabell, but a flood of phone calls and mail from skeptical kids who could tell the difference forced producers to re-hire Keeshan a few weeks later. He was fired again (along with almost all of the rest of the supporting cast of *Howdy Doody*), when he led an uprising for more money minutes before going on the air live in December 1952.

Bob Keeshan was only twenty-eight years old in 1955 when he and producer Jack Miller created *Captain Kangaroo*. Television was a new addition to most American homes; there had never been a generation of children exposed to home-video entertainment before. This series was designed to give kids a gentle alternative to the frenetic nature of most juvenile shows of the day (of which *Howdy Doody* was one of the worst offenders). Watching an episode of *Captain Kangaroo* from the early '60s, one is struck by the achingly slow pace and overall gentle nature of the show.

A Saturday-morning version of *Captain Kangaroo* with a different Treasure House set (supposedly taking place in the basement) ran from 1956 until 1968, with a year off in 1964–65 when Bob Keeshan starred as *Mr. Mayor.*

TVpartyer Todd Kelson tells us: "The real story of *Mr. Mayor* is interesting. Apparently CBS, Keeshan, and another group held the actual rights to *Captain Kangaroo.* CBS and Keeshan started *Mr. Mayor* to force out the third party. Both programs were sort of first cousins in terms of the types of characters and format. If the third party had not gone peacefully, the captain would have bitten the dust and the mayor would have taken his place all week. The dispute was settled, and it was *Mr. Mayor* who went gently into that good night. I was told this many years ago by my dad, who was the set decorator on *Kangaroo* from 1962 until the early '70s and again at the very end of his run in the '80s (and during the brief run of *Mr. Mayor*).

"As a young child my two brothers and I were probably the only children ever to see (and get to play in) what I consider to be the *real* treasure house—by which I mean the *Kangaroo* prop room at the CBS Broadcast Center, where aisles and aisles of 'teeeerriffic' toys and props were kept."

Regular features on *Captain Kangaroo* included visits from zoo animals, Mr. Green Jeans' zany inventions, Bunny Rabbit (a hand puppet) and his carrot scams, and a torrent of falling ping-pong balls brought on whenever Mr. Moose asked the captain a knock-knock joke (the dropping of balls came along with the punchline, which was usually "ping pong balls").

"Tom Terrific" was a regular cartoon segment created specifically for the *Captain Kangaroo* show that aired from the '50s through the '60s. Designer, director, and former UPA executive Gene Deitch created "Tom Terrific" with imaginative scripts and stylized designs to hide the fact that the animation was so simple—necessary for tight daytime kid's

Bob Keeshan was seen as Captain Kangaroo in the Tom Arnold movie *The Stupids* in 1996.

79

TV budgets. The scripts were tongue-in-cheek and the music was minimal as well, just a single accordion.

In the stories, Tom had the ability to change into any shape he could imagine in order to save his loveable but lazy wonderdog Mighty Manfred from the clutches of the villainous Crabby Appleton and assorted do-badders in the three five-minute segments that made up each story arc.

"'Tom Terrific' was one of my favorite segments of *Captain Kangaroo*," TVpartyer Ricky Waller writes. "The villainous Crabby Appleton sang a song that I will always remember and it went like this: 'My name is Crabby Appleton, I'm rotten to the core, I do a bad deed every day, and sometimes three or four. I can't stand fun for anyone, I think good deeds are sappy, I laugh with glee, it pleases me, when everyone's unhappy!'"

By 1968, the show's pace had quickened a bit to reflect the shorter attention spans of kids now used to a steady TV diet. A new cartoon feature starring Lariat Sam was added, along with travelogues of the Captain and his Dancing Bear touring the great cities of the world. In the '70s, stars like Marlo Thomas and Carol Channing would often visit the show and in 1980 Bill Cosby became a semi-regular. Slim Goodbody (John Burnstein) also joined the show in 1980 as a man wearing a bodystocking with the major human organs painted on it.

In 1981, CBS cut the running time of the show from one hour to a half-hour and moved the Captain from his traditional 8 AM timeslot to make way for the *CBS*

Morning News. The new series, *Wake up with the Captain,* was broadcast at 7 AM, then bumped to 6:30. A year later, the show left the weekday morning schedule altogether and began running for an hour on Saturday and Sunday mornings at 7. CBS cancelled *Captain Kangaroo* in 1984, so Bob Keeshan took the show to PBS where it ran for several more years.

Today, Bob Keeshan is a public speaker and children's advocate. The NEA recognized his achievements by awarding him the National Education Association Award for Advancement of Learning through Television in 1982.

THE BANANA MAN MYSTERY:

"Please help me. I swear I saw a phenomenon on *Captain Kangaroo*! His name was the Banana Man and he would pull watermelons, more watermelons, this and that and a little bit of everything from his coat. Then, finally, he would start pulling bunches upon bunches of bananas from his coat.

"He did not speak but only would say 'Wow' in soprano. I sat there mesmerized by this strange man. Finally, at the end of his act, he would take his props in the background and turn them into a locomotive with cars following. I think he even generated smoke from the front of the locomotive. Who was he?"
—Terry Koch

"The Banana Man (Mr. A. Robbins) was an old vaudevillian. Only problem was, so was his costume—which was so complicated, it could not be cleaned. Every few years (when the set was updated or something) they had to get him back in to retape his bit, and the entire studio stank to high heaven so badly no one wanted to be near it."
—Todd Kelson

"There's a TV special that I've been looking for and you guys are the only ones who could dig it up—it was called *Time to Change* from 1986, and it was produced and hosted by a post–*Captain Kangaroo* Bob Keeshan.

"It was about how 'men should get in touch with their feelings' and that kind of touchy-feely type stuff. Anyway, the amazing part of this thing came when Scott Baio and McLean Stevenson were playing a father and son on a fishing trip. Keeshan appears behind them and says something like, "Little do they know that a crate of luggage from a overhead plane will soon kill them both," then a pile of suitcases lands on top of them a la the sixteen-ton weight from *Monty Python.*

"We then see Scott Baio's ghost saying stuff like: "Dad! Dad! I never got the chance to say 'I love you!'" Then Stevenson's ghost runs around, saying the same type thing. It ended with a close-up of Stevenson's sweaty face, while he moans, ". . . my son . . . my son."

"I would say that I hallucinated this whole thing, except a friend of mine also saw it. People think we're pulling their leg when we tell them about it."
—A Reader

The Old Rebel Show

Host of one of the longest-running kid shows of all time, George Perry was on the air for WFMY-TV in North Carolina for an astonishing twenty-seven years—1950–1977.

"Every day we had the kids in the audience walk through the door on the set and give us their names. This we simply called the 'name game.' If it was a large crowd, their name was about it. If it was a smaller group, often the Old Rebel would ask questions like what school or what town were they from. We had kids from southern Virginia to just outside of Charlotte and everywhere in between.

"As far as funny stories go, they range from kids fighting in line to falling down to crying babies to those who felt the only way they could be heard was to scream their name at the top of their lungs into the microphone. Being a tape-delayed program, we could stop production if needed, so these events usually were not seen the next day.

"I have heard stories from the old days when the show was live—stories about kids telling on the boy who broke wind when the Old Rebel asked them why they were laughing.

"We also had a daily Birthday Spotlight. Children from all over the state (as well as Virginia, it seemed), would send in their pictures. I can't even guess how many hundreds of those we showed over the years.

"I do feel there is something very nice and friendly about a local show of this type. The nature of the beast that is broadcasting has changed so much in recent years that local stations can easily and cheaply buy a packaged program from a syndicator rather than create one themselves. Unfortunately, they don't have a local flavor and children today don't seem to have any more loyalty to one station than to any other. Every television station is just another spot on the dial to them. Children can't go visit the station anymore and they don't have any local heroes."

—Jim Wiglesworth, "Jungle Jim" co-host from 1968 to 1976

Tune to the
OLD REBEL AND PECOS PETE SHOW
for the code ciphers to use with the
MAGIC WHEEL CODE CARD
Decode the mystery message. Then send to the Old Rebel and Pecos Pete Club, WFMY-TV, Greensboro, N. C.
Outer circle for the first of the code ciphers

83

CAPTAIN SATELLITE

by the captain himself,
Bob March

The creation of
Captain Satellite sprang
from my youthful pas-
sion for science fiction.
As a boy I devoured
magazines such as
*Galaxy, Flash Gordon,
Buck Rogers,* etc.

1958 was fortuitous time for the
emergence of a television program with a space
theme; it was the year the Russians launched the first earth
satellite, named Sputnik. This started the "Space Race," an effort on the part
of the United States to dominate the last frontier.

When I see the high-tech computer-generated special effects of today I am green
with envy. The first set for Captain Satellite's space ship was a hodge-podge created
from pie plates fastened to the wall, along with garden hose to simulate wiring,
and a dismantled pinball machine.

Over the ten years the program aired, the set evolved into a flying saucer.
Thanks to film footage from NASA we were able to simulate a blast-off which,
for the time, was quite realistic.

I wanted audience participation, so I created a game called "Space Lock," a
contest where kids would send in a drawing depicting a space theme. If their picture was selected to be displayed a prize was awarded. The winner would choose
one of three keys to open Captain Satellite's "Space Lock," which contained a
really grand prize.

Captain Satellite was live television, which made for some hilarious and sometimes scary moments. Animals would get loose and start savaging the set or Santa's
reindeer would relieve themselves on camera.

The crew would attempt to catch the captain off guard. One day when no children were scheduled to appear on the program, KSFO personality Don Sherwood
(who was taping his weekly variety show in the studio next door) provided a memorable moment. The captain strolled over to open the Space Lock. The door slid

"Imitation is the sincerest form of television." —*Fred Allen* open and there stood a beautifully posed nude model (courtesy of Sherwood). The captain broke into hysterical laughter. Of course the camera had been positioned not to show the model to the TV audience.

Captain Satellite and all the other children's show hosts were a very special part of growing up in the Bay Area. Through their weekend personal appearances (at parks, markets, theaters, etc.) they would autograph a picture for you and in many cases you could appear on their programs.

I am still working with children in an entirely different capacity as a mental health counselor at juvenile hall in Sacramento. As a licensed marriage family therapist I find it extremely rewarding to help troubled youngsters make changes in their lives.

The children of the '50s and '60s lived in a simple time; they were fun to have on the show and meet in person at appearances. Today's children are being inundated in a flood of violence and overstimulation of primary instincts. In some ways they grow old faster.

Enough sermonizing.

"I remember, when the show was cancelled, KTVU gave the captain a big send-off, with many well-wishers dropping by for the final voyage of the Laser 2. Bob March later hosted the morning edition of *Dialing for Dollars,* on which he would run old sitcoms like *The Patty Duke Show.* During the breaks, he would phone unsuspecting people 'from the nine Bay Area phone books' to ask them if they knew the 'count and the amount.' Occasionally someone did, and won a modest jackpot.

"March also had a tiny cameo at the beginning of *Magnum Force,* which was Clint Eastwood's second Dirty Harry movie. He played the councilman who had 'no comment.' I think it's safe to say that Bob March will be best remembered as Captain Satellite!"

—Mike Humbert

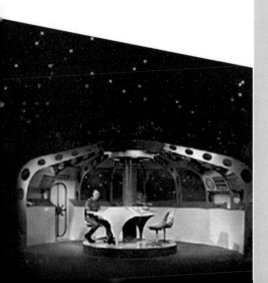

"I worshipped *The Mighty Hercules* so much that I named my new pet guinea pig after him! My mom also brought home a female guinea pig to keep Herc company. I named her Sharon. They made a lovely couple. Well, Hercules the Guinea Pig also 'had the strength of ten ordinary men' and the libido to match, because he spent more time on top of Sharon than I spent watching TV! My parents would sheepishly skirt the subject when I asked what they were doing.

"Anyway, good old Hercules eventually loved poor Sharon to death; she died from too much of Hercules's lovin'. Poor Hercules missed his wife so much that he too died within a month of his dearly departed.

"That's how I remember the *Hercules* cartoon." —*Manny F*

LA favorite Chucko the Birthday Clown

[SEEN ON LOCAL KID SHOWS]

87

Sally Starr

"I never missed the *Sally Starr* show. My mom learned not to serve dinner before 6 PM because she knew there'd just be a scene at the dinner table with me crying about missing Aunt Sal.

"The other day while I visiting a friend, she made her kids turn the Three Stooges off because they were 'so violent' and I protested saying, 'We grew up on the Three Stooges and we're fine.' Her reply to me was, 'Yeah, but we had Sally Starr to tell us not to do those things to each other!' Recently, going through some old family photos, we found a picture of me in my Sally Starr cowgirl outfit taken one Christmas evening. I was so proud! My sister and I laughed ourselves silly over it but I wouldn't trade that picture for anything. God bless you, Aunt Sal. I still love you!" —*A Viewer*

"There was a time when I could not imagine life without being able to watch Sally Starr on TV after school. I remember having mixed feelings about our summer vacations in Wildwood Crest because our family always rented bungalows without a television. The idea of missing our gal Sal was unbearable. I can also remember the thrill when we got our first UHF adapter and we were able to watch *Wee Willie Webber* on channel 17. This was my first experience with *Marine Boy, Prince Planet*, and, of course, *Speed Racer!* Ah, to be nine years old in Philly, in 1969—it was a real treat!" —*Tim Smithers*

"Sally Starr, along with Gene London, were the royalty of Philly kid's television. Aunt Sally and Gene were on sometimes seven days a week and no one got tired of watching them. All of these performers were great in their time and made an impact on our generation, but Gene and Sally more than any of them were probably our second parents, providing morals and guidance you didn't get at home and school.

"Sally Starr started at about 4 PM in the afternoon (after *American Bandstand*) till 6 PM. The old show was called

Popeye Theater and featured a giant cut-out of Popeye wearing a cowboy suit. (I wish I had that now!!) Her opening line was 'I hope ya feel as good as ya look to your gal Sal' and she closed with 'May the Good Lord be blessing you and your family, bye for now!' She never talked down to her audience; you knew she was sincere.

"Sally's show was mostly famous for Popeye in all his reincarnations and the Three Stooges (shorts, cartoons, and Stooge guest shots), but throughout the years the viewers also saw Warner Bros and H/B cartoons, *Bullwinkle, Clutch Cargo, Space Angel, the Funny Company, Ramar of the Jungle, the Lone Ranger, Andy Clyde* shorts, *Doodles Weaver, Beetle Bailey, Krazy Kat,* and *Snuffy Smith* cartoons too.

"She used to plug Good and Plenty, Cocca Marsh, and Gino's. If she flubbed her lines, she would bend her cowgirl hat and say, 'I made a boo boo!!' It was great when the Stooges were on because I was proud that Larry Fine was from Philadelphia."
—*Will Hill*

"Concerning Sally Starr, she is still active in the Delaware Valley and has a Sunday morning country and western radio show on 92.1 FM in Vineland, New Jersey. She makes many local appearances, too. For a while, she hosted a weekend western movies show on Channel 65 before the station went 'Home Shopping.' She lived in Florida for a while, but moved back to New Jersey after losing her home and belongings in a tragic fire several years back. Our Gal Sal is alive and doing well in the Philadelphia area."
—*Mike Brady*

Love, Luck & Lollipops!

—*Philly's Gal Sal*

Top right photo: Jacqueline (left) and her sister Peggy Ulatouski
Photo taken circa 1957 in Atlantic City, NJ.

Gigglesnort Hotel!

THE CURIOUS WORLD of BILL JACKSON and his DIRTY DRAGON

by Rick Goldschmidt

There is an undisputed champion in Chicago children's broadcasting and he goes by the name of Bill Jackson. His talent went far beyond hosting a children's television program. He was and still is a performer, artist/cartoonist, puppet sculptor, character designer, teacher, voice actor, and producer/director, among other things. In short he is an amazingly talented man who is appreciated by many. He is also very modest and is quick to acknowledge all the many people who helped him along the way on his road to *Cartoon Town* and beyond.

If you lived in Chicago, you certainly remember his cast of puppet characters, which included *Cartoon Town*'s postmaster Dirty Dragon, Mother Plumtree, Weird, W.C. Cornfield, the Lemon Joke Kid, Dr. Doompuss, Wally Goodscout, The Old Professor, Mertz, the Martian Meanie, the Thumptwangers, Foo-Foo, and many, many more! B.J. was Mayor of *Cartoon Town* and one of the most personable guys you would ever want to dial up on your television set. He inspired many a young artist with his Whozits (cartoon easel drawings of famous cartoon characters), and he started many a backyard carnival for the Muscular Dystrophy association. In short, a wonderful guy on and off the screen.

"When I came to Chicago, we did a show called *Clown Alley* and I played a character called Freckles

CLOWN ALLEY
Bill Jackson as
Freckles

the Clown on WBBM Channel 2. It was the best-kept secret in Chicago television (laughs)," says Bill Jackson.

Bill started his television career in Fort Wayne, Indiana, and was on a show called *Popeye and the Little Rascals Club.* While in Fort Wayne, he made a wonderful silent movie tribute to the old Max Sennett comedies (*The Big Apple Caper*) in which he played a Chaplin-type character. The piece looks remarkably like it was shot in the period it represents and was re-aired on *Cartoon Town* occasionally. "We had a great deal of fun with that one!," says Jackson. "The police department was very cooperative. The car was loaned to us. The whole cast was made up of crew members from that station including the art director, who was a big help. We didn't have a whole lot of money to do it but we sure put a lot of time and effort into the production."

After his beginnings in Fort Wayne, he moved on to Indianapolis and began to develop a cast of puppet characters. A character named Dirty Dragon was born along with the Blob (an ever-changing clay character with a language of his own) and the ever-popular Thumptwangers "You're Dag Bird Right." *Clown Alley* began in 1965 and the Sunday version of the show, *Here Comes Freckles,* followed in 1966.

His puppets were taking on a look of their own and were about to become a legendary part of Chicago television history. "I designed the characters and made the heads. The process would begin by sculpting the heads in clay and then molding them into latex rubber puppets. I would then paint them. I didn't do the bodies though. The clothing was a little more complicated than just using children's clothing or something like that. Various tailors and seamstresses would sew the many costumes my puppets wore," says Jackson.

After moderate success with *Clown Alley,* B.J. (as he was now known) became mayor of *Cartoon Town* on February 26, 1968 and the rest is history. The memory of seeing B.J. trying to land his Red Derby on his head at the beginning of each show will forever be ingrained in my memory. There are so many facets of *Cartoon Town* that are legendary. The characters were wonderful!

Dirty Dragon was a disgruntled postman who blew so much smoke out of his snout that it would often fog up the entire television picture. Weird was a hilarious, boisterous character who brought more comedy to the show than any other puppet. the Old Professor and Mother Plumtree were full of good-natured banter and could be incredibly sentimental at times. Bill Jackson's character designs and portrayals should have been enough to boost *huge* ratings at the UHF station Channel 32, but that wasn't the case initially.

"When I was at Channel 32, we always had to do much more promotion than you would think would be necessary. At the time, 32 had the White Sox games on and they weren't winning many games. Our promotions girl at the time was a

"If you are going through hell, keep going." —*Sir Winston Churchill*

woman named Kathy and at the time we were doing many personal appearances. We created this whole 'Dirty Dragon for President' campaign. I remember telling Kathy, right before we were to appear at Mayor Daley's Back of the Yards Fair, 'If this doesn't work out, we are going to have to pack it up.' We were at that point. Rick, I am happy to say that we broke all attendance records that day! I was brought into the fair by helicopter and I had the pilot wear a Lemon Joke Kid costume, because on the last show I was kidnapped by the Lemon Joke Kid! It was great fun!," says Jackson.

B.J. and Dirty Dragon became household names, touring all around Chicago and its surrounding suburbs and promoting the appearances each week on the show. When they played the Paramount Arts Center in Aurora, artist Ron Murphy recalls, "He brought a kid up out of the audience and dressed him up as a cowboy and called him Tex. Tex threw his horse off the stage to B.J.'s disbelief. I saw that same kid the next day and asked 'Tex' why he threw the horse." B.J. also sold

"I remember *Gigglesnort Hotel*! My brother and I would watch it every sunday morning. I was young, about six or seven years old. What I do remember and what fascinated me most was when Bill Jackson use to paint; it was like magic to me how the picture would just appear by a few strokes of his magical paintbrush. Sunday-morning shows back then were the best. We will never see shows that creative anymore, it's sad. That show was a part of my childhood. I will never forget it." —Sheri

"Thank Merciful God someone else remembers this show!!! I grew up in Albany, Georgia and it use to come on afternoons in the early '80s there. I think it was on WTBS before it became the 'Super Station.'

"I remember Maynard the Crow as the repair person. Maynard had a girlfriend crow named Myrtle. Maynard was also a musician (guitar, I think) and he sang a song about her. There was this one episode where Myrtle was acting timid or shy about something, I think it was going on stage in front of an audience with Maynard to play in his band, and she finally came around in the end. The song went something like 'Myrtle was a turtle 'til she came ah-right outta her shell.'

"I recall a two-part-or-more epic where the bellhop, the Blob, and some other characters went to another planet. I remember they were locked up in a dungeon. Blob showed up looking like a monster and scared all the guards away. The bellhop and the princess of the planet fell in love but he had to go back to the hotel. When they got back, no one believed them.

"The Lemon Joke Kid would fly in on the lemon-shaped blimp and throw down lemons like bombs. If you read the painfully bad joke written on it, it would blow up and you'd be 'puckerized.' The trick was not to read it, but someone always inadvertently did.

"Finally, the title character was called Commander Gigglesnort or Admiral or Captain, I don't remember which, and was dressed accordingly. I remember him on top of the roof, 'steering' the building with a ship's wheel. And when he'd laugh, he would suck all the air back kind of like he was about to sneeze, and then snort. Hence the name.

"Again, thanks for helping me open a very tightly sealed vault which had remained hidden in the back of my mind. Whew!"
—Tramm Wigzell

red plastic, felt-covered derbies at the show for around a dollar a piece. Audience participation was always an important part of the stage shows.

For a short time on the show, kids would write in for a phone call from B.J. to do a Whozit on air. B.J. would draw a popular character and the kid caller would get to guess the cartoon. If he did guess right, he was awarded a large pencil with Dirty Dragon's likeness on it.

Maurice Lennell Cookies was a sponsor of the show and Bill was the perfect salesman for this product. He would always say, "Look for the box with the boy in the cookie jar on it."

I can remember that as the cookie of choice in my neighborhood.

One of the most memorable features on the show was the appearances made by the Lemon Joke Kid. Bill's shows never carried any violence in them but they did have a great deal of excitement and the Lemon Joke Kid was his way of mixing up the show. When the kid would come to town a dark cloud would linger in the sky and lemons would fall. His bombs were his bad jokes. Bill alluded to the fact that this might be Weird in the Lemon Joke Kid's costume, but it turned out to be his lookalike cousin.

B.J. made a couple of Christmas specials during this period. The first was *Please Open Me before Christmas* (which was actually a Thanksgiving special to put

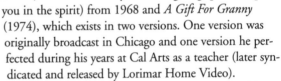

you in the spirit) from 1968 and *A Gift For Granny* (1974), which exists in two versions. One version was originally broadcast in Chicago and one version he perfected during his years at Cal Arts as a teacher (later syndicated and released by Lorimar Home Video).

"I like the first one better story-wise. We were able to up the production in California, but we changed the plot and characters quite a bit and I think we were more successful the first time around in those areas. I am thinking about putting the first version out on home video," says B.J.

Cartoon Town eventually became *The B.J. and Dirty Dragon Show* and B.J. ultimately changed his suit color from red to blue (just like the famous Bozo of *Bozo's Circus* fame). Competition became fierce during his timeslot. WGN began running reruns of *Batman* and *The Flintstones* and a decision had to be made. Since the live stage shows were so popular and *Bozo's Circus* was having great success with its audience participation format, it was decided to make *The B.J. and Dirty Dragon Show* a stage show and use "road show" costume versions of the characters.

Something was missing. The show was still lively and fun, but it was missing the warm and homey qualities that made it popular in the first place. Realizing the show was failing, B.J. urged the powers that be to go back to the old format and they did. After returning to the old format the show eventually signed off the air on July 27, 1973. It made a brief return in the town Carefree Corners (aimed at pre-schoolers) on WGN from September 1973 to August 30, 1974, but the end of an era had reached *Cartoon Town*.

Bill Jackson can be found at *www.dirtydragon.com*

Bill Jackson brought back the same characters and added a few more in his critically acclaimed and highly successful series *B.J.'s Gigglesnort Hotel*, which ran for three years (seventy-eight episodes) beginning in January of 1975. This is a very entertaining series where B.J. operates and runs a hotel for Mr. Gigglesnort and brings back our favorite characters from *Cartoon Town*.

Creatively, it wasn't as successful as *Cartoon Town* because there was no longer the freedom or the spontaneity of humor that existed at WFLD. "We had to stick to a format and get across a message. I think I enjoyed myself more in the early days of *Cartoon Town* but *Gigglesnort Hotel* is a HUGE success. I put out three recent volumes of the series myself and they are sold at the Museum of Broadcast Communications."

The last show that included these characters was a series called *Firehouse Follies* that ran from 1979 to 1980. Instead of running around in a hotel, they were running around in a firehouse. Bill went out to California after this show and joined the staff of Cal Arts as a teacher and administrator for some twelve and a half years. During this time he launched many careers in the entertainment field. He

"Oh my lord! I've got to send this to my sister!! We've been branded as loonies for even mentioning this show. No one ever believes it's real.

"We live in Portland, Oregon and remember long long ago in the late '70s watching this wacked-out show early in the morning. Like almost before sunrise. I think they put it on so early because it was just so weird.

"I don't know that I'd go so far as to say it was Satanic but I do remember one morning I was feeling very ill. Some sort of stomach flu . . . anyway, we went down to watch *Gigglesnort Hotel* and I just kept getting sicker and sicker . . . I was sure it was the show using 'evil powers' on me to make me sick . . . then I just couldn't help myself; I threw up and felt like I was dying. I was absolutely convinced the show did it to me and I never watched it again.

"For over ten years now I've been talking to everyone I know at some point and asking if they remember this bit of TV history. Nobody, and I mean *nobody* has any clue what I'm talking about. Thank you for grounding this bit of my memory in reality. "—Nathan S

"I enjoy reading everyone's memories of their shows . . . but Satanic? That's kinda extreme . . . I guess I know what they mean now by 'younger and more sensitive viewers,' but never mind.

"Personally, I had a huge crush on Bill Jackson. Between his good looks (at least what I thought were good looks during my latency years), his artistry (the caricatures he did were really impressive to a kid who couldn't draw a straight line), and his sculpting of poor Blob, I thought he was the ultimate in one! I always remember being so happy that such a talented person had a job where people could see what he did so well.

"I can't even guess how many years it took to realize that the superimposed sounds of the Blob during his sculpting sessions was the SAME darn tape every time. B.J. reacted sympathetically when he sounded upset, encouraging when Blob gave that kinda raunchy, 'ho,ho,ho' laugh, and seemed continuously interested in keeping Blob happy during his 'remodelings.'

"Dirty Dragon was the perfect antihero. I never understood why he was so popular at the time. Always on the edge of a fiery rage, he indeed jeopardized all the mail in Cartoon Town, forcing B.J. to walk on eggshells in his quest to first get his mail, then protect the rest from getting FIEEEE'd on. Now and then, they took turns reading viewer mail. When I sent in a letter, I gushed like mad about how wonder-

never really talked about his past efforts during this period, but every now and then a student from Chicago would recognize him from his past.

Bill was honored by the Museum of Broadcast Communications on April 5, 1995, and there was a huge turnout of Bill Jackson fans to pay tribute to his incredible body of work. Bill was quick to turn the attention to all of the people who worked behind the scenes to make him look good. This is typical of the wonderful man to which everyone paid tribute. The man we all knew and loved on the screen is the same man that you meet in person.

The work of historian/artist Jim Engel in bringing the focus back on B.J. cannot go unnoticed. He assembled a wonderful magazine called *The Little Theatre Screen* in the summer of 1994 and was instrumental in making the *Evening with Bill Jackson* at the Museum of Broadcast Communications a reality and hosted the proceedings. Most importantly, when it looked like B.J.'s puppets might not be housed properly at the museum, Jim single-handedly constructed and designed a wonderful permanent display for B.J.'s puppets for the rest of Chicago to enjoy.

Responding to the many inquiries at *TVparty.com* over the last few years, Bill said, "I am just so pleased that they remember! The business is a very fickle thing, it really is, and I am just so overwhelmed that they remember and care. What a beautiful thing!"

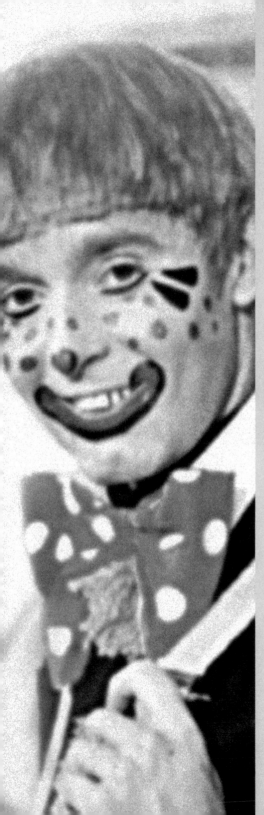

ful I thought B.J. was. I remember getting a postcard back, with an autograph thanking me for a '*very* complimentary' letter . . . now I wonder if I promised him my firstborn, my chastity, or what . . . I remember my heart breaking once when I saw him wearing a wedding ring . . . sigh.

"As an adult, I remember one campaign waged by B.J. and the Dragon, called FIE on Tailgators! They railed against how dangerous a habit it was and how it could result in terrible things for both the perpetrator and the victim of this behavior. Now that I drive, the slogan comes back to me at least three times a week! They were also into criticizing litterbugs and many other of the civic annoyances adults encounter. I daresay B.J. used the show (in very small part) as a bully pulpit, though I never heard a soul's complaint about that.

"I remember Mother (Pearl) Plumtree, the old lady puppet, and when she married the old guy puppet, Fenster, or Fester. I think they also called him Grandpa or something? And, of course, Wally and Weird . . . Wally wore a Scout uniform a lot, and had a very femmy voice, very much the 'Bert' to Weird's 'Ernie.' There were some wild plot twists where they Doppelganged into Frankenweird and WolfWally, but I usually avoided watching the show when they went that way . . . They were strange enough in their usual forms!

"B.J., wherever you are, I'd still love a shot at ya. Hehehe!"

—Jussamagin, Romeoville, IL

"With kids of my own and a 'grown up' existence I sometimes forget what it was like to be a kid. Thanks for you guys reminding me. I *loved* Dirty Dragon and the Lemon Joke Kid!

"I loved B.J. I remember he had a show before *The Gigglesnort Hotel* that I can't remember the name of, that had Dirty Dragon and some of the other characters from the *Hotel* on it, and he would draw cartoons and things. I seem to remember that there was a neighborhood of some sort he would walk through.

"It was good to remember that time in my life. It was a younger, simpler time. It was a time when the characters didn't have to break down into pieces and become something else, or when you didn't have to go into debt getting all of the paraphernalia to go with the show. It was a time when things could just be funny for funny sake . . . no cause, no deeper meaning, just plain funny. Whoever thinks it was Satanic needs some help. Thank you, Bill, for years of laughs and some really GRRREEEAAATTT memories!"

—Sincerely, Gina

97

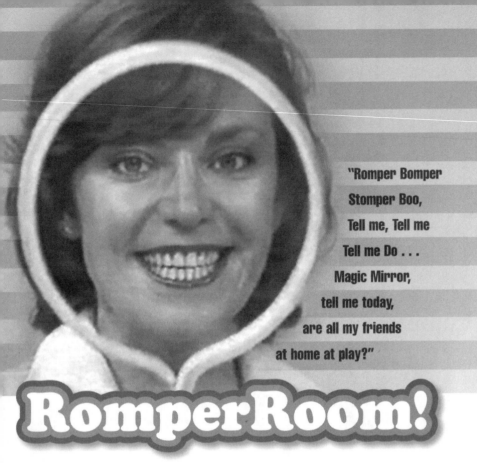

"Romper Bomper
Stomper Boo,
Tell me, Tell me
Tell me Do . . .
Magic Mirror,
tell me today,
are all my friends
at home at play?"

RomperRoom!

"I was sitting in Honors Physics today, and it was very wacky. We had kids doing whatever they wanted, and lots of noise. The teacher bobbed his head and quietly said, 'Please, can we stop the Romper Room?'

"The phrase soon caught on, and was said every time we got too 'insane.' We eventually made a banner with a stop sign, and it said, 'The Romper Room' and put it outside the class. We even have a magic mirror."

—Sincerely, Brian Rutherford

Romper Room was a preschooler that ran for a period of almost forty years in every major market in the United States. Beginning in 1954, the show was sold to stations in two ways—in standard syndication and as a franchise so that locals could have their own hostess (there were 150 in all by 1970). The series was developed by Bert and Nancy Claster, who trained many of the local hosts around the country.

The syndicated version of *Romper Room* was originally filmed in Baltimore, Maryland, (later moving to Chicago), and starred Miss Nancy (Claster) with a studio-classroom of seven young children. She wasn't slated to host, but the woman they originally hired backed out at the last minute and Nancy Claster (who had a teaching degree) eagerly stepped into the role and into TV history. She was replaced in 1964 by her daughter, Miss Sally.

All of the regional hosts, many of them former kindergarten teachers, spent the half-hour basically the same way—reciting the Pledge of Allegiance, reading from books, and teaching the alphabet, along with stressing proper manners and core values in a gentle way with repetitive sing-a-longs and games.

Occasionally, the kids on the show would get a bit nuts; some wouldn't communicate at all; others would take over the whole program and there was nothing the poor hostess could do but deal with it because they were on a cramped set together for thirty minutes—live. Every episode ended with the hostess gazing into the Magic Mirror (actually an empty mirror frame) and saying (changing the names each day): "I see Mary Ann and Bobby and William and Virginia and Hannah and all of you boys and girls out there!"

Shocking scandal: when the kids on *Romper Room* said the Pledge of Allegiance, it included the words "under God"!

TVparty viewer Dixon Hayes adds: "I watched *Romper Room* on stations in Birmingham and Atlanta. It was the first educational TV show to have a direct impact on me, because I am told my first complete sentence was the Pledge of Allegiance, which I learned from *RR*.

"One thing I remember is the near-complex I developed from never hearing the hostess call out my name at the end of the show, as she looked into her magic mirror (Dixon is an unusual first name, obviously). Once she even called out the names of my sister and three other kids on the block ('I see Chuck, and I see Michelle, and I see Cathy, and I see Stacy . . .') and my sister lorded it over me for years."

Videotapes of *Romper Room* episodes are exceedingly rare; the tape itself was so expensive that stations routinely erased each day's show for the next. TVpartyer V. Scott was a guest on *Romper Room* on WOR-TV in New York in 1976 and was given a copy of the program, saving it as a treasure all these years.

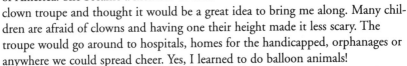

Ms. Scott (right) sent a copy of the tape to TVparty (where we can preserve it in digital format) and told us about her day on *Romper Room*:

"My Aunt Kathy was working for Ma Bell and volunteering for the Telephone Pioneers of America. She became a member of their clown troupe and thought it would be a great idea to bring me along. Many children are afraid of clowns and having one their height made it less scary. The troupe would go around to hospitals, homes for the handicapped, orphanages or anywhere we could spread cheer. Yes, I learned to do balloon animals!

"The day we taped, some of the employees of WOR-TV were making a decision about going on strike. The host of *Romper Room* (Miss Mary Ann) was unhappy and it shows. Being five, I didn't notice much but my mother and aunt told me about it years later. Most of the people were short tempered but were still nice to us. Poor woman, she was trying to be gracious to all those kids and worrying about her job at the same time.

"The first segment had them singing the days of the week. Miss Mary Ann had to hold up two cards because one of the kids hadn't shown up yet. He came in

later in the show and she scolded him for being late. I found out that he had been late all week and was a general problem. Backstage, Miss Mary Ann told the crew that he would not be allowed on the set if he was late again.

"I watched most of the show from backstage. My Aunt said I squirmed the entire day. The other clown on the show was the meanest person I had ever met. She used to say nasty things to me to get me to cry or mess up my lines during sketches. She said something to me before our first segment that upset me so much, and the mean clown had hurt my hand from holding it! After our first segment, we went backstage to a very small dressing room and put on our makeup and costumes. People from WOR kept coming in and introducing themselves and telling us how nice we were for working with the handicapped. I couldn't have cared less! I wanted to go and watch the show. I was also very upset because Mr. Do Bee was not there. He was my favorite.

"After the show, the cast and crew ran around frantically to get ready to do the news. We watched part of it but all they did was talk and it was really boring. Well, at age five it was boring."

Brian B. in Lynchburg, Virginia remembers the show this way:

"I lived and breathed *Romper Room*! The tie-ins were heavily marketed when I was little, so I made sure to own the Romper Stompers (upside-down plastic yellow pails with green tubing which you'd tug to make them stay under your feet—Ralph Nader must have overlooked these).

"Also, I had the bottom-weighted inflatable Romper Room Punching Clown. He was bigger than I was, and would return my punches with a daunting smack. Still, he was from *RR*, and so he was cherished.

"For drawings we had mailed in, my brother and I each received the special thank-you post-card with Do Bee in the corner and an *actual* hostess signature! My brother's was blue and was signed by "Miss Jane" (or some sweatshop worker) in blue ball-point pen. My postcard was green (much prettier, with better xerography) and was signed by "Miss Sally" (blue ball-point, again), whom my brother was by this time too old to worship.

"Routine and order were the keys to this show's 'comfy' factor, so installments were only memorable when they were also somewhat frightening. When you'd see a kid throw a tantrum, and then become conspicuously absent after the commercial break, it could make the Juice and Cookie Time seem even more gloomily like communion rites.

"I particularly remember when I was five or six, that the Big Red Phone (which looked like a presidential hotline) rang on one show. My beloved Miss Sally answered it, and dramatically effected a fake conversation with the Fire Chief. 'Oh, really? That's terrible! Yes, I'll be certain to tell the Children-at-Play!'

"After hanging up the phone, she gathered the wide-eyed kiddies 'round and solemnly told them the fire chief's news: Somewhere, a child had *looked at the sun* and had *had his eyes damaged*! So we must *never* look at the sun! She was so heavy about it, that I now reason I must have been watching a franchised version from our local affiliate, and was being treated to a fake Miss Sally. She was simply too spooky to be national. And who even knew that sun-staring was within the fire chief's jurisdiction? My fake Miss Sally made sure that *we* knew!

"For better or worse, this show shaped me (and they call GenXers jaded!)."

You can really see how different it is for kids today when you compare *Romper Room* with a recent episode of the *Maury* show, which airs in many markets on the same stations at the same time of day that *Romper Room* once aired. On *Maury*, the host introduced a parade of dangerous, foul-mouthed pre-schoolers for the

Before cookies and milk everyone on the show would say a prayer, "God is great, God is good, and we thank him for our food."

audience to boo and hiss at before they were whisked off to detention centers. And without even saying the Pledge of Allegiance!

If we're now watching images of post-toddlers hustling off to bootcamp, one can only imagine what scenarios the next generation of television will bring for our children.

MAURY REACHES OUT TO TRAVIS!

Punch, Punch
Puncher Ball
Punching's so much fun
Use your wrist
Hand and fist
And keep it on the run
Punch, Punch
Puncher Ball
Is really something to see
The roly-poly Puncher Ball
Keeps coming back to me!
—*Song for the*
punching clown

Miss Louise, NYC's Romper Room hostess circa 1969.

Former Hostess Updates:

"My name is Molly McCloskey Barber and I was the hostess of *Romper Room* after Miss Mary Ann in NY. In 1981, I travelled to Baltimore to replace Miss Sally on the syndicated version of *Romper Room*.

"The name was changed to *Romper Room and Friends*. We taped 100 episodes and they ran in syndication until 1992. I then moved to NY and hosted *Romper Room and Friends* from 1982 until we went out of production in 1987 on WOR, which then became WWOR. They were wonderful years and I really enjoyed being Miss Molly."

—Have a great day, Miss Molly

"I was the *Romper Room* teacher in LA from 1975 to 1989 on KCOP-TV. I was called Ms. Soco and I absolutely loved doing the show. Parents called or wrote in to get their kids on and I scheduled three boys and three girls for each week.

"I made sure that the kids were between four and five years old. Younger kids could not keep up with the other children and six-year-olds acted too cool by then. I also made sure that we had a good ethnic mix, since this was LA, after all.

"Even after twelve years off the air, I still get recognized by my *Romper Room* graduates, as I call them. They are now in their late twenties or early thirties. It's really wonderful when this happens because it means that I was a part of their lives and I may not have changed all that much."

—Socorro Serrano, "Ms. Soco"

In 1967, everyone was singing, **"McDonalds is our kind of place."** As the fast food chain became a national phenom, they wisely decided to target kids in their advertising. That was smart—for the first time in history, children had some say in what the family purchased and ate for dinner.

An advertising agency is 85 percent confusion and 15 percent commission. —Fred Allen

Quisp

"The Qwazy cereal from outer space!" Quisp had a feud going with Quake over who had the best cereal, but they both tasted exactly the same; they were just shaped differently. Still, kids "voted" by purchasing their favorite and Quaker Cereals was the winner. Quake left the marketplace in the '80s but Quisp has always been around, it just isn't generally available in most areas. Ask for it.

The Cheerios Kid

"He's got Go-Power!"

The Cheerios Kid was introduced in the early '60s and was only recently retired.

In the early sixty-second commercials, everything rhymed and the Kid went from saving the entire community to rescuing just his girlfriend Sue (when he only had thirty seconds).

In the politically correct '80s, girlfriend Sue didn't need rescuing—she would eat Cheerios along with the Kid and kick some major butt herself!

Trix Cereal

Everyone knows that Trix are for kids. They should, after forty years of the same slogan. That's what you call staying on message!

David Cassel tells us:

"In the '70s, they had an election as to whether or not the cruel Trix-withholding children should give the Trix rabbit some Trix. I remember voting—kids all across America did—and, in fact, the Trix rabbit did win the right to have a box of Trix. (The post-Nixon era '70s was a time of sweeping reform.)

"They aired a commercial in which the Trix rabbit ate his box of Trix. And then realized that he would never, ever, get another one.

"The end.

"The only thing more existentially disturbing was the way kids used to torment Sonny the Cuckoo Bird with his obvious psychological addiction to Cocoa Puffs."

Shenanigans (1964–65) and *Video Village, Jr.* (1960–61) were two shows that featured kids as pawns on a giant game board.

Video Village, Jr. was a CBS Saturday-morning game based on the prime-time and daytime game *Video Village* (1960–62), which featured adults playing on the big board. *Shenanigans* starred singer/dancer and comic actor Stubby Kaye, one of Broadway's most versatile and talented performers (he had great success in *Guys and Dolls* and *L'il Abner*). A role that would go to Nathan Lane today would have gone to Stubby Kaye in the '60s. Stubby also appeared as a regular on game shows in the '50s like *Pantomime Quiz* (ABC 1958–59) and *Stump the Stars* (CBS 1962–64), and sitcoms *Love and Marriage* (NBC 1959–60) and *My Sister Eileen* (CBS 1960–61).

Shenanigans featured announcer Kenny Williams as Kenny the Cop, who participated in the games and helped to keep things moving along. He played the same role on *Video Village, Jr.* and another kiddie game hybrid, *Storybook Squares* in 1969 based on *The Hollywood Squares*.

Stubby Kaye was in the films *Cockeyed Cowboys Of Calico County* (1970), *Sweet Charity* (1969) and *Cat Ballou* (1965).

"*I remember a Saturday morning kid's show called* Shenanigans *that was a life-sized replica of a real board game. The kid contestants were the game pieces and moved along the squares on the board, which were all basically like booths at the midway of a fair. My favorite was the 'Pie in the Eye' where you had to throw a cream pie into this big eye as it blinked and opened.*"   —Ben Corr

Game Shows For Kids!

The object of *Shenanigans*: two kids compete on a three-dimensional game board, landing on spaces that direct them to perform a stunt or receive a prize. Money was given out as "Shenanaganzas," which were redeemable like trading stamps. The program was sponsored by game maker Milton Bradley and the trials the kids went through to get to the end were mostly based on Milton Bradley games like Operation and Time Bomb.

The commercials were solely for Milton Bradley products as well, which proves that Saturday-morning toy tie-ins go back a long way. In the ultimate bastardization, you could also buy the *Shenanigans* home game—from Milton Bradley, of course. Not so coincidentally, Milton Bradley also made the home version of *Video Village*.

After a well-received first season, *Shenanigans* was renewed for a second term. Returning after a summer hiatus, ratings declined and the show was pulled in December 1965. Stubby Kaye died in 1997. *Shenanigans* was his last regular TV gig and he was rarely seen even as a guest star after 1966.

Stubby Kaye was last seen in *Who Framed Roger Rabbit*.

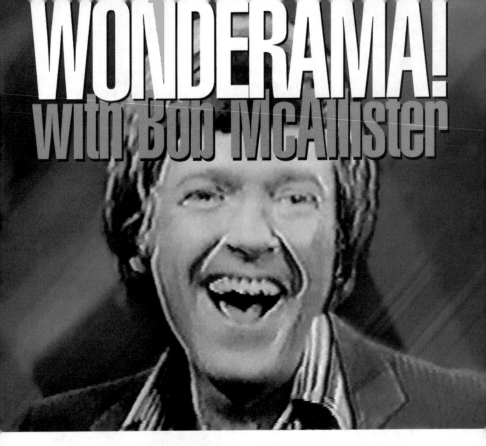

WONDERAMA!
with Bob McAllister

Wonderama *was the nation's local kid show—delivered every week via cable TV over the Metromedia Superstations.*

Host Bob McAllister assaulted the senses for three hours every Sunday and made a lot of friends over the years! McAllister passed away on July 21, 1998, so we present these testimonials and memories from some of his many friends, coworkers, and fans in his honor.

As it is with memory, things you read here might not be 100 percent accurate, as the mind often colors outside the lines.

BEFORE WONDERAMA THERE WAS BALTIMORE

Before Bob McAllister hosted *Wonderama*, he did a local TV show in Baltimore called *The Bob McAllister Show*, which was produced in the mid-'60s on station WJZ. Is there any one besides myself that remembers this show? I had the pleasure of being on it back in 1966. I have written WJZ in Baltimore, and, of course, nobody there ever heard of the show. —*Joe Rizzo*

I grew up in Washington, DC, in the early '60s and watched Bob McAllister's show on WJZ-TV 13 from Baltimore. I remember his characters Thurman, Prof. Fingleheimer (Fingleheimer song: "the more you

fingle, the less you heimer"), and Mike Fury, who was a super-hero character who proclaimed that he was "courteous, kind, obedient, cheerful, thrifty, friendly, brave, and a goody."

When Bob left for *Wonderama,* WJZ did a final show in which Bob talked about the Mike Fury character. In order to make him fly, they strapped him to the top of a Westinghouse van and drove around the Baltimore beltway. Supposedly the van was only available once a year so all flying was taped on that day.

The Baltimore show was fun and I felt that Bob lost something when he moved to *Wonderama* in New York. There was no real mention of his death in the *Baltimore Sun* other than a few short lines and no mention of his work on WJZ.

The *Washington Post,* in an article surprisingly larger than the *Baltimore Sun,* mentioned his role on *Wonderama,* as well as work in Baltimore and Norfolk.
—*Wesley*

When I was about three in the mid-1960s, my father worked at WJZ-TV in Baltimore and got me on *The Bob McAllister Show.* On my own appearance I followed him around and asked him so many questions he could hardly do the show. My father told me that he once ran into McAllister after a taping and McAllister described that day's group of kids this way: "They weren't just shitting in their own pants, they were shitting in *each other's* pants!"
—*A Reader*

BOB & CRANCY

I too remember Bob from his morning shows on WJZ in Baltimore in the 60's. His Mike Fury bit was a fave in my school. I think he even showed *Diver Dan* shorts on the show. I'm sure he showed those goofy *Mighty Hercules* cartoons ("Herc, Herc! Wait for me!" said the centaur).

Bob also hosted an afternoon adult program called *People Are Talking* while at WJZ. It was your basic man-on-the-street interview show filmed at Lexington Market and other local places. Kind of like talk radio today. It was the coolest show on when I was in seventh grade. Bob would occasionally sing his song, "I Want to Take a Bath in Bath, New York, the Cleanest City in the State."

Bob was a great magician, and you could run into him on Saturday afternoons at Phil Thomas's Yogi's Magic Mart on Charles Street. I was also way into performing magic tricks in seventh grade too. Bob created some very cool tricks. One I remember buying from Phil and performing was a color-changing scarf trick in a spotted can. You'd have to see it, but it was a funny trick. We would watch *Wonderama* after he went to NY, but those shows never quite clicked with my Junior High crowd.

Baltimore television of the '50s and '60s was pretty good. We had the Buddy Dean dance show after school (I dated one of the dancers, Faith Worschofsky. She wore long, blonde hair that was ironed straight! And *very* short skirts!) John Waters immortalized the show in *Hairspray,* changing the name to *The Corny*

Collins Show. And then there was that strange little fifteen-minute show after the news on WBAL with these really clever puppets. It was called *Sam and Friends* brought to you by Esskay. The puppeteer behind the show's name was Jim Henson—I wonder what ever became of him?
—*Mark Salditch*

WONDERAMA YEARS

My parents sent in a ticket request for Wonderama when I was eight years old. I got my ticket and went on the show when I was 14. I felt like an idiot sitting in the middle of the audience with kids whose requests must have been put in when they were still in the womb. I have to admit, though, that I had a great time. Until I had to go back to high school the next day and face my friends who had seen me on the show waving my hands back and forth at the opening of the show like I was trying to guide a 747 to the runway.

I'm thirty-eight years old now. I went to my twenty year class reunion this past November and guess what the first topic of conversation was when I got there? And I've still never seen an aardvark.
—*Tom Larkin*

I remember *Wonderama* vividly. McAllister came out as a character called Dr. Fingleheimer on occasion.

There was also a contest called "What is it?" in which he would hold up an obscure object and the audience would try to guess what it was (one was an Ugli fruit). After the audience was stumped, a voice with a thick Yiddish accent would say, "What the heck is it?" and McAllister would give the answer.

The audience dance segments were interrupted by the Disco Kid, who would run in with a song request, although I recall that the song stayed the same for weeks on end.

Some of the guests I recall are: Michael Palin and Terry Jones, who were in town to promote *Monty Python* on PBS, as well as the *Big Red Book*. The kids were com-

The biggest stars appeared on *Wonderama*.

pletely bewildered by them, a pratfall or an explanation of the game "Pass the Bengal Tiger" notwithstanding.

Stephanie Mills, when she was in *The Wiz,* Stan Lee of Marvel Comics, who appeared with Spider-Man, who did a dance called, "The Spider-Man." A contest was held for the kid who did the dance the best. I regret to say I remember part of the dance!

Mel Blanc was conscripted to do a contest—the kids had to guess how many voices he could do in a minute. He did eleven, ending with Jack Benny's Maxwell.
—*A Reader*

I have an LP by Bob McAllister called *Kids Are People Too.* The copyright date is 1971 and it says that all the songs are written by "Susan & Robin McAllister's daddy: Bob." The list of songs include: "Kids Are People Too," "Fingleheimer Stomp," "I Wish, I Wish (The Animal Song)," "Exercise," "Abracadabra (Instrumental)," "Heavy, Heavy," "(Have You Heard Any) Good News," "The No, No Song (eh-eh-eh)," "The Make-up Song," and "Ecology."
—*Randy Ralston*

Wonderama was on Sunday mornings on KTTV 11 in Los Angeles and I recall watching Joe Frazier, Muhammad Ali, David Essex, ABBA, Bay City Rollers, Maria von Trapp, Jerry Lewis, and Bob McAllister asking an eleven-year-old audience member who his favorite music artist is, the child's response being, "The Grateful Dead." Bob's expression was one of being oblivious to who they were or are. Adam Corrolla of *Loveline* waxes nostalgic of *Wonderama* on occasion, and it cracks me up hearing him sing the exercise and aardvark songs.
—*Ethel*

It seems many people remember Bob McAllister fondly. Bob used to live in my home town of Pelham, New York. Every Halloween, he put on quite a show for the neighborhood kids. I remember the elaborately carved pumpkins and waiting in line for a quick show that was performed inside his garage. I was really impressed when R2D2 was there one year along with a magician. There was also a witch flying in circles around his back yard. I watched that witch for quite some time and never did figure out how it was done. We never saw Bob on those nights, but we did see him around town and he always took the time to say hello to kids and to sign autographs.
—*Robert Pflugfelder*

Above: On *Wonderama,* Bob breaks up Muhammad Ali and Joe Frazier before their big title match, to be held the next day.

I loved *Wonderama* and remember it as one of the happiest points of a rather confused and messed-up childhood. (My parents divorced right during that time.) Unfortunately, my memories are scattered. I remember his New Milford performance, and having him come through the crowd to pick kids to go on stage. We were mobbing him pretty badly, and he came to my row. In my enthusiasm in waving my hand towards him to be picked, instead of coming within feet of Mr. McAllister, I came within inches—and he rightly told me, "Get your hand out of my face!" He ended up picking the sister of my best friend, two seats away—it was a ball-and-blanket game. I just remember *really* wanting one of those balls (they looked neat under the purplish lighting.)

He didn't do autographs that day, but we managed to convince an assistant to bring a photo of him we'd bought back to him while he was eating lunch—I didn't get to see him, though. I can imagine it would be difficult, being mobbed like that show after show.

I had the album *Gee It's Great to Be a Kid,* but lost it somewhere along the way. All I remember of it is loving it immensely, and the second song being about a magician.

One show featured three cartoonists, one of which was the fellow who does *Hagar the Horrible* (Johnny Hart). They had a drawing contest, to see who could draw each other's characters the fastest.

I never got to do it while he was around, so I'll do so now. Thanks, Mr. McAllister, for some of the best, happiest memories of my life. May we meet on streets of gold, and may you pull a coin from my ear.

—*Walter White*

I remember *Wonderama* keenly because I not only watched it every Sunday but appeared as an audience member three times (my sister, cousin, and I were on it in the late '60s)! What a fix!

My aunt was good friends with Bob McAllister so it was only natural that after enough whining I was able to score my first-time-ever appearance(s) on television.

The first two times, my sis and I got zilch (if you discount the stomachache from consuming candy and RC Cola all day). So my aunt let into Bob M. The next time I was on, I not only got to play the "Snake Charmer" in the Snake Cans game, but he awarded a Deluxe Spirograph to my sister (I came away with a fire engine, and assorted toys that, piled up, were taller that I was).

Snake cans!

I'll never forget the first time we participated in the "Aardvark Song"—where the kids were asked to bring and show off unusual items from home. I brought in a large leather-bound book from the 1800s (unusual enough to have all the kids ask to check it out) and my little sister brought an oversized wooden salad fork and spoon. I was embarrassed by my sister's conception of "cool," but it made Bob McAllister hysterical with laughter.
—*Jonathan Tessler*

I had the pleasure of speaking with Bob McAllister personally. My son had a magic project to do for school (at that point I didn't know that he was also a magician, that was in May or June of 1994). A friend of mine gave me his number. I called, expecting to get a secretary, but to my surprise he answered his own phone! I remember asking for him; when he said, "Speaking," I almost fell off my chair! I too had watched *Wonderama* and *Kids Are People Too* and couldn't believe I was speaking to him directly (I was star struck!). He was so helpful with information, and even told me that he held meetings for young magicians in New York City on Sunday afternoons! It was truly my pleasure!
—*Ileana G*

I was saddened to hear of the passing of Bob McAllister, but only slightly more-so than I was to see him on a tiny stage at New Jersey's Six Flags Great Adventure in 1993. He was doing the same shtick to the same schmucks (okay, we watched for awhile), and I would not have imagined him to be ill. The small audience seemed either to be the morbidly curious or old-timers like us (we were about thirty) dragging their kids to see what they used to watch every Sunday for three hours on Channel 5 (before it became Fox). Strangely enough, the kids were eating it up.

An even better story from New Jersey dates back to when I was about eight (1972). My parents got us tickets to see *Wonderama* at the Paramount theater in Asbury Park (now actually making a comeback after years of neglect). I don't know if they were as stupid as my younger brother and I were or if they were just going along with the game, but we all seemed to think we were going to be on TV. Instead, it was just a scaled down version on the Paramount's hard cement floor with kids packed into a few old bleachers. I recall being very disappointed not seeing any cameras. I also don't remember old Bob being very friendly. We still

"Ass, gas or grass, nobody rides for free." — *Bumper sticker from the '70s*

watched the show religiously, though, and I told all my friends that I was on *Wonderama*. Don't tell my wife I wasn't.

—Marc Natanagara

When radio humorist Jean Shepherd appeared on March 31, 1974, it marked the only time in the show's history that the studio audience's parents were seen on camera. They wanted to be part of Shep's storytelling session. Later in the show Jean performed a musical number ("Hot Buttered Popcorn") by hitting his head repeatedly. The kids guessed how many times Shep hit his head to win prizes.

Early in the interview segment Jean was heard saying "I know what *that* kid's thinking." To which Bob replied, "Easy, Jean. We're a children's show"

—*Pete Delaney*

Here's some information that you probably didn't know. Arthur Forrest, the producer of *Leeza*, also produced *Wonderama* for a while—definitely in the '70s. I met him at the Daytime Emmys in 1996, when both of us were nominated (for different shows).

McAllister actually put out an album called *Kids Are People Too* (his big signature line), and did album signings around New York in the early '70s. One of those signings occurred at Mays' Department Store near Lake Success, NY. He was appearing promptly at ten in the morning and the kids were lined up outside the store. When the doors opened, there was a stampede to the table where Mr. McAllister was. The line went around the store and outside, but I waited patiently until finally I talked to Mr. McAllister and got my autographed copy.

I went on *Wonderama* about three times and here's some information regarding tapings. The show was staged at WNEW/Metromedia television studios at 205 East 67th Street in New York, just a few blocks down from the old Jim Henson shop. Overall *Wonderama* tapings were pretty long. You arrived midweek at 9 AM, and the taping would take about eight to sometimes ten hours.

They didn't supply lunch, only snacks. During each break, McAllister would step away from the kids (my guess is that a few got on his nerves) and smoke like a chimney. I remember once or twice he snapped at some kid who was being annoying. Other than doing his bit for the camera, he never seemed to be interested in the kids at all. Maybe it might have been the pressure of an eight-hour long taping.

The big *Wonderama* basement where they did all the dancing was, in fact, just the other side of the same studio set. All they did was aim the cameras in the other

I know these pictures look fuzzy—but almost no footage of *Wonderama* exists!

direction and pulled out those four dancing platforms and turned on the color lighting.

At the end of the show, many kids ended up going home with just a bag of junk like Silly Putty, Lender's Bagels, Good Humor Ice Cream, Krause's Hot Dogs, and some other crud. Very few won the toys. But as a kid I ate it all up cause it was a thrill, and the memories are still good. At the end of the show, they would set up for the *Ten O' Clock News* (which was done live in the same studio) and they brought you down from the fifth floor by elevator. The parents must have had the worst part—sitting in a small room for the whole day watching it all on the monitor.

Oh yeah, a few other facts: When *Wonderama* finally left the air (1977), McAllister did a national show on ABC called *Kids Are People Too!* He exited the show after a few months because of creative differences (he was replaced by a younger man). A few years ago I saw an ad on television selling a *Magic Tricks by Bob McAllister* kit. And he looked much the same as I remembered.

A funny story was relayed in a 1997 interview with Rocky Allen of WPLJ in New York. McAllister recalled that Maria Von Trapp of the Von Trapp family (*Sound of Music*) and Richard Rodgers (Rodgers and Hammerstein) were both guests on Wonderama when the elderly Von Trapp eagerly asked the kids how old they thought she was. One kid screamed out, "Ninety-three!" Rodgers leaned in and said, "Serves the old bag right," to McAllister's delight.

—*Brian Mitchell*

WORKING ON WONDERAMA

I worked on *Wonderama* from 1974 to '78, and was in fact Bob's assistant.

Now, I am VP of a record label in NY, and I am a little bothered by the incorrect info about the eight-hour tape days at WNEW in NY. At each break, I would go out, take the mic from Bob, and speak to the kids in the audience to keep them entertained. TV is not easy to make, and it takes time and patience. For a number of years, we fed the kids. But the hot lights and excitement caused upset stomachs, so we stopped, and just gave them snacks. You know, if one kid threw up, it would cause a chain reaction. Not good.

The taping didn't start until 1 PM. I don't know where the person who wrote in came up with 9 AM, but we weren't even allowed to have parents or kids line up until after *Midday Live* went off the air at noon. Also, the parents who didn't have to stay were kept in a spacious room on the third floor (Kluge Hall), with easy chairs and a couple of big monitors and soft drinks. We tried to make those who

"We must never forget that art is not a form of propaganda; it is a form of truth." —*John F. Kennedy*

did stay comfortable. Very often, I would go down with other staff members, and allow those parents to come to the fifth floor and peek into the studio and/or control room. Against the rules, but nice to do.

Bob didn't smoke like a chimney. He smoked on occasion, and did quit long before he died. Brian Mitchell sounds like a man who's miffed he didn't win Snake Cans. In fact, there was a seven-year wait for tickets, and he should consider himself lucky for having been on three times. Bob never "snapped" at a kid. He truly loved kids. Not just hype, but really did. And the bag of junk the kids got when they left were souvenirs. Not gold nuggets. The memories of being there is what counted. The kids were treated well. Very well. They left with smiles on their faces.

Bob, who owned the right to the name *Kids Are People Too* (written by Bob and Artie Kaplan), was replaced on that ABC show by Michael Young but retained the ownership of the name.

Richard Rodgers actually said, "That serves the old bitch right."

The correct name of his video is *Bob McAllister's Amazing Magic*, changed from *Bob McAllister's Blockbuster Magic*.

Bob's dog Ralph was a Hungarian poolie trained by Lew Burke who lives in Carmel, NY—a frequent guest on *Wonderama* with his dog Buddy.

There were seven Metromedia stations—New York / Boston / Cincinnati / Minneapolis / Los Angeles / Kansas City / Washington, DC.

The Disco City song changed every week. It was selected by associate producer Jan Bridge.

Message to Marc Natanagara—Sorry you were disappointed by the hard floors. Surely not as hard as your head.

Additionally, I worked with Bob on all of the "Live" weekend shows he did around the country—the non-televised charity events. Ninety percent of them were for charity—mostly Women's American ORT (Organization for Rehabilitation and Training). I negotiated the deals, and worked with him at the shows along with Jan Bridge.

Bob would make a small fee—barely enough to cover his expenses. We would supply the entire show—all of the props, toys, games, etc. All of the money above and beyond his fee would go to the charity, including a large percentage of the money from the sale of the merchandise—bagel necklaces, pins, albums, etc. We did many, many each year—almost every Saturday and Sunday in New Jersey, Maryland, DC, Virginia, etc. On the very rare occurrence that the turnout was

The Jacksons sang *Enjoy Yourself*.

light, Bob would return *all* of the money to the charity and forgo his fee. How many in the entertainment industry can make that claim?

Bob and I (and Ralph the poolie) drove from NY to LA the first week of July, 1976, arriving in LA on July 4, 1976. We had worked out a deal with ORT to stage eight shows in the Los Angeles area over a two-week period. We were in places like Van Nuys, Tarzana, Culver City, etc. A few years later, I moved to LA and lived there for fifteen years (in the Woodland Hills area) and every time I drove by one of those high schools where we performed, it brought back great memories of a fun and successful fund raising trip. We drove in Bob's big yellow/gold Dodge van, packed with toys and props, and while we were there car customizer George Barris painted the outside of the van to read *Kids Are People Too*. It was quite a sight. Driving home to New York, you would not believe how many people around the country recognized Bob, and made contact with us on the CB radio. His CB handle (name) was "Wonderama Man."

The only real disappointment on the coast was a show we did in San Diego. We never realized in San Diego very few folks had ever heard of *Wonderama*. Although there was a nice sized crowd, Bob returned his fee for that show to add to the ORT's take.

After I moved to LA in 1978, and Bob was no longer hosting *Kids Are People Too*, he came to stay with me for a couple of weeks in the early 1980s, and did a week's worth of shows at the Magic Castle for packed houses every night. It was great to be there, and great to work again with Bob in front of the likes of Cary Grant, David Niven, and a who's who of the entertainment industry—all loving the show he did. He geared the live *Wonderama* and magic show to adults, and everyone had a ball. Castle owner Milt Larson was thrilled.

More random *Wonderama* notes:

Around 1975, Monty Hall flew Bob out to LA to host one episode of *Let's Make A Deal*—not to replace Monty, but to serve as an audition for a new game show Monty was producing called *Carnival*. A few months later, Bob was back in LA to host the *Carnival* pilot, which was terrific, but, like most pilots, not picked up. Bob was disappointed, as he felt this could have been his first real network job.

Producers of *Wonderama* over the years included: Art Stark, former producer of *The Tonight Show Starring Johnny Carson*; David Brenner (yep, the same one); Artie Forrest, who I believe just concluded directing *Rosie O'Donnell*, and directs *Leeza*; Dennis Marks, who last I heard was working for Marvel; Norman Blumenthal, former creator and producer of the original *Concentration*. Chet

"Outside of a dog, a book is man's best friend. Inside of a dog, it's too dark to read." — *Groucho Marx*

117

Lishawa was the director of *Wonderama* and the *Channel 5 Ten O'Clock News,* and is now a director for the Fox News Network.

Associate producers included Jan Bridge (major force for *Wonderama* being on the cutting edge of the music business in the '70s; Jan now works for Sony Music), and Gary Hunt (now a partner of Hunt-Jaffe Productions in LA). Other staffers included Anna DeSimone and Neme Schlesinger (Where are you now, guys?). Other *Wonderama* guests included—Marcel Marceau, Neil Sedaka, Edward Villella, Roberta Peters, Jacques Cousteau, Leroy Neiman, Johnny Bench, Reggie Jackson, dancer Ann Reinking (was on the same show as the Jacksons), ABBA, Bay City Rollers, Dick Clark (Anna and I appeared on that show in *The 25,000 Peanut Pyramid),* Rodney Dangerfield, Charlie Strauss and the cast of the original *Annie,* Mark Wilson, Harry Blackstone, David Copperfield, Dick Van Dyke, and literally a hundred more.

That's it for now.

—Don Spielvogel

I was always a major *Wonderama* fan as a kid, so I wrote a letter to Arthur Forrest, the show's director, when I was twelve years old to ask if I could come down to the control room to watch the taping. He said yes, and this became my routine every six months or so.

My father would take me to the studio by subway, then come back and pick me up, some six hours later. I always wanted to be a cameraman on *Wonderama,* but the show went off the air when I was twenty-one and I never made it.

I did, however, become a cameraman at ABC, and worked with Bob on *Kids Are People Too.* We talked about the days I came down to Metromedia to see the show, both as an audience member and an observer in the control. That show really helped me make up my mind about being a cameraman.

I'm forty-three now, and still talk to Arthur and his son Paul. I've won two Emmys for my camera work and also became a director on a daytime soap at ABC. I have Arthur Forrest, Bob McAllister, and *Wonderama* to thank for my twenty-five year career at ABC. Shortly before his death I had talked to Bob about doing a kids show again. That show will never be produced now . . .

—Howie Zeidman

My most fun memory of this show is twofold: Assistant producer Jan Bridge did the music for the show and used a song by a Cleveland, Ohio, band named Circus for six weeks in a row. It didn't help sell the song ("Stop, Wait & Listen"), but it

Bob McAllister was seen in the TV movie *Herbie Day at Disneyland* (1974) with Bob Crane and Helen Hayes.

sure put me in good with the band. Ironically, the show never played in Cleveland.

Bridge was a buddy of mine and I recall helping him move from one apartment to another. For this deed, he gave each of his helping a friends a thank-you gift: records, rock and roll stuff, etc. Me, I got fifty Burger King coupons—the kind they gave out on the show. Those 1974 BK coupons got you a Whopper (which *did* really take two hands to hold) a big order of fries, and a big Coke.

It took three years to eat through those coupons. Twenty-five years later it still kills me to pay for Burger King food!

—*Pete Kanze / WARY Radio*

What a hoot!! I remember as a kid seeing Mel Blanc on *Wonderama* and being in awe of him. I made it my lifelong goal to do voices for cartoons, in particular Porky Pig. Well, I've been voicing Porky as well as many other characters for a while now. Thanks for the memories!

—*Bob Bergen*

Wonderama became the show that it was because of Bob McAllister and his excellent talents. Whenever I think about the show, it's Bob who comes to mind first and foremost.

My brothers and I were on the show in May of 1970 and at that age it was really a big thrill. The majority of what was said about the experience people had while being on the *Wonderama* set is accurate. When I was there in 1970, then, too, Bob was snapping at people off camera. This doesn't imply that he hated kids, just that he seemed to be under the stress of deadlines, etc.

The taping may not have started at nine in the morning, but actually started at 12:30 PM and continued until 6:45 PM on Wednesdays and Fridays. This is per a 1970 letter sent to my mother from WNEW's June S. Hamilton, who worked in the ticket department at the time. Either way, it's still quite a bit of time taping for a kid.

The prizes were simple and the whole set for that matter was cheap, period. But it was a very original show which was hosted by a very talented man. He really knew how to entertain children, which may explain why he had such a great number of viewers. His job there must have been very demanding on him, but he never showed it, not on camera anyway. Regardless of whether or not his career was as successful as some of his guests were, Bob left a great memory with many people and in the long run that's what really matters.

—*David Ferreira*

Hi, I'm Susan, Bob McAllister's oldest daughter. I have enjoyed reminiscing at your Web site. My dad was the first one to show it to me. He got a kick out of it also.

Dad enjoyed much fame in his career, particularly in the '70s. The story of his rise to that period is fabulous; he got his start in what I would call the "old school" of television. He took many risks that paid off and eventually landed him *Wonderama*.

What was even more telling of his sterling character, however, was the grace with which he accepted the decline of his fame in the last few years. What may not be common knowledge is that Dad was a true magician at heart, and managed quite well for himself through personal appearances and teaching magic both at Stuyvesant and at magician conferences. He was an innovator in this field, inventing whole new concepts in magic. He had these big, thick fingers that didn't look like they would be adept at sleight of hand (which was his specialty). They would fumble through a trick (or so you thought) and something amazing would bound to life. The following is a quote (from *The Merry Heart* from Viking Press) we found in his address book . . . my sister Robin read it at his funeral:

"WHAT IS MAGIC? Is it not the production of effects for which there appear to be no causes? Behind all magic there is an explanation, but it is unwise to seek it too vigorously; there are lots of things in life which are more enjoyable when they are not completely understood. A good piece of magic is a work of art and should be respected as such; it is a flower, not an alarm clock, and if you pull it to pieces to find out what makes it work you have destroyed it and your own pleasure."

Our family is still sorting through the shock of his passing. It came quite unexpectedly two weeks ago, from lung cancer he didn't know he had. Since then, I promise you, my grandfather clock chimes an extra chime every hour, and I am tempted to say as I have so often in the past, "How'd he DO that?"

—*Susan McAllister*

ster, 63, TV Host and Magician

S Jr.
.ed his
without
host of
w, then
yester-
ttan. He
s decade
Brown-
a."
se was a
he would
d been di

llister re-

Sonny Fox
Second host of
Wonderama

I have many memories of, and much detritus from, *Wonderama*. I have recently dug it all up and organized it as part of a book I am currently trying to write. My book will start in the dim recesses of growing up in Brooklyn in the depression years, and include the many forms and shapes—the agony and the ecstasy—of a loooong career.

Perhaps the knowledge that we always had a standby mop in the *Wonderama* studio will be of interest. Since the young audience was incarcerated for over five hours while we taped (on Thursdays) the Sunday mini-telethon, one could always count on at least one kid wetting his/her pants and one kid throwing up. Came with the territory.

The number of my "kids" (now forty-five to fifty-five) who continue to seek me out, mostly via the Web site is astonishing. The most amazing thing is the vividness of their recall. When your audience is young, all the experiences seem to occupy more space in their minds.

Hell, I can still sing the theme song of Uncle Don, who was my Sonny Fox on radio each evening in the 1930s.

—Sonny Fox

**Sonny Fox is
Sr. VP of Population
Communications International.**

SHRIMPENSTEIN!

Was this the craziest kid show of all time?

"*Shrimpenstein* was on KHJ Channel 9 in LA from about late 1966 until sometime in 1968 or '69. The hosts were Gene Moss (Dr. Von Shtick) and Jim Thurman (voices). Shrimpenstein was a miniature Frankenstein monster (a ventriloquist dummy created when jelly beans were thrown into the Monster Machine—no, I did not make this up).

"The show was in color and I still have my Shrimpenstein Value stamps and a 45 record of the opening theme sung by Gene Moss in a bad Boris Karloff imitation. Moss and Thurman did advertising campaigns, mostly for radio. Moss later did voiceovers for LA's Channel 2 News and Disney/Touchstone Pictures preview voice overs. Thurman also wrote and did voices for *Sesame Street*.

"*Shrimpenstein* was funny and irreverent, which probably led to its downfall, as they made fun of the sponsors (McDonalds) and the cartoons on the show (the very limited animation Marvel superheroes)."   —*Sincerely, Mike G*

"The zany little *Shrimpenstein* puppet was built by renowned artist Wah Chang. Chang was responsible for all sorts of stuff, like the props and weapons in the original *Star Trek*. Moss and Thurmon went on (not much later) to do a short-lived

"You're never too old to become younger. " — *Mae West*

Johnny Carson–esque talk show on KHJ as well as writing and voicing the cult favorite *Roger Ramjet."*   —*Robert Hill*

"Gene and Jim were fired from *Shrimpenstein* and replaced by KHJ announcer Wayne Thomas for a few months preceding Shrimpy's demise. Wayne-o just didn't have it!

"The late-night talk show thing during the summer of '67 was called *The Moss & Thurman Show OR the Thurman & Moss Show OR the OR Show.* Broadcast Monday through Thursday at 10 PM on Channel 9, they had a three-piece combo headed by Stan Worth (along with Whitey Mitchell on bass and Allan Goodman on drums).

"They had screwy guests (I think Brother Theodore may have been on) as well as an actual notable person from time to time. They had a studio audience, first come first serve, and audience members would bring big poster signs. It was silly and fun.

"Thereafter, Gene and Jim concentrated on their advertising career for a while . . . Der Weinerschnitzel is my personal favorite ("Der Weinerschnitzel, weiner-schnitzel, dis must be the place. Just drive right in and put a great big hot dog in your face"). We'd watch out for various commercials they'd be in or do voiceovers for—Gene's Coffeemate ("Rounds out the flavor of a good cup of coffee"—the square cup morphing to round), and Jim as the VandeKamp's Fisherman, all decked out in yellow slicker.

"As has been noted, they started doing voices on *Sesame Street,* and Jim eventually became a writer for the *Electric Company* and, I believe, won an Emmy. Most recently (although it has been awhile) I picked up their voices on *MathNet* on PBS."   —*Ann R.*

Sadly, Gene Moss died in July 2002.

The creator of Shrimpenstein speaks!

The zany comedy team of Gene Moss and Jim Thurman put the *Shrimpenstein* show on the map, but they were not the creators of the character Shrimpenstein or the show.

I, Mike Dormer, being of semi-sound mind, dreamed up the little squirt while seated at my stylish plastic kitchen table in the mid-'60s in Ocean Beach, California.

Lee Teacher, my creative cohort at the time, and I have the copyright as proof. Our pal at Capitol Records, producer / packager Fred Rice, suggested that we cook up some cute monster characters for merchandising, and when he saw Shrimpy, the fuse was lit. Fred, Lee, and I honed him visually, then we took the idea to KHJ and pitched the "suits" there on a TV show.

Teacher and I had been doing rock radio promo stuff at the station with a guy named Don Berrigan, so we had an "in." KHJ bought the idea and we started to knit the show together. Fred had worked with Moss and Thurman before on record albums, so they were plugged in as actors. Teacher and I became instant TV writers.

The Shrimpenstein puppet was cleverly crafted by noted sculptor and puppetmeister, Wah Chang. I designed the Shrimpy set and all the goofy machines used on the show, and our crackerjack stage crew built everything in record time. Teacher and I also wrote the *Shrimpenstein* theme song lyrics.
—Mike Dormer

Jot was a series of five-minute short subjects produced and written by Ruth Byers for the Radio and Television Commission of the Southern Baptist Convention. The first batch of thirteen segments debuted in 1965. They were non-secular but projected a strong religious message.

Lessons in obedience, honesty, and virtue were reinforced through feelings of guilt, balanced with words of wisdom from Jot's parents and an implicit forgiveness from God.

In the first segment, Jot steals a cupcake from his mom and goes through a psychedelic, freak-out guilt-trip. In most of these morality plays, it's Jot's conscience that speaks loudest, a concept that may be forever lost on modern audiences.

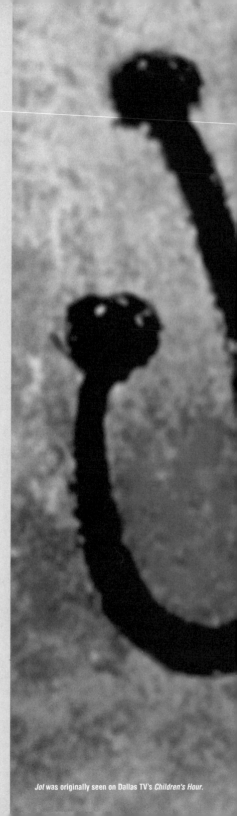

"Until I found your mention of the animated religious cartoon *Jot,* I was becoming increasingly afraid that my recollection of the surreal show was just a bizarre hallucination.

"Watching *Jot,* with its stark, modern-art-influenced abstract-minimalist design (characters were simply blank round circles set against a plain, single-color background) combined with often disturbing, yet subtle religious themes (which seemed to gently hint at the virtues of totalitarianism), was a near-hypnotic experience which inexplicably always seemed to be able to draw my attention away from more enlightening fare such as *The Pink Panther Show.*

"Oddly, the Dali-esque claymation and fatalistic tone of *Davey and Goliath* had that same power . . ."

—MQ

Jot was originally seen on Dallas TV's *Children's Hour.*

twin cities farewells

by Julian West

Roger Awsumb had wanted to be a radio performer since he was a youngster growing up in Saint Paul, Minnesota. After a stint in the Army, stationed in Japan, he graduated from Macalester College with a B.A. in speech and radio. His first professional job was at radio station KDLM in the northern Minnesota town of Detroit Lakes, where he created a children's program called *Storytime Express.* In 1952, Roger had the opportunity to transfer to the Twin Cities and enter the then-new field of television. For a time he worked at WCCO-TV, Channel 4, but in 1953 he joined WTCN-TV, Channel 11, where he did just about everything: announcing, floor managing, directing—and starring in a new children's show called *Lunch with Casey.*

Roger had decided to portray the famous railroad engineer Casey Jones on the show because, he said, "He's such a well-known figure and railroading is romantic for children." Created in an era when many children went home from school to eat lunch, as the name implies *Lunch with Casey* aired during the noon hour and it quickly became a lunchtime tradition throughout the Twin Cities area. During the first few years of the program, Casey's sidekick was Joe

the Cook, a wild-eyed mustachioed manic chef of Greek heritage and dubious culinary skills, played by Chris Wedes.

Meanwhile, WCCO-TV badly needed a strong entry in the kidvid sweepstakes. It's not surprising that the station turned to a proven performer like radio veteran Clellan Card.

Although Clellan's kid appeal had been noted as early as the 1930s, he had always considered himself an entertainer of adults. Not that there was anything off-color in his routines; it's simply that most of his humor was aimed at grown-ups.

Clellan was recruited to play a variation of his wacky Scandinavian character Axel, a familiar voice on radio since 1937. To play Axel's dog Towser, Clellan enlisted the aid of a young actor and director named Don Stolz, who was building a reputation at the Old Log Theater in the suburb of Excelsior. The pairing proved to be a winning combination. The chemistry between Clell and Don would be a key factor in the success of the new show.

Clellan, Don, and director Harry Jones worked out the basic premise of the Axel program, probably during the summer of 1954. They realized that visuals were crucial in the new medium of TV. Axel's costume, like the outfits worn by the classic movie comedians, was simple yet memorable. A train engineer's cap perched high on his head, the brim sticking straight up. A bushy mustache erupted from beneath Axel's nose, making him vaguely resemble an idiotic Adolph Hitler (but apparently there were no complaints from viewers). He wore a T-shirt with wide black-and-white horizontal stripes, intersected by a pair of broad suspenders that held up his baggy olive-green khakis. To make absolutely sure that his pants stayed up, Axel added a long rope belt that dangled almost to his knees.

Right from the very first program, Axel also brandished his magic spyglass. Allegedly a telescope, even a small child could see that it was nothing more than two cardboard tubes, one nested inside the other. Yet, somehow, Axel's spyglass worked—probably because he so convincingly claimed that it did. He affectionately called it his flute and carefully put it away after each use, so that "nobody could steal it." He often talked about it as if it were the latest in modern technology, and spoke of turning up the "candlepower" to increase its range. Once, he claimed that he could see "even out to Esther Williams's house out to California out dere." The distances seemed to grow greater and greater as time went on, until eventually Axel declared that, using his spyglass, he could look "clean around the world"—and see himself!

The telescope worked beautifully as a transitional device. Every time Axel squinted into it, he directed the audience's attention to the next cartoon, short subject, or commercial. Though its appearance would change over the years, Axel's spyglass became an indelible part of his goofy gestalt from the moment he first peered through it.

Director Harry Jones decreed that Axel's dog Towser should remain unseen by the viewing audience, except for his paw. "I figured that if you really saw [Towser], all you'd see was some kind of a dumb dog outfit that would never convince anybody. I always felt very strongly that kids liked [to use their] imagination. I mean, what did Towser really look like? Well, we never ever showed Towser on the air."

Viewers only saw Towser's huge mottled brown paw—actually a sort of gigantic mitten that fit over Don's entire arm. Yet despite being almost completely unseen and unable to talk to boot, the mutt was vividly brought to life by Don Stolz. A canine of indeterminate breed, Towser was Axel's most trusted friend, and, like any dog, he was loyal and eager to please. Although he couldn't speak English, he definitely could communicate, using an amazing variety of barks, arfs, growls, howls, yips, yaps, and yelps. At times, it almost seemed as if Towser could talk.

On one show when he asked Towser, "What aminal is the best timekeeper?," the dog uttered a staccato series of barks in reply. Axel shook his head, saying, "No, I think you have the wrong idea there. Try again, please." Towser barked again and Axel laughingly exclaimed, "Yah, he's right, a watch dog! Oh well, speaking of time, I s'pose that's the windup!"

Director Jones conceived the setting for Axel's shenanigans: a ramshackle tree house atop a large tree in a forest. "My main philosophy, if you want to be artsy enough to call it that," he noted modestly, "was that if you're going to do a kids' show, the setting is very important." In retrospect, Harry's choice seems utterly perfect, a felicitous blend of reality and fantasy. To kids, a tree house offered a genuine refuge from the grown-up world, a place where adults seldom ventured. *Axel's Treehouse* was an idealized version of that childhood daydream, with the intimate atmosphere of a clubhouse. Anyone with a television set could join the gang. "It is entirely imaginative," Clellan declared in 1957. "We've put Axel, a crusty old guy who likes kids, in a treehouse. It's a good setting for kids' imagination and lends itself to the stories I tell or the films being run."

Unlike many kids' TV shows, *Axel and His Dog* did not include a 'peanut gallery' full of breathless, restless youngsters. It was felt that seeing the show in the studio would shatter the illusion for kids.

At 5 PM on Thursday, August 5, 1954, *Axel and His Dog* aired for the first time. According to Don Stolz, it nearly turned out to be the last time as well. Like virtually all television programs of the era, it was broadcast live. Cast and crew had a quick run-through to determine the basic positions for the two floor cameras, but there really wasn't a proper rehearsal. There was no script—the show was always basically ad-libbed. WCCO-TV had been running promotional announcements for the program during the summer, inviting kids to send in jokes for Axel to read on the air. This had netted a stack of postcards chock-full of gags, knock-knocks, and riddles. In spite of the hectic atmosphere, the first show proceeded pretty smoothly—until Axel decided that it was time to read some of those jokes that the kids had sent in.

Plucking a letter from the pile, he read aloud: "Why does the chicken cross the road?" Perhaps chuckling at the notion that the first joke on his new program would be the world's oldest chestnut, Axel read the punch line before he realized what he was saying: "Because she's laying the farmer on the other side!" Miraculously, the show wasn't immediately cancelled.

A few kinks needed to be worked out as well. The most critical one concerned the cast of characters: despite Towser's eloquent barking, it rapidly became apparent that Axel needed a sidekick who could actually speak English. Since the show already had a male dog, the logical counterpoint was a female cat. Like Towser, the pussycat's puss was never seen onscreen; only her white paw appeared. Harry dubbed the new character Tallulah, after throaty-voiced aristocratic celebrity Tallulah Bankhead.

Naturally, Don played the role of Tallulah. Unlike Towser, who was all blundering guttural affability, Tallulah was temperamental, whiny, and high-strung. She spoke in a high-pitched voice that was often difficult to understand, but she usually seemed to be complaining about something. Thanks not only to her ability to speak but also her moody and volatile personality, Tallulah could respond to Axel's hijinks far more potently than Towser ever could. The verbal jousting that characterized the relationship between Axel and his cat was an important factor in the success of *Axel and His Dog*. Clellan and Don were able to give free rein to their funnybones and they delighted in trying to top each other.

Although Axel was apt to say anything at any time, the Saturday morning version of *Axel and His Dog* was especially wild. "This was all live, you have to remember that," Don noted. "Clellan was a night person, and I certainly was, operating a theater, and half of the floormen were night people, and I'll tell you, anything could happen on that show at that hour of the morning."

Mary Davies, who played Carmen the Nurse for many years, laughed about one New Year's Day when she got home early in the morning after an evening of revelry, and she just happened to tune in Axel's show. By this time, a gawky Birdie puppet—a long-necked spotted fowl with huge fuzzy eyebrows and uncertain taxonomy—had been added to the program. On this particular morning, the Birdie had an ice-pack on its head and was reeling back and forth, obviously hung over. Suddenly, Axel turned to the bird and asked, "Say, Birdie, can I get you a tuna-fish malted?"

Another Saturday morning, near the end of the program, Axel said to the kiddies, "Well, we've been up here in the Tree House for about an hour now, and you've been up for a while, but I'll bet that your parents are still in bed. I think it's about time that they got up, too. So, get a glass of water, go into their bedroom and throw it in their faces, and say, 'Good morning! Time to get up now!'"

After the show, Don turned to Clellan and said, "I don't think you should have done that." Affecting an air of unconcern, Clell brushed him off, saying, "Oh, don't worry about it."

The two of them had just walked into Clellan's office when the telephone rang. For some reason, Clell was reluctant to answer his phone, so Don picked it up and intoned, "Clellan Card's office." The woman on the other end of the line snarled, "Put that son of a bitch on!" Don gingerly handed the receiver to Clellan, who answered with great aplomb, "Hellllloooo?" That, however, was the only thing he had a chance to say, as the woman launched into a furious tirade—because, of course, her child had done exactly as Axel had instructed.

In 1958, Chris Wedes left WTCN-TV for Seattle, taking Channel 11's clown character J.P. Patches with him. He became a venerable institution in the Pacific Northwest. His replacement was a gifted performer and talented mimic named Lynn Dwyer, who had previously been a skater with the Ice Capades—on *Lunch with Casey* he was known as Roundhouse Rodney. Roundhouse's manic personality contrasted perfectly with Casey's pleasant quiescence. He might appear as Tarzan spouting one-liners, a life-size female windup doll, or do his dead-on Jimmy Durante impression. Every year at Halloween, an evil witch would shrink Roundhouse and trap him in a pumpkin—probably so Lynn could take a vacation! Just in time for Halloween, Casey would carve the pumpkin, rescue Roundhouse, and restore him to normal size.

Each day Casey would have lunch delivered by a local restaurant like Shakey's Pizza or McDonalds. Guests like Bob Duerr, animal handler from the St. Paul Como Park Zoo, or a musical act would sometimes entertain. Occasionally they produced musical segments that could best be described as early music videos, featuring Casey and Roundhouse lip-syncing to novelty tunes. A particular standout was a nutty song called "I Love Onions."

Casey Jones   Roundhouse Rodney

"LUNCH WITH CASEY"   WTCN 11

Back on WCCO-TV, it had been established that Axel's Tree House existed in a mythical place called

Magic Island. That fanciful isle became the locale for all of Channel 4's growing list of children's shows: *Johnny .44!*, with Jack Hastings as a cowboy bunking at the Lucky Horse Shoe Ranch: *Popeye's Club House*, originally featuring unlikely sailor Mel Jass; and *Commodore Cappy*, starring John Gallos as a nautical geezer who piloted an atomic submarine called "The Crazy Carrot," and sounded like a cross between Lionel Barrymore and, according to Gallos, "Walter Brennan in heat."

In the fall of 1959, John Gallos appeared as a new character: Clancy the Keystone Cop, who had a voice that owed a lot to Bob Hope's mustachioed sidekick Jerry Colonna ("Aaaaahhh, yes!"). Two years later, he metamorphosed into the drastically different futuristic Clancy the Space Cop in a vain effort to exploit the space race. After just one season the Space Cop vaporized, but Gallos returned as the modern-day Clancy the Cop on Tuesday, September 3, 1963. Unlike his predecessors, this contem-

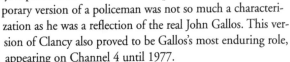

porary version of a policeman was not so much a characterization as he was a reflection of the real John Gallos. This version of Clancy also proved to be Gallos's most enduring role, appearing on Channel 4 until 1977.

The new show, set in a small detective agency, was called *Clancy and Company*. Aspiring theater actor Allan Lotsberg was the "Company." "John needed somebody to talk to," Allan said, "because we found out at that time [that] teams work a lot better than somebody talking into a lens—and if you've ever done that, it gets real lonesome out there."

Allan was originally recruited to handle a witch puppet named Vivian Vulture on the new Clancy show. After a week or so, director Harry Jones persuaded him to appear on camera as well. The next day, Clancy walked over to the portrait of Sherlock Groans, the founder of the detec-

tive agency, and tweaked his nose. The picture slid up, a big door opened, and a wheeled box came rolling onto the set, carrying a silly little guy dressed in a hound's tooth checked suit, his legs akimbo. "Ah! It's Willie Ketchem!" Clancy exclaimed.

Willie quickly became an integral part of the show, his youthful, bumbling exuberance balancing Clancy's reserved and somewhat obtuse persona. Later, Allan developed other characters for the show, notably Willie's Auntie Ketchem, who persistently called her nephew's superior "Clanky," and Wilfred the Wiener Wolf, a furry puppet with a predilection for a particular sponsor's products. *Clancy and Company* often had actual storylines, usually centering around a silly mystery or a lighthearted adventure. The yarn might be told in one self-contained episode or strung out over several weeks, depending on the strength of the material and the needs of the moment. Allan and director Jones usually developed the rough plot, which Clancy and Willie would improvise on from day to day until the tale reached its resolution.

Meanwhile, Don Stolz had left *Axel and His Dog* around the spring of 1962, due to his increasing workload at his ever more successful Old Log Theater. Mary Davies, a talented singer who as Carmen the Nurse had been making sporadic appearances on

the show since 1954, was eventually chosen to co-host the program. Under Carmen's influence, Axel's show became a kinder, gentler program. Some viewers felt that it lost some of its edge.

Another factor in the mellowing of the program may have been Clellan Card's declining health. Diagnosed with cancer, Clell—ever the trouper—continued to do the show between hospital visits and bouts of chemotherapy. "He tried so hard to keep going," Mary remarked with a mixture of admiration and melancholy. Ultimately, though, the reality of his situation was inescapable. One day—probably in mid-March 1966—Clellan came in to do the show, but found that he was physically unable to continue. He knew that he'd finally reached the end of the line. As he slowly made his way off the set, he told Mary flatly, "I won't be back." She'd been dreading the moment for

some time, but when it finally came, she became quite distraught. "What should I do?" she implored him. "What do you want me to tell the kids?" "Aah, tell 'em I'm going around the world," he grumbled, and walked away.

"That was the last time I saw him," Mary murmured sadly. Clellan Card finally succumbed to cancer on April 13, 1966. Mary Davies carried on with the show, eventually moving it out of Axel's Treehouse and into Carmen's Cottage.

In the years immediately after Clellan's death, live-action children's shows remained profitable for local stations. Although the networks had discovered that they could make more money on cartoons than on comparatively expensive live children's television productions, it was another story at hometown affiliates. A low-budget children's show still made sound financial sense for local stations. Sponsors clamored to get their products onto the kids' shows. They loved having local hosts announce their commercials, because they were incredibly effective hucksters, or children were incredibly gullible consumers—or perhaps a bit of both. In any case, when products were promoted by local favorites, kids bought them in droves.

Some saw this as exploitation. A group of concerned parents formed Action for Children's Television (ACT), spearheading an effort to clean up kids' TV. In an effort to protect children from all sorts of alleged evils, ACT began to pressure the National Association of Broadcasters to enact sweeping reforms. Finally, in 1972, the NAB Code was amended to say:

> Children's program hosts or primary cartoon characters shall not be utilized to deliver commercial messages within or adjacent to the programs which feature such hosts or cartoon characters. This provision shall also apply to lead-ins to commercials when such lead-ins contain sell copy or employ endorsement of the product by program host or primary cartoon characters.

This new amendment became effective on January 1, 1973. Even though the NAB Code was a collection of nonbinding principles that stations abided by in a rather desultory fashion, in this case compliance was assured because no one wanted to appear to be taking advantage of children.

"Children have more need of models than of critics." —*Carolyn Coats*

Although the directive didn't eliminate commercials from kids' shows, in one stroke it erased the incentive for sponsors to support local kiddie show hosts. That, in turn, meant that TV stations no longer had a reason to go to the trouble of mounting a daily or weekly children's production. Local stations could fill airtime with relatively cheap cartoons, just as the networks already had, or with syndicated programs that had no local connection. From coast to coast, kids' show hosts were abandoned. The NAB Code reforms had been enacted with the best of intentions, but ironically the net result was that local children's programming became virtually extinct, and was largely replaced by mindless, violent, poorly-animated cartoons that all too often were little more than half-hour advertisements for action toys.

In the Twin Cities, the impact of the new commercial regulations was immediate: after almost nineteen years on the air, Channel 11's *Lunch with Casey* was summarily cancelled. The show's hosts had been rendered utterly expendable to Metromedia, Inc., the conglomerate which then owned WTCN-TV. A storm of protest from the local community ensued, but Metromedia stood fast. Casey pulled into the station for the final time at noon on Friday, December 29, 1972—just days before the NAB amendment was due to take effect.

It was a bittersweet finale. Regular chef Hank Meadows gave Casey a pumpkin pie, animal man Bob Duerr presented him with a mounted South American butterfly, and Minnesota Twins legend Harmon Killebrew "poked in his balding head to mutter a farewell." People from the Como Zoo brought Billy the monkey and Peaches the skunk to say good-bye; Billy expressed his condolences by stomping through the pie. Minneapolis Mayor Charles Stenvig put in a surprise appearance, toting a bag of McDonald's hamburgers. He announced that he had signed a "Bring Back Casey" petition, which unfortunately had no impact whatsoever. Hizzoner promised Casey a distinguished service award, chomped on a burger, and departed.

After reading the list of kids' birthdays for the final time, Roundhouse and Casey bid their audience farewell. Roundhouse declared, "To all the gang out there, if we caused you to laugh a little, we were pleased. If we got you to learn something, we were honored. But if we caused you to think, then this has been perfect."

Then it was Casey's turn. "Well, it's been a long time. Thanks to everybody here and I hope we'll see you," he said, his voice breaking. "Just thank you all very much." An audience had accumulated in the studio as the show progressed, and at the end they burst into applause. After the broadcast, Roger Awsumb quit his other job in WTCN-TV's announcing booth and left the station forever.

At WCCO-TV Channel 4, the kids' shows lasted longer but the end finally came. One day, the station announced the wholesale cancellation of its long-running children's programs to make way for the hot *Donahue* show. On Friday, March 25, 1977, *Carmen* and *Clancy and Willie* made their exit. In the opening of her final show, Carmen shuffled stiffly onto the set, her eyes puffy. "It's a very special day on Magic

"Cauliflower is nothing but cabbage with a college education." *—Mark Twain*

Island," she declared without enthusiasm, "and I'll get to that with a little story for you later." After some uninspired bits and a *Little Rascals* episode, Carmen told a little fable: "About twenty-seven years [ago], a beautiful young girl wandered into WCCO television, walked over to a piano, and started singing a song on a show, and immediately fell in love, not only with the people on that show, but with people [on] many, many shows to come.

"And that beautiful young girl is still beautiful—" she paused and sniffed in a exaggerated way, "albeit long in the tooth—however, twenty-seven years is a long, long time to have a wonderful time and a wonderful love affair with great and wonderful people. I am the gal who came in, and today is the day that I am going to leave WCCO Television, and I will be leaving as Carmen . . . I'm going to miss you, and I know you'll miss Carmen, but that's the way it goes. Time moves on."

"There is so much I could say," she continued, smiling bravely, "and there's so much love I would like to express, but most of it for those daddies and moms who were little kids twenty-four years ago when Carmen came to join you for the first time, who now have little kids themselves. I just want to say 'Thank you.'"

Steeling herself, she went into the wind-up. "WCCO Television, that's the place to stay. God bless you. I love you." She blew a kiss and abruptly got up from her desk. "Remember me!" she called out plaintively, as she quickly walked off the set.

Following a commercial break, the final installment of *Clancy and Willie* began. The centerpiece of the program was Clancy's histrionic telling of "Casey at the Bat," a recurrent highlight of the show. Typically, near the end of the program Clancy and Willie would talk to the kids in the studio, but on that melancholy occasion there was no audience. Instead, Willie soberly informed viewers, "This is the last day. We are closing the Agency here at old WCCO Television." He then introduced Clancy for the last time.

"It has been a real pleasure and a privilege to have been a part of many of the routines in many homes around the Twin Cities, and Minnesota and Wisconsin, for lo, these past many years," Clancy declared. "We've had a lot of laughs over the years, we've had some ups, we've had some downs—and it isn't over yet, because I know I'll be looking for you on other programs here on Channel 4. I'd like to close with an Irish blessing that I think Clancy would enjoy:

"Wishing you always, Walls for the wind, And a roof for the rain, And tea beside the fire. Laughter to cheer you, And those you love near you, And all that your heart might desire. May the road rise to meet you, May the wind be always at your back, May the rains fall soft upon your fields, And until we meet again, May God hold you in the palm of his hand."

As he recited the verse, the camera slowly moved in until at the finish Clancy's face filled the screen. He gazed steadily into the lens, forced a sad little smile, and said simply, "Good-bye."

Roger 'Casey Jones' Awsumb died on Monday, July 15, 2002, at his home on Bass Lake in Merrifield, Minnesota.

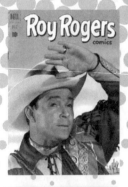

DELL COMICS ARE GOOD COMICS

Dell published a line of comic books based on TV shows and other licensed characters from the 1940s until the 1970s, when the novelty of television programs wore off and reruns became all too plentiful.

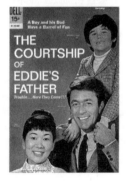

Dell Comics were not subject to the Comics Code.

"Comic books, first of all, are junk. To accuse them of being what they are is to make no accusation at all;

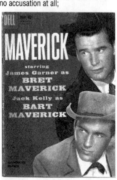

there is no such thing as uncorrupt junk or moral junk or educational junk." —*Jules Feiffer*

Dell Comics were more expensive than other comic books because of licensing costs—and no ads.

I WAS A TV CHILD STAR

by John Eimen

Former child actor and McKeever and the Colonel *co-star John Eimen shares his memories of working in the television industry during the '60s.*

I was involved in TV from the age of six. I started as an extra for the first year or so, on such shows as *Ozzie and Harriet, Leave It To Beaver, The Millionaire, Bachelor Father,* and *Petticoat Junction.*

The first *Leave It to Beaver* I did as an extra. I had only been in the business for a short time and hadn't yet progressed to speaking parts. It was either the very first or the second episode, so the show had not been on TV yet. It was a classroom scene and I was just a kid in the class with the Beaver.

A few years later I was on an episode called "The Long Distance Call," where the Beaver talked to Don Drysdale of the Dodgers on the phone and ran up a big phone bill. As I recall, my scene took place just outside the classroom, where I, the Beaver, and maybe somebody else from our class were talking about how he "was going to get it" when his dad found out. I've never seen this episode since I grew up and hope to catch it sometime. Tony Dow and Jerry Mathers were so unassuming, such genuinely nice guys—it was so refreshing to find that success and fame hadn't spoiled them in the least.

Ozzie and Harriet: The whole Nelson family was unassuming, kind, considerate . . . even when Ozzie was directing, he never got heavy-handed or lost his patience, even when dealing with a bunch of kids who, at times, could get slightly out of control. Harriet bought me an ice cream cone in the commissary after I dropped the one I had. Looking back on it now, it makes me feel so good to know what fine people were involved in the business—their family values were no act at all.

Lassie was a transvestite, a male dog posing as a female.

In the first couple of years I also appeared on *Fury*, *Lassie* (with Jon Provost), three different shows with Frank Sinatra (*Telephone Time*, a live Thanksgiving special with guest Dean Martin, and the movie *Ocean's Eleven*, where my bit part ended up on the cutting room floor).

Fury was filmed on location. Peter Graves was the star, of course, and Bobby Diamond and a boy named Jimmy Baird were co-stars. (Bobby played the son of Peter Graves.) I mainly remember lunch brought out by catering for the entire cast and crew, out in the dusty, hot hills—and the yellowjackets and bees swarming all around the area! I believe that Bobby Diamond became a star gymnast at U.S. Grant High School (a few years before I also attended the school).

I was crazy about Soupy Sales when I was a kid—and I had a chance to work with him on *McKeever and the Colonel* and on a pilot he made called *Where There's Smokey*, where he played a fireman. After he guested on *McKeever*, he invited us to watch him tape one of his shows. I was in heaven!!!

I did a lot of westerns—*Lawman* (Episode: "Yawkey") and *Have Gun—Will Travel*, a couple of *Wagon Train* episodes, *The Rebel* (with Nick Adams), and *Tales of the Plainsmen* (with Michael Ansara).

The scariest shows for me were the live shows—back when you didn't get a second chance. I did the live commercial segment of a Danny Kaye special (with guest Louis Armstrong) where I was warned in advance that Danny just might not give me the exact

John Eimen

Television
Leave It To Beaver (Twice)
Ozzie and Harriet (Four Times)
Twilight Zone
Wagon Train (Twice)
Have Gun—Will Travel (Twice)
The Untouchables
Lassie
Bachelor Father
Wendy and Me
Love, American Style
Lawman
The Lloyd Bridges Show
Profiles In Courage
G.E. Theater
The Rebel
Tales of the Plainsmen
Walt Disney Presents: Gallagher
Walter Winchell File
Petticoat Junction
Going My Way
Angel
Grand Jury
Frank Sinatra Show
Betty Hutton Show
Oh Those Bells!
Believe It or Not

Weekly Co-star of
McKeever and the Colonel
(as Cadet Monk)

Pilots
Dr. Kate (as Jane Wyman's son)
Time Out for Ginger
Where There's Smokey (Soupy Sales)

Live TV
Day In Court
The Danny Kaye Special
(with Louis Armstrong)
The Dinah Shore Show
The Frank Sinatra Thanksgiving Special
(with Dean Martin)
The Bells of Akatsuki
(in Japan)
11 PM (Japanese Late-Night Variety Show)

Model
Carnation Instant Milk
(as the original Milk Mustache)
"Stay In School" Ad
for an Insurance Company

Commercials
The original Alpha Bits commercial
Sugar Frosted Flakes (with my band)

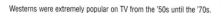
Westerns were extremely popular on TV from the '50s until the '70s.

This is the
Instant that's
delicious
for drinking!

cue—as it turned out, he didn't, and it threw me for a brief moment. (I had also been advised not to talk to him right before the show, as he was a nervous wreck, waiting for the show to start.)

The Alpha Bits commercial I was in had three kids—two girls and a boy—at a carnival. The lines were: "Let's go see the Alpha Bits Man"; "Will he do his tricks?"; (the littlest girl)"What's a trick?"—The song went, "Alpha Bits spell energy, from a to z with a capital E; gee those letters just happen to be, better than any other cereal happens to be." We dubbed the music over at Glenn Glenn Sound, in Hollywood. They had to change my part because I couldn't hit the low note on the word "energy"—instead, they changed it so that I just shouted the word!

There was a little cafeteria next to the place (or it might have been inside the studio, I'm not sure). The Three Stooges were sitting in there, having lunch! I really wanted to meet them but didn't want to go over and bother them. My mom told the waitress to ask them if they'd sing Happy Birthday to me (*even though it wasn't really my birthday!*). The next thing I knew, there they were, singing to me! What nice guys. I got their autographs, too.

One classic advertisement I did was for Carnation Instant Milk back in early 1959 (*Life* magazine, February 2, 1959). That was the earliest (that I know of) model with a milk mustache—long before the current dairy board campaign.

McKeever and the Colonel

McKeever and the Colonel ran during the 1962–63 season on NBC. Cadet Gary McKeever (Scott Lane), with the help of fellow cadets Monk (Johnny Eimen) and Tubby (Keith Taylor) make life miserable for the Colonel (Allyn Joslyn) of a military school.

It always amazes me that so many people remember *McKeever and the Colonel*. It was only on for a year, but it was back in the days when we used to do a lot more episodes for a season than they do now.

McKeever and the Colonel ran from September 1962 to June 1963.

For a show that was on for a short time, they had a few products that were related to it—"McKeever's Retriever" was basically a baseball mitt with a long rubber band and a ball attached to it. I'd be highly surprised if anyone was dense enough to buy one! We (myself, "McKeever" and "Tubby") did at least one commercial for Stratego, the board game Bamboozle was based on the series, and I just recently found a *McKeever and the Colonel* comic book. It was a real kick to do the show.

Alan Joselyn (the Colonel) and Jackie Coogan (Sgt. Barnes) were real veterans of the business and also loved to joke around. It was because of Jackie Coogan that we have our current child labor laws, as you may know. He was "The Kid" with Charlie Chaplin in the '20s. He made a fortune as a small boy but his parents robbed him of it. For some reason he was especially nice to me and I'll always remember his many kindnesses.

"The Colonel" was a good man, too, but aside from the scenes we did together he spent little time with any of us. The other adult regular on the show was Elizabeth Frazier. Even though we were only about twelve years old, all three of us thought she was an absolute babe. There is one still photograph I have of McKeever explaining something to her, where it looks like he's about to feel her up. It was hysterical to us at the time.

Both Scott Lane and Keith Taylor were very smart. I was just an average kid but I had worked in the business for a long time and was very comfortable and unassuming. I lost touch with both of them after the show was cancelled. I had seen Scott on an episode of *The Patty Duke Show* and I heard that he appeared in something else after he grew up. Keith played Piggy in *Eating Rauol*, a movie where he was the main course for dinner but beyond that we didn't hang out together after that. We didn't live near each other and we were all too young to drive.

On *Wendy and Me*, I actually got to dance with Connie Stevens. George Burns was the other star of the series. I remember they pulled me aside when I got there and advised me not to say anything about Gracie, who had recently died. I did an episode of the *Gallagher* series (Walt Disney) where I

The picture to the right is from *Gallagher*.

played a bully trying to make Gallagher pay me to pass by—and did some other roles, too.

I was on an episode of *Petticoat Junction* called "Kate's Day in Court." For some reason, I had trouble getting clearance into the lot and was about five minutes late. I was grown up and on my own and my heart sank that I was blowing it!!! But Bea Benaderet was absolutely wonderful. The director was mad when I first got there, but Bea took care of that. She was one of the warmest and nicest people I'd ever worked with.

I went to Valley Junior College and was in the theater arts department, doing plays and also writing music for some productions. I was in many bands from high school onwards, and in college. I was in a band with Ed Begley, Jr. (later of *St. Elsewhere* and still a good friend). We used to play for parties in the San Fernando Valley, including some for the Dodgers and (at that time) the LA Rams.

My days at Valley were a big reason I didn't continue in the business as an actor for long as an adult. The people in Theater Arts were such a talented bunch—there was Ed Begley, Jr.; the first time I ever saw him I was so impressed with his abilities as an actor. And Michael Richards—Kramer!!!—I was in awe of him. He did things like *Waiting for Godot* and other productions and was a close friend of Ed Begley, Jr. They even did some improv things together as a duo at the Troubadour and other local clubs.

I was simply not in the same league with performers like these—and began to reconsider what I wanted to do. So I found my little niche there mostly doing smaller parts and also music for some productions. Ebbie Smith was also there at that time. He eventually would write the screenplay for the movie *Falling Down*. And there were others who were just extraordinary—Marty Christopher, Robin Bach, Jan Fischer, Bart Williams, Bill Malloy—some you may not know, but they were simply incredible. That sort of set me towards doing more in music, where I had more confidence in my abilities as an adult.

I continued performing in bands in LA, finally ending up in a group that performed at supper clubs around Beverly Hills and West Hollywood (The Larry Sargent Trio). It was very good but I was hardly keeping alive. At about this time (1974) a friend of mine set me up with a blind date—a girl studying English in the US, from Japan.

We started dating and ended up getting married in Japan with a traditional Shinto ceremony at a shrine and staying in Japan for ten years. We then moved to Seattle, where I'd never even visited but had

If I had done any research at all for this book I'd know who that wrestler is.

heard that it was a great place to raise a family. We had a difficult time starting over there. I even worked for one year (three months at a time) aboard factory trawlers in the Bering Sea of Alaska as an interpreter / liaison between the American crew and the Japanese technical advisors. Just the other day, I read several crew members died in those waters out in the Bering Sea.

I sought work on dry land after that. I got a job with a major American law firm, running the office services center for all their back-up needs in copying, mail, faxes, etc. About six years ago another interesting opportunity came my way. Northwest Airlines was looking for Japanese speakers to become Flight Attendants.

Within two weeks I was in training in Minnesota and I became a Flight Attendant in April of 1995. I'm based out of Detroit and still live here in Seattle.

My older son, Daniel, will graduate from the University of Washington with a

degree in engineering and a minor in Japanese this June. My younger son, Chris, is the current celebrity in the family. He's in magazines a lot as a professional bike rider under contract to the K2 Corporation. There's even a "Chris Eimen" Bike now (called "The Biker"). Midori teaches Japanese at two high schools here in Seattle.

For me, my acting days were a positive experience overall. The kids, the crews, the grown-up actors, and just about everybody I came into contact with were professionals doing their jobs with warmth, intelligence, and a huge amount of humor.

Despite the horror stories of kid actors who turned to drugs and alcohol and became bitter about their lives, a lot of them were probably like me—they loved the opportunities they'd been given and the chance to meet and work with so many wonderful people. I think the ones who had the most trouble were those who felt that "I was never a child but I played one on TV . . ." They were the ones who probably had no normal life at all outside of the soundstages. I'm so happy that wasn't me!!!

—*John Eimen*

The Hathaways
Friday nights at 8 PM
ABC / 1961–1962

In *The Hathaways*, Peggy Cass and Jack Weston portrayed the typical Los Angeles suburbanite family—with three kids who happened to be trained chimps.

The chimps (named Enoch, Charlie, and Candy) are taken in by real estate agent Walter Hathaway to help out Walter's pal, a theatrical agent played by Harvey Lembeck. Simian silliness ensues.

The Hathaways featured the Marquis Chimps, a performing troupe well-known for their appearances on *The Ed Sullivan Show* in the '50s.

Not to be confused with *Me and the Chimp* (1972).

TV's Most Sexist Show?

My Living Doll starring Bob Cummings (*Love That Bob*) was one of the craziest sitcoms ever—bizarre even for the '60s.

Cummings portrayed Dr. Bob McDonald, a psychiatrist who cohabitates with a live-in robot/patient played by Julie Newmar. Of course, she initially arrives at the doctor's penthouse apartment wearing only a bedsheet.

Robot AF 709 was paired with Dr. Bob specifically to learn how to become the perfect woman. In 1964, this meant learning to cook, clean, and be enticingly obedient.

Behind the scenes, the two co-stars hated each other and fought often, leading to Cummings storming off the set and leaving the production for good with five episodes left to film. A popular star up to that point, he was rarely seen on television again.

My Living Doll
Sunday nights at 9 PM
CBS / 1964–1965

Some women like to be called dolls—I've just never met one.

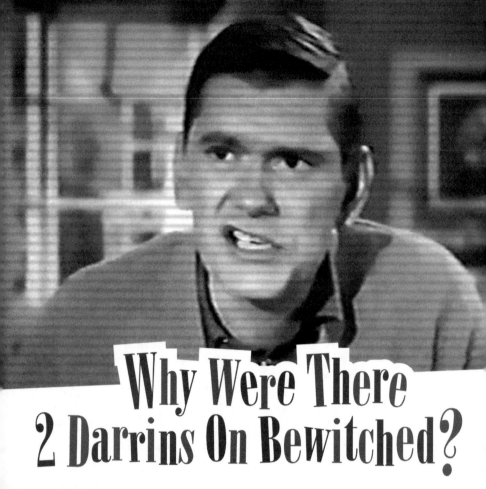

Why Were There 2 Darrins On Bewitched?

Why did Dick York quit one of the best jobs in television, co-star of the sitcom *Bewitched,* and then seemingly drop off of the face of the earth?

The Dick York Darrin was the better of the two as far as I was concerned; I liked his skittish, perpetually exasperated reactions over the cocky, angrier Dick Sargent Darrin that followed. For my money, Dick York played panic better than any other actor on television.

But Dick York had a secret that the producers didn't know when they hired him; he was chronically ill and addicted to painkillers. A severe back injury on the set of the film *They Came to Cordura* in 1959 left him with a habit for pills to relieve the excruciating pain he would have to endure for the rest of his life.

In 1962, Dick York was cast in the TV series *Going My Way,* a comedy/drama starring Gene Kelly as Father O'Malley and Leo G. Carroll as Father Fitzgibbon.

"Television enables you to be entertained in your home by people you wouldn't have in your home." *—David Frost*

The experience was a good one for York, but his back condition flared up so often during production that special ramps were built to make maneuvering the set easier for the actor. Despite high critical acclaim, *Going My Way* was cancelled in the fall of 1963.

In September 1964, *Bewitched* debuted on ABC with Elizabeth Montgomery as housewitch Samantha Stephens alongside Dick York as her hapless husband Darrin. The series shot to the number-two position in the Nielsen ratings by first season's end. *Bewitched* was so popular that ABC began re-running it weekday mornings for two years starting in 1968 and on Saturday mornings beginning in 1970.

Dick York played the role of Darrin for five years, through black and white and color, through the honeymoon, intense in-law meddling, and on into fatherhood. For all of those years the show stayed in, or hovered around, the top ten, and throughout all of that time York suffered from a roller coaster of pain and painkillers. With the actor in such bad shape, situations were contrived to allow him to be lying down or reclining as much as possible. Because of the nature of the program *Bewitched*, occasionally scenes arose that would tax even a man in good physical condition.

On one such occasion, the crew was setting up for a special effects shot focusing on Dick York suspended fifteen feet in the air beside Maurice Evans, who was playing Darrin's warlock father-in-law. It had been a bad day already for the show's co-star; he was on a cycle of taking pills at night to sleep and receiving shots of novocaine and cortisone in his back during the bad days to keep working. Technicians were setting a little tiny spot that was supposed to be filling in his eyes, passing their hands back and forth in the light to see where it was falling. York was quoted as saying:

"Somehow all that flickering made me feel weird and I'm sitting on this platform up in the air and Maurice is sitting there too and I'm trying to go over my lines; they don't mean a damn thing. But I know that they're a stickler for these lines being exactly the way they're supposed to be. If this line is 'bibbetty wham bang whoppo,' that's what you better say. Anyway, I'm running these lines back and forth and they're making less sense to me and this light is flickering off and on and I turned to Gibby, a friend of mine on the set, and I say 'I have to get down,' and I put my hand on his shoulder and he said, 'Sure, Dick.'"

At that point the poor guy passed out and had to be rushed to the hospital. Painkillers and witchcraft incantations—sounds like a lethal combination to me.

While recuperating in the hospital, Bill Asher (*Bewitched* producer/director and Elizabeth Montgomery's husband) paid the stricken star a visit. Asher pointedly asked York if he wanted to quit the show, and York replied yes. After that point, work dried up for Dick York and he faded into obscurity.

Meanwhile, Dick Sargent took over the role of Darrin Stephens on *Bewitched*. While he looked a lot like Dick York, Sargent played the part with a more defiant

Elizabeth Montgomery also played Sam's sister Serena, but the part was credited to "Pandora Spocks."

stance against his witchy in-laws. The first script that Sargent filmed was called "Samantha's Better Halves," actually a remake of a Dick York episode. In it, Endora splits Darrin into two personalities—one gregarious, the other all business. It was decided against broadcasting this as the first "new Darrin" episode because Sargent was so nervous during the filming.

Another sound reason to delay the episode—Samantha utters the phrase, "But I only want one Darrin" and other comments along those lines. There are those who believe this script was a purposeful jab from the writers directed towards Asher and Montgomery for not standing by Dick York in his time of need.

In an effort to distract viewers from the switch in husbands, another baby was hastily added to the Stephens' household, Tabitha's little brother Adam. Thereafter, the character of Darrin Stephens became more of a puppet for Endora (Agnes Morehead) or the kids as they cast the spell of the week on him or conjured up some famous person from a book for him to chase after.

Bewitched dropped in the ratings from number eleven in 1969 (the last Dick York year) to number twenty-four in 1970 (the first Dick Sargent year). The next year, the show dropped out of the top thirty and the next year marked the end of an eight-season run.

Dick York remained on his back for a year after leaving *Bewitched* and fell on hard times soon after. Bad investments left him broke, and his teeth rotted out (a common problem for drug abusers), so he and his wife were reduced to cleaning houses for a living. In a tragic twist of fate, the actor found out later in life that offers had been coming in for him all along, but because his listing with the union was somehow messed up, he was never notified.

Buoyed by this news, in 1982 Dick York got his life together, got his teeth fixed and went back to work, guest-starring on *Fantasy Island* and *Simon and Simon*. He also did a clever TV movie called *High School, USA* featuring a large cast of former classic sitcom stars. His comeback was short-lived, however, and he devoted most of the rest of his life to fighting his life-threatening illnesses and helping the homeless. Dick York died in 1992.

Honey West

Friday nights at 9 PM
1965–1966 / ABC

Honey West was a sly combination of *Man from U.N.C.L.E.* and *77 Sunset Strip* from the Four-Star Studios, produced by a young Aaron Spelling (*Dynasty*) and written by TV's finest genre writers, William Link and Richard Levinson (*Rockford Files, Columbo, Murder She Wrote*).

Honey (Anne Francis) inherited her flourishing private eye business from her dad. She also got his partner in the deal, rough-and-tumble (and, of course, handsome) Sam Bolt, played by John Ericson. There was a simmering attraction between the two but Honey West's only true love was adventure—and her pet ocelot, Bruce.

Anne Francis really delivered as the high-kicking PI. Incredibly effective in the role, Francis never overplayed the character as was the style of the day. She displayed an unmatched, unmistakable aura of cool that captivated the boys and started little girls rethinking what they might want to be when they grew up.

Honey West was a judo/karate master who tooled around town in a cool little white sportscar like a super-'60s

Barbie doll, dressed to the nines with scarves, dark sunglasses, and leopard-print coats (costumes by Nolan Miller, later of *Dynasty* fame). She even had her own mobile spy unit disguised as a TV repair truck, with high-tech mini-cameras and microphones. Don't break up with this chick!

Even when the stories fell flat, those go-go-era Four-Star shows (from Warner Brothers) were entertaining to watch, with top notch production values, attention to stylistic detail, superior art direction, jazzy music, and well-designed main titles that gave new meaning to style over substance as it applied to television.

Honey was more than a match for her many wily opponents, but by far her most deadly foe turned out to be *Gomer Pyle* over on CBS. He proved fatal to her ratings.

Honey West had tongue planted firmly in cheek but was out of step by 1965. The Warner Bros' style of private eye shows like *77 Sunset Strip* had fallen out of favor for more gimmicky offerings from Twentieth Century Fox like *Lost in Space* and *Batman*.

Honey West was first featured on an episode of *Burke's Law*, also a Four-Star Studios show.

H*who was* ank?

We get a lot of requests for a show called *Hank*, a situation comedy that ran on NBC, Friday nights at eight beginning in September, 1965.

Dick Kallman played Hank Dearborn, a young man determined to get a college education despite the economic hardship brought on when his parents were killed in a car accident, leaving him to raise his baby sister. Hank would take all kinds of odd jobs on campus, in the laundry room, driving a self-serve general store/truck, whatever it took to find out who wouldn't be attending classes that day. Resourceful Hank would then sit in on classes disguised as a student he knew would be absent, employing a number of elaborate deceptions to avoid detection by the school's staff.

Western University's registrar Dr. Royal (Howard St. John) made it his obsession to track down whoever it was auditing classes illegally, never suspecting it was the boy his daughter Doris (Linda Foster) was dating.

Hank was one of those clever sitcoms that never found a large audience, a show just begging to be remade. It was up against a hit on CBS (*Wild, Wild West*) and a miss on NBC (*Tammy*). Like most good shows in the '60s, *Hank* lasted only one season. Typical episode (and the plot of the pilot): Hank is seen dashing to class by the coach and gets asked to join the University's track team.

TVpartyer Bill Smith tells us: "One of the things that made *Hank* a rarity among 1960s shows was that the final episode actually wrapped up and resolved the series. The registrar finally caught Hank, but because of his superior academic performance and talent on the track field, they awarded him a scholarship to the college.

"The last line of the final scene of the final episode had his little sister watching Hank walking off hand-in-hand with his girlfriend (the registrar's daughter) and saying, 'There goes my brother—the registered student.' This is the only '60s show I know of that ended in this way."

After *Hank*, Dick Kallman turned from TV to the legitimate stage, first in LA with a starring role in the Los

My brother's name is Hank.

Angeles Civic Light Opera's production of *Half a Sixpence* from September 13 to October 29, 1966, later moving to New York where he pursued acting roles and opened a small shop.

This message came from someone who wishes to remain anonymous:

I knew Dick Kallman. No one ever touched me the way he did; he was the greatest personal love of my life. I must tell you that I have not talked about or even shared my feeling with just but a few close and intimate friends.

Dick Kallman loved publicity. Dick was the most spontaneous person I ever encountered in my life—what a delicious ham he could be at times. Once his agent sent him to an audition and got the address confused with a voiceover call and Dick ended up at a Mattel Toy voiceover audition by mistake.

Always one to make the most of where he was, he asked to audition anyway—the voice they wanted was that of a grandmother type . . . Yep, you guessed it: he got the voiceover and the checks came for years, as that ad ran longer than any other Mattel ad ever . . .

Did you know about the Batman *episodes Dick was on? Dick had the lead in* Babes in Toyland *on Broadway at seventeen and was one of the last contract players at Warners Bros.*

Dick was stabbed to death in 1980 during a "drug induced" robbery—while most of the articles mention he was murdered in his apartment, it is my belief that he was abducted by someone on drugs looking for money and forced back to the apartment . . . clearly it was a robbery and a very violent one.

I never sat foot in our home again. I left everything I owned in it to be sold. Frankly, when I saw this write-up last evening I cried uncontrollably for longer than I ever remembered. I was away from NY at the time on business . . . something that has haunted for twenty years . . . never being able to forgive myself.

I do not know if you are fortunate enough to have someone special in your life . . . but, friend, know this . . . Love can last a lifetime, so the sages say—but treat it gently, oh my friend, for a lifetime can last but a day.

"*I thought I was the only one who loved Hank, the drop-in. In my university years I actually shadow-audited an entire year's lectures on . . . guess what? Subliminal Seduction (prof. Wilson Bryan Key) at the University of Western Ontario.*" —J Lamb

Twenty-seven-year-old Charles Lonnie Grosso was convicted of the killing and sentenced to twenty-five years to life in prison.

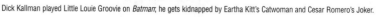

Dick Kallman played Little Louie Groovie on *Batman*; he gets kidnapped by Eartha Kitt's Catwoman and Cesar Romero's Joker.

Yo Mama the What?!?

With the unprecedented success of *Bewitched* and *The Man from U.N.C.L.E.* in 1964, the three networks unleashed an assault of way-out, fanciful shows in 1965. *I Dream of Jeannie, Lost in Space, Get Smart, Green Acres, The Smothers Brothers Show* (the sitcom where Tommy came back as a ghost to haunt his brother), *F Troop,* and *Wild, Wild West* were just some of the weird programs that debuted in 1965.

Outlandish as some of those were, *My Mother the Car* has been held up to ridicule as possibly the worst television series of all time. NBC was the butt of many jokes for putting the show on the air in the first place, then leaving it there for an entire season. Still, *My Mother the Car* was probably worth it to the network as fodder for *Tonight Show* punchlines over the next three decades.

My Mother the Car followed the antics of lawyer Dave Crabtree (Jerry Van Dyke from *Coach*), a typically flustered sitcom family man who is looking around the used car lot for a family station wagon when he makes a startling discovery—his mother has returned from the grave as a 1928 Porter convertible automobile.

He (naturally) buys the car against the wishes of his family, who (naturally) think he's gone crazy. Maggie Pierce was cast as wife Barbara and Cindy Eilbacher and Randy Whipple played the 2.5 kids. Avery Schreiber appeared as the show's villain, Capt. Manzini, a ruthless car collector who feels an unnatural, violent urge to own the Porter for himself. Ann Sothern (*Private Secretary*) was heard as the voice of Mom.

Just like another popular sitcom of the day (*Mr. Ed*), the car won't talk to anyone but Dave, so (naturally) hilarity ensues when everyone continually doubts dear old dad's sanity. Kids tuned in but critics were merciless. "*My Mother the Car* tried combining the U.S. fascination with cars, sex, and mom," a scathing review in *Time* magazine went, "But something happened in casting: Mother (who returns to earth from celestial regions, using the car radio as a voice box) is an invisible Ann Sothern; and as for hero Jerry Van Dyke, he has finally answered the question, what is it that Jerry hasn't got that Brother Dick has?"

My Mother the Car was the brainchild of Allan Burns and Chris Hayward, soon to be the multiple Emmy Award–winning creators of *He and She* and *The Mary Tyler Moore Show.* Maggie Pierce was particularly good as the wife and anything with Ann Sothern can't be *all* bad!

So why wasn't the series cancelled sooner if it was considered such a flop? Probably because it was effective in drawing the young viewers. The competition on the other networks were all adult dramas (*Rawhide* on CBS, *Combat* on ABC).

But networks were looking for overall large numbers, not specific audience seg-

Jerry Van Dyke turned down the role of Gilligan because he thought it was too silly.

ments like they do presently, or *My Mother the Car* might still be on today!

"You mentioned a Randy Whipple as one of the kids. For the past several years or so, he's been an anchor at KVAL Channel 13 in Eugene, Oregon. His biography at kval.com says he 'played Jerry Van Dyke's son on an NBC sitcom.' Of course, he now goes by Randall, but I remember watching him on KVAL's news when I was enrolled at the University of Oregon."
—*Bill Griffiths*

"I was a high school classmate of Randy, and even performed in the school musical with him. He was pretty tight-lipped about his work on *My Mother the Car* but trouble seemed to follow him, on TV anyway.

"It seems that he was responsible for breaking Red Skelton's finger in a live sketch on his famous TV variety show. Red went on and finished the show, but Randy didn't work in TV for quite a while after that.

"Not too many kids in TV get two 'bad breaks' in a single career. (His third strike in showbiz came when he infected me and the entire cast of *The Music Man* with rubella one week before opening night.)" —*A Reader*

Run, Buddy, Run

This dizzy and typically '60s sitcom starred trumpet player Jack Sheldon (occasional band member on the *Merv Griffin Show*) as a guy on the run from comical criminals.

The plot: Buddy Overstreet is enjoying a steam bath when he overhears a big-time mobster (played by Bruce Gordon of *The Untouchables*) planning the death of a colleague.

When he's discovered hiding by the gangstas, Buddy is paranoid and on the run. Basically a sitcom version of *The Fugitive*, this kid fave was wedged between *Gilligan* and *Lucy* on CBS Monday nights from September 1966 to September 1967.

Jack Sheldon was also a regular on *The Cara Williams Show* and *The Girl with Something Extra*, but is best known today as the vocalist on several classic *Schoolhouse Rock* tunes.

Bruce Gordon (below) was the Tony Soprano of his day, playing this same mobster character as a guest on dozens of sitcoms like *The Lucy Show* and *Sanford and Son* over the next three decades.

Someone at NBC took the term reinCARnation a bit too literally.

THE BIG
SUPERHERO BUST

TV goes camp with Batman, Green Hornet, Captain Nice, and Mr. Terrific!

As 1964 rolled around, National Periodical Publications (also known as DC Comics) was about to make a momentous decision. The venerable comic book publisher had been in business for decades, pumping out the comics kids loved best. *Superman. Wonder Woman. The Flash. Justice League of America. Batman.*

Batman, see, that was the problem. That comic book line had stopped making a profit some years earlier. *Batman* and *Detective Comics* (where the character debuted in 1938) were going to get canned after thirty years on the stands.

As a last-ditch effort, the books were assigned to the editor of DC's science fiction line, Julius Schwartz. His mission—move *Batman* into profitability within six months or else. The team he assembled did the trick, turning the Caped Crusader into more of a high-tech sleuth and less of a costumed clown. Colorful villains like Catwoman and The Joker were resurrected and given new life in stories by John Broome and Gardner Fox, illustrated by Carmine Infantino and various artists under the "Bob Kane" byline.

That same year, 1964, *Shindig!* debuted on ABC-TV. A prime-time rock music show that featured live (not lip-synced) performances by the biggest acts, *Shindig!* was a sensation at attracting the youthful crowd the network was courting. The show did so well, it was expanded to an hour midseason and, in the fall of 1965, split into two half-hour shows a week. This two episodes a week format was not unheard of; ABC had been doing it for a few years as a way of milking their hottest shows. *Peyton Place* was broadcast two nights a week in 1964 and three nights in 1965.

Unfortunately, the audience deserted *Shindig!* after that first season, leaving two gaping holes in ABC's already desolate schedule. In an act of sheer desperation, they rushed one of their most promising shows forward for a midseason debut. This was a risky move because, while there had been other shows that premiered in the winter, they were never terribly successful. None of them. Ever.

Batman starred Adam West as the Caped Crusader and Burt Ward as his youthful sidekick, Robin. West had last been seen on *The Detectives* (1961–62); Burt Ward was an unknown. Proving to youngsters at an early age that life isn't fair, *Batman* was scheduled opposite *Lost in Space* on CBS.

Together with screenwriter Lorenzo Semple, Jr., executive producer William Dozier crafted a show that could be enjoyed by adults as well as kids. *Batman* debuted on January 12, 1966. Within the first few weeks, the telecast was attracting 55 percent of the viewing audience, with a surprising two-thirds over the age of eighteen.

They called it "camp," ironic comic perfection. The key to *Batman* was in the lead actors playing outlandishly fantastic situations with a straight face, and the stunt-casting of hot TV personalities like Julie Newmar (as the Catwoman) and aging movie icons like

The Batmobile is a modified 1955 Lincoln Futura.

Cesar Romero (as the Joker) and Frank Gorshin (as the Riddler). Before long, every star in Hollywood lined up for an opportunity to be the costumed kook-of-the-week on the top show in the nation. "These people [stars] would call up, or send their agents around, saying, can't so and so be on?" William Dozier bragged to a reporter. "Gloria Swanson, I remember, called me from New York, but we couldn't find the right part for her. Everybody came out of the woodwork; we never had to go after those people. A lot of them I had known personally, and they would call and say that they would love to do one of those because 'my kids want me to do it.'

"Up to twelve years old, they take *Batman* seriously. From thirteen on, we've got them chuckling in their beer." Indeed, Dozier (who was also the show's announcer) instinctively knew this pop-art froth had a short shelf life, but just how short? Network rivals were betting *Batman* was another Hula Hoop craze. "They gave it only ninety days. I gave it two years."

At the end of just six months, Bat-mania was in full flower. Seventy-five million dollars worth of Batman books, capes, toys, coloring books, bubble gum cards, and weaponry had been sold, with Batman's face plastered on every conceivable product whether it had any relevant practicality or not. Never before had the world been bombarded by such a ridiculous assault of loosely branded products. Batman candy. Batman bicycles. Batman lunch boxes. Batman bath soap. Batman race cars. Batman lamps. Batman every-damn-thing-you-can-think-of.

And those *Batman* comic books DC almost stopped publishing two years earlier? They could barely keep up with demand; any comic book with Batman on the cover could be counted on to sell up to a million copies a month. Editor Schwartz had done his job well, since many of the plots for the TV program were taken directly from his four-color stories.

Batman changed the course of television in a profound way by proving that a program could debut midseason and still be a hit. From 1966 forward, all three networks began seriously programming a second season.

"*Batman* will fade, of course," Dozier correctly predicted in the *Saturday Evening Post*, at the height of the show's popularity. "We won't keep all the adults we have now. We have to think ahead." Dozier was right to be concerned about audience erosion; he reasoned that adults would soon defect once the novelty wore off. By the fall of '66, *Batman* was the number-one show in the nation, but adult ratings had dropped to half what they once were. Not surprisingly, ABC was more than willing to give the producer another slot on their fall schedule—*Batman* was the biggest hit in the network's history.

To recapture lost adult viewers, Dozier decided to try the superhero genre without playing it for laughs. To achieve this, he revived one of the most successful superheroes from the radio era, the Green Hornet.

The Green Hornet was originally a product of 1930s radio and not comic books. Other than that

The Lone Ranger was the Green Hornet's great uncle. They were created by the same person, George Trendle.

minor distinction, the similarities to Batman were many; wealthy Britt Reid, crusading newspaper editor (whatever happened to them?!?) and his butler Kato are secret nighttime crimefighters. They patrol the city in their souped-up car and capture do-badders with high-tech weapons and old-fashioned karate chops.

Keeping with the winning formula, another detective show cast-off, Van Williams (*Bourbon Street Beat, Surfside Six*), was hired for the lead role. Kato was embodied by relatively unknown martial-arts master Bruce Lee, who went on to movie icon status and an early, mysterious death. Paid only four hundred dollars per episode, the real reason Lee got the part was that he was the only person who auditioned who could accurately pronounce the name Britt Reid.

On the very first episode, the Green Hornet and Kato delved into the mystery of "The Silent Gun," a flimsy story about gun that made no noise. The next week, they faced a strangler, the next a killer pet leopard. The overall pedestrian nature of the scripts became quickly apparent, pointing up the inherent problem with this series. Why have two fantastically clad heroes in a blown-out muscle car when all they're after are two-bit burglars, bootleggers, and common kidnappers?

In an attempt to generate some buzz, the Green Hornet and Kato appeared on two episodes of *Batman* in March 1967. When the heroes / adversaries squared off against each other, Bruce Lee expressed extreme displeasure that he had to let Robin win their match. The Gung Fu athlete wanted to really let loose on Burt Ward and kick his pampered TV-star ass all over the lot.

Dark, moody, serious, and slotted on Friday nights (where no fantasy show had ever done well), *The Green Hornet* wasn't the hit ABC was looking for. Ironically, the series had everything it needed to be a smash; the concept was there, the production looked great—they had only to unleash Bruce Lee. That would happen later, in another medium.

CBS and NBC were determined not to make the same mistake when they launched their superhero rip-offs. They would make darn sure their offerings were as silly as they could possibly be.

TV CROSSOVER: Where did Otis from *The Andy Griffith Show* do his drinking? Some of it was done on the train, apparently. That's where he encountered Mr. Terrific in the super-guy's pilot episode. At least Otis didn't drink and drive!

Mr. Terrific on CBS was the story of nerdy Stanley Beamish, who works for the Bureau of Special Projects in Washington, DC. As part of his job, he swallows an enormous jaw-breaker-sized "Power Pill" developed by the government that turns him (and only him) into a superhero with tremendous powers—for one hour. Trouble comes when the pill wears off and timid Stanley is forced to face the crooks without his super-abilities. Mr. Terrific can even fly during his brief hour of power but he has to flap his arms to do it!

Also appearing on the series were Dick Gautier (Hymie the Robot from *Get Smart*) as gas station attendant Hal and John McGiver as head of the government bureau that watches over Stanley. Typical plots: Stanley finds himself with a miniature transmitter implanted in his tooth when he visits a spy dentist; while the president's plane flashes an SOS, Stanley is busy seeing a psychiatrist about his temporary inability to fly; in another episode Stanley impersonates a safecracker who is his exact double. I told you they were typical plots!

You can still see *Mr. Terrific* occasionally. Several episodes were combined to make a TV movie called *The Pill Caper*. Unfortunately, because the main character gets his powers by taking drugs, this series itself was never offered by the studio for syndication.

Mr. Terrific debuted on CBS January 9, 1967. That very same night, immediately after it went off the air, in fact, *Captain Nice* hit the airwaves over on NBC, brought to you by the creators of *Get Smart*.

This steroidal sitcom starred William Daniels (that old guy on *St. Elsewhere*) as Carter Nash, a police chemist who develops a serum giving him basically the same powers as Mr. Terrific, except Captain Nice didn't have to flap his arms to maneuver the friendly skies. Oh, and it was Carter's mom who made his dopey-looking costume.

The pilot was written by series creator Buck Henry. Alice Ghostley co-starred as Nash's mother and Ann Prentiss portrayed policewoman Candy Kane, the Lois Lane love-interest type. In one episode, Captain Nice battles a psychotic doctor who kidnaps Candy Kane, injecting her with a lethal tropical poison. In another, Carter tries to become Captain Nice, only to find his mother drank all of the formula.

When *The Green Hornet* proved a disappointment, Dozier filmed two dreadfully lame "campy" pilots featuring comedic versions of *Wonder Woman* and *Dick Tracy*, but they went nowhere. Hurting for fresh ideas, the TV producer went back to Julie Schwartz and

Carmine Infantino (remember them?). Dozier told them that sinister Catwoman was the public's favorite character on *Batman* but she couldn't be on every week. What could be done? The comic book guys came up with Batgirl, designing a form-fitting costume similar to Catwoman's with an added cape and groovy Bat-cycle for Dozier to copy. A zippy pilot episode was produced for a *Batgirl* series, with Yvonne Craig, a favorite of summertime beach movies, cast to fit the super-heroine's tights.

As the 1966–67 season rolled to a close, superheroes were falling by the wayside. Bat-mania was wearing off like a bat drug. With ratings in the cellar, *Captain Nice* flew off the screens on August 28, 1967, the same night *Mr. Terrific* flapped his last.

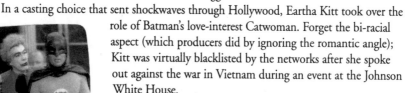

ABC realized they needed a way to get the spark back into *Batman*, renewed for a third season but down to just one night a week. Rather than risk a spinoff, Batgirl was added to the roster of *Batman* in the fall of 1967. With more lead characters, less time for story, and a week between cliffhangers, the formula wore paper-thin. Still, there were third season highlights like Batman and the Joker in a surfing contest, Ida Lupino as the entrancing Dr. Cassandra, and Anne Baxter as Queen of the Cossacks teamed with Vincent Price as Egghead.

In a casting choice that sent shockwaves through Hollywood, Eartha Kitt took over the role of Batman's love-interest Catwoman. Forget the bi-racial aspect (which producers did by ignoring the romantic angle); Kitt was virtually blacklisted by the networks after she spoke out against the war in Vietnam during an event at the Johnson White House.

Bat-ratings were down in 1968, and adult viewership dwindled to a mere 10 percent. With only kids watching and the show consistently over budget, the decision was made to cancel *Batman* and take the money and run—straight to afternoon syndication of the reruns. NBC discussed picking up *Batman* for a fourth season and a deal was almost struck, but they backed out because of the expense of rebuilding the Batcave set, which had been destroyed just days after the cancellation notice came down.

Ironically, while *Batman* had been saved in the comics by making him more serious, the TV program and unbridled exploitation made the character a buffoon in the mind of the public. When the Bat-fad passed, sales of comic books in general plummeted. *Batman* comics in particular took a beating, leading to the near extinction of the character (and the entire industry) a decade later.

In a bizarre twist, *Captain Nice* co-star Ann Prentiss (sister of Paula from *He and She*) was convicted by a Santa Monica, California, court of battery in 1998 for assaulting her eighty-six-year-old father, solicitation of murder, assault with a firearm, and making terrorist threats toward Richard Benjamin, her sister's husband and TV co-star. Calling Captain Nice!

The movie *Boogie Nights* had a party scene with an extra dressed in a Captain Nice costume.

It's *About Time* ran from September 11, 1966, until August 27, 1967, and starred Jack Mullaney and Frank Aletter as two astronauts who break the time barrier and end up in prehistoric times.

It's About Time was produced by Sherwood Schwartz, creator of *Gilligan's Island* (then in its third year on CBS) and *The Brady Bunch*.

The astronauts take up with cave dwellers played by the great Joe E. Ross ("Ooh, Ooh!"— Officer Toody from *Car 54, Where Are You?*) and Imogene Coca (*Your Show of Shows*). Also seen: Mary Grace as daughter Mlor; Pat Cardi as Breer, their son; Cliff Norton as Boss; Kathleen Freeman as Mrs. Boss; and Mike Mazurzsky as Boss's henchman Clon.

Like *Gilligan's Island*, situations were played for broad laughs and the show was universally panned by critics but loved by children.

The series shifted direction mid-season to try to build ratings—the cave people and Astronauts returned in the spacecraft to modern times. The focus shifted from the space-travellers to Coca and Ross as they confronted life in twentieth century New York City.

"I remember watching this show and loving it! I was only eight years old at the time. I wasn't very good at lyrics, and I remember singing the theme song like this:
'It's about time,
it's about space,
it's about time
I slapped your face!'"

—James Salhoff

IT'S ABOUT TIME

One of the best theme songs ever!

Jack Mullaney and Frank Aletter

Joe E. Ross and Imogene Coca

This show was never popular in reruns—too few episodes to syndicate.

IRWIN ALLEN'S
TIME
TUNNEL

ROBERT COLBER

There was an Irwin Allen–produced science-fiction series on the air every year from 1964 to 1970. One of those years, 1966, he had three series running concurrently on two networks: *Voyage to the Bottom of the Sea* (ABC, 1964–1968), *Lost in Space* (CBS, 1965–1968), and *The Time Tunnel* (ABC, 1966–1967).

Allen was from the old school, starting out as an announcer on LA's KCAL radio, entering television briefly at first, long enough to be credited with inventing the first celebrity panel show in the late '40s. In the '50s and early '60s he produced lightweight theatrical feature films like *Double Dynamite* and *A Girl in Every Port* starring Groucho Marx, the sci-fi cult classic *The Lost World, Five Weeks in a Balloon,* and *Voyage to the Bottom of the Sea.*

It was *Voyage* that brought Irwin Allen back to television in 1964. By using existing sets, miniatures, and special effects from the film, he was  able to bring big-budget excitement to the small screen for the first time. The longest-running Irwin Allen series, *Voyage to the Bottom of the Sea* started out as a serious adventure series with cold-war overtones and realistic underwater sequences, later degenerating into a weekly monster-costume fashion show.

In 1965, *Lost in Space* took TV sci-fi to new

"Two American scientists are lost in the swirling maze of past and future ages during the first experiment of America's greatest and most secret project—*The Time Tunnel*. Tony Newman and Doug Phillips now tumble help-lessly toward a new fantastic adventure some-where along the infinite corridors of time."

—*opening to* The Time Tunnel

LEE MERIWETHER

JAMES DAR

heights and new depths at the same time. The story of a family set adrift in space due to the machinations of a villainous stowaway, the first few episodes of LIS stand out as thrilling entertainment even if the scientific underpinning was a bit shaky.

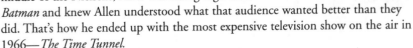

Though Irwin Allen's programs fell in the mushy middle of the Nielsens, ABC was riding high with *Batman* and knew Allen understood what that audience wanted better than they did. That's how he ended up with the most expensive television show on the air in 1966—*The Time Tunnel*.

Directed by Irwin Allen himself, the pilot (which cost a whopping five hundred thousand dollars, tying with *Batman* as the most expensive of that time) told the story of Dr. Tony Newman (James Darren) and Dr. Doug Phillips (Robert Colbert), two research scientists who become entrapped in a top-secret portal through time.

The first adventure had Tony and Doug captive aboard the Titanic hours before it struck an iceberg. That opening episode was one of the best science-fiction dramas produced in the '60s. The pacing was exciting throughout, the Emmy-winning special effects colorful and hypnotic, and guest star Michael Rennie performed admirably as the doomed ship's laconic captain. To demonstrate the wider possibilities the series held, Tony and Doug dive from the deck of the Titanic at the show's conclusion only to materialize inside a rocket capsule about to be jettisoned into the atmosphere. Every show ended with the two time-travellers in a cliffhanger situation to entice viewers to tune in next week. This was a technique Irwin Allen had pioneered with *Lost in Space* the previous year, and a trick the producers of *Batman* picked up on as well.

At the controls of the Tunnel were Whit Bissell as General Heywood Kirk and John Zaremba as Dr. Raymond Swaim, both veterans of many "B" horror movies; Lee Meriwether as Dr. Ann McGregor; and Wesley Lau as security officer Jiggs. *The Time Tunnel* was unique in the fact that the regular supporting cast almost never got to work with the two lead actors. Consequently, they had little to do but yell "Tony!" and "Doug!" at the tunnel while frantically mashing the buttons and twisting the dials on the surplus NASA computers that made up most of the set.

Several times the men had to push poor Ann out of the way so that they could turn the dials and push the buttons while she had a panic attack on the sidelines. It's no wonder she was so stressed—just like all of Irwin Allen's inventions, the Time Tunnel exploded every time you used it.

The Time Tunnel emergency sequence.

Maybe one reason *The Time Tunnel* is so fondly remembered is the subliminally sexual quick-cut sequence that comes every time there's a Time Tunnel emergency. First you see the pulsating, phallic power core of the complex, then the deep inner corridor, a close-up of the power core, and then the camera rests on the tunnel itself, spitting sparks and smoking profusely. Hello!

As the season progressed, our heroes entered into a gunfight with Billy the Kid, searched for Tony's father during the bombing of Pearl Harbor, fought in the War of 1812, become imprisoned on Devil's Island, and landed on the scene at General Custer's last stand. By mid-season, more far-out plotlines found Tony and Doug rescuing Ann from futuristic kidnappers, fighting space aliens in 1885, and following a criminal through several centuries into a beehive of the future.

Along the way, kids at home got to learn a lot about history. For instance, it was Nero's ghost who made Mussolini so evil and it was Robin Hood who forced King John to sign the Magna Carta after a mortar attack on his castle. I remember being *very* disappointed when Halley's Comet came back around in 1986 and it was so small you could barely see it. On *The Time Tunnel*, it filled the sky!

"There was absolutely no pressure on us to depict history accurately." *Time Tunnel* series writer Robert Duncan told an interviewer. "Once we entered that combination of aliens from outer space woven into historical episodes, there was no need for accuracy."

Irwin Allen's brand of 'science' fiction was popular fare during the '60s; you just had to forget the major lapses in logic and enjoy the ride. When writers

Monogram had a best-selling series of models based on the Irwin Allen Twentieth Century Fox properties. Say what you will about weak plotlines and slim characterizations, the machinery looked cool!

Allen acquired the rights to a sci-fi novel by Murray Leinster called *Time Tunnel* and loosely adapted it for his TV series bible.

After the show debuted, Leinster wrote a book based on the TV premise. He also wrote three *Land of the Giants* novelizations while that program was on the air.

A *Lost in Space* book was commissioned and released in 1967. It's a rare find today.

Comic books with exciting photo covers from Gold Key were popular, as were lunch boxes and other tie-ins.

or directors objected to a major lapse of basic common sense in the script, Irwin Allen's edict was simple: "Don't get logical with me. This is a running and jumping show."

Allen would direct only the pilot episodes of his TV series himself. A consistent problem became his tendency for blowing his wad during the first quarter of the season and then hacking out the remainder.

Fortunately for the writers, *The Time Tunnel* was able to take full advantage of the large stock footage library at Twentieth Century Fox to provide blue screen and cut-away shots where elaborate historical settings or large numbers of extras were needed. Too often it was obvious that the plodding scripts were written around some old film clip of marauding medieval hordes or a trojan horse, with an obligatory fistfight or two written in for good measure.

Writer Robert Duncan explained it this way: "We approached one of the leads with the idea of providing more substantial material, only to have him ask us to keep his speeches short. He wanted simple lines like 'Let's go!' or 'We have to get out of here!' so we did." At the end-of-season wrap party spirits were high as cast members said their goodbyes for the summer, relieved that their show was renewed for a second season.

TVpartyer OM tells us what happened next: "*Time Tunnel* wasn't cancelled due to bad ratings. Granted, it had the Friday night 'slot of death,' but the ratings were no worse than *Star Trek* depending on what was showing on the other two channels. In fact, ABC was internally hailing it as the one true success in what was a really *bad* season for them. Not one of their shows was in the top-twenty end-of-year averages and the only new show that came close for even one week was *The Time Tunnel*.

"Why cancel it then? Well, someone at ABC pushed for a series called *The Legend of Custer* and managed to get enough of his fellow execs laid sufficiently to allow the series to not only get on the '67 fall schedule but to get additional promo funding. The only problem was that the fall schedule had been decided (but not officially announced) and there was no room for an additional one-hour drama. The exec in question argued for dropping *Time Tunnel* on the grounds that 'Irwin Allen's giving you phony history lessons wrapped inside cheap sci-fi schlock. *Custer* was the real thing!' The argument apparently held just enough water to get Project Tic-Toc shut down for good.

"On a side note, *Custer* was ruthlessly nuked by the critics and denounced by various Amerind and Native American groups. No other western save for *The Men from Shiloh* two years later was so ruthlessly derided and *Custer* was thankfully shitcanned after only one season."

The Time Tunnel was Irwin Allen's favorite of all of his series, but with three productions going simultaneously in 1966–67, his team at Twentieth Century Fox was stretched far too thin. "The set was definitely not a place to take our kids or relatives," Duncan recalled, "They were always behind schedule and fuming. They were under pressure to make up time." I have to assume that was said with some degree of irony.

1966–67 was season two for *Lost in Space* and three for *Voyage to the Bottom of*

Jonathan Harris (Dr. Smith) guest-starred on *Land of the Giants* as a Pied Piper trying to lure little boys away from their homes.

the Sea. Both suffered greatly from hastily-written scripts and diminishing production values during this period—and those shows could ill afford any slide in quality. Partly to blame for this deterioration was the success of *Batman*, another Twentieth Century Fox property. If, as some were saying, the key to *Batman's* success was that it was so bad it was good, Irwin Allen seemed to think he could make his shows god-awful to be great. As a result, *LIS* and *Voyage* were reduced to hosting the freak of the week in 1966: lobsters, carrots, frogs, and houseplants all took on humanoid form that season, appearing along with assorted fairy tale characters, werewolves, and space vikings. If you want to know the reason why people who are serious about their science fiction *hate* Irwin Allen, those wretched episodes stand out as shining beacons.

Competition on the other networks severely split the available audience for a show like *The Time Tunnel* as well. Viewers had *The Man from U.N.C.L.E.* on NBC and *The Wild, Wild, West* on CBS to choose from, this on a Friday night when most young people were out doing other things anyway. *The Time Tunnel* slipped into history on September 1, 1967. When *LIS* and *Voyage* returned for a new season in 1967, the quality of both shows was (somewhat) improved, but it was to be the last season for both.

In 1968, *Land of the Giants* took over the 7 PM Sunday-night slot held by *Voyage* since 1964. *Giants* was *Lost in Space* redux, right down to the built-in villain, but little people running around in a big weedpile, occasionally encountering a gigantic stiff hand, stray cat, or garden weasel made for dull sci-fi. This bewilderingly bad series meandered through two seasons before getting the giant axe. The '60s were over and Irwin Allen was destined for even greater success in the next decade, becoming known forevermore as "The Master of Disaster."

The Man from the 25th Century
[Irwin Allen's lost sci-fi pilot]

This series that never sold (was to have) starred James Darren as an earthling stolen as an infant by aliens, who super-charge him and return him to earth to prepare for an invasion—only to have the multipowered earthling turn against them. John Crawford, who played aliens and weirdos on *LIS, Voyage,* and *Time Tunnel*, played Darren's interplanetary ex-boss with the big head.

A twenty-minute film was made to show ABC execs what the show would be like, but this pitch looked more like a rejected episode idea for *Lost in Space* than a fully realized concept.

Irwin Allen produced *Code Red* with Lorne Greene and Adam Rich in 1981.

The Valley of the Jolly Green Giant

(It's all been developed
into condos and
time-shares now . . .)

Glad Wrap

"Calling Man from Glad!" No need to phone
the cops, this was the way marital disputes were
handled in the '60s. Typically, man and wife
would argue over sandwich freshness and the Man
from Glad would jet in to save the day.

When economic conditions worsened in the
1970s, domestic calls became more frequent and
the Man from Glad was overwhelmed. Eventually,
the government was forced to step in, leading to
our current 911 emergency system.

MADVERTISING?

1970 Chevy Nova

When an automaker chooses a spokesperson, they look for someone strong, dependable, and trustworthy. A person of solid integrity who reflects the stability and honesty of the car company itself.

That's why Chevrolet chose football great O.J. Simpson to appear in their 1970 Chevy Nova commercials. In the TV ads, the Nova was compared feature by feature with O.J. Simpson—as in: the Nova has more horsepower than O.J. Simpson and the Nova has more padding than O.J. Simpson.

Here's another comparison—if the Nova ever killed anybody it was probably an accident.

O.J. advertised Chevy, but made his getaway in a Ford Bronco.

THE BEER WITH A PAST

The Blitz-Weinhard Brewery closed in 1999.

NOLO CONTENDO

Demographics was a relatively new concept being put into practice by the networks in 1970. All of a sudden, it didn't matter to the big three how many people were watching their shows; what mattered was who those people were. If the audience didn't fall between the ages of 18 and 49, then they were considered "bi-modal" (on one side of the numbers or the other) and the show was gone. The thinking thirty years ago was that kids and old people made good people ratings, but it's a combination that did little for advertisers because kids and seniors didn't have any disposable income back then.

Alas, the Nielsen top twenty was a sea of bi-modals in the late '60s, and the networks weeded them out rapidly. *Dragnet, Daniel Boone, Petticoat Junction, Jackie Gleason,* and *Red Skelton* were all top-rated programs in 1970 when the networks bit the bullet and cancelled the lot in favor of shows they hoped would appeal to more urban viewers, like *The Mod Squad, The Interns, The Flip Wilson Show, The Young Lawyers,* and *The Young Rebels.*

The Young Lawyers was *The Mod Squad* without guns, the story of a group of Boston law students committed to helping those who can't afford real lawyers with their "Neighborhood Law Office." In keeping with '70s tradition, the cast was ethnically diverse. Aaron Silverman (played by Zalman King) was the passionate Jewish idealist, Pat Walters (Judy Pace) the street-wise black woman, and David Barrett (Lee J. Cobb) their more experienced (WASP) advisor, a successful barrister who left a prestigious practice to help these young mavericks make a go of it. The plots were of the slumlords/police brutality sort at first, later moving into more serious courtroom cases mid-season. *The Young Lawyers* lasted one season.

That same season, *The Young Rebels* was seen at seven o'clock Sunday nights, occupying the timeslot left empty by the cancellation of *Land of the Giants.* This was the story of four freedom-fighting teens in Chester, Pennsylvania, struggling against "the man." In this case, "the man" wasn't the Nixon administration; it was the British circa 1777.

Louis Gossett, Jr., starred as Isak Poole, a blacksmith and former slave who buys his freedom to team up with the long-haired son of the town's mayor, supposedly good-for-nothing Jeremy Larkin (Rick Ely). Unknown to most, Jeremy is the leader of a secret cadre of rebel fighters, consisting of his girlfriend Elizabeth Coates (Hilary Thompson) and inventor/explosives expert (and Ben Franklin look-alike) Henry Abington (Alex Henteloff). Together these youngsters form the "Yankee Doodle Society" to do everything in their power to to harass the British occupying forces—steal their cannons, foil their battle plans, and look for any useful information to help the revolutionary government. Philippe Fourquet frequently appeared as young General Lafayette, the only outsider to know their secret identities.

The Young Rebels is one of TVparty's most requested shows, but it only lasted a half-season. Turns out the young audience the show was attracting was *too* young; the network had unwittingly churned out another bi-modal.

Insert bad lawyer jokes here.

MEAN,
T....
HE
G.

E FILE
TED
THE
THIEF
N....
VERY
RING
CH
DEATH

BUT *WHY?* WHY WOULD HE STEAL THE FILE? WHY WOULD HE TRY TO IMPLICATE AN INNOCENT PERSON?

N.L.O.
NEIGHBORHOOD
LAW
OFFICE

FOR THE *GLORY* OF IT ALL! YOU HEARD BARRETT. WE'RE FAMOUS NOW. THE LEGAL BEAGLES WITH A *BOMBER* AFTER THEM. THIS WHOLE THING COULD SET UP A LAWYER *FOR LIFE!*

Pete Duel's Unexplained Suicide

by Sam Hieb

ABC was attempting to capitalize on the success of *Butch Cassidy and the Sundance Kid* with a Western adventure series featuring two amiable outlaws trying to go straight.

Alias Smith and Jones premiered on January 21, 1971, starring Pete Duel as Hannibal "Joshua Smith" Heyes and Ben Murphy as Kid "Thaddeus Jones" Curry.

Heyes was a silvery-tongued safecracker and card sharp, while Jones was a dead-eye gunslinger, who, in spite of all the banks and trains he robbed, never shot anyone. Desiring to lead upstanding lives, Heyes and Curry are promised a pardon from the governor if they can stay out of trouble for one year. In the meantime, however, they will remain wanted.

"That's a good deal?" Heyes smirks.

For three television seasons Heyes and Curry were chased across the American West (many scenes were filmed on location in Moab, Utah) by posse, bounty hunters, and fellow outlaws looking to settle a score. Despite their earnest attempt to lead honest lives, circumstances would often dictate that they fall back on the tools of their former trade to get themselves out of trouble.

Alias Smith and Jones was able to capture a fair audience with its catchy theme song and unique opening credit sequence in which a gravelly-voice narrator provides unique insight into the adventures of our likable anti-heroes. Sally Field joined the show for two episodes as Clementine Hale, a fun-loving rogue who simultaneously spelled pleasure and trouble for the guys. *Alias Smith and Jones* wasn't able to displace NBC's *The Flip Wilson Show* from the Thursday eight o'clock time slot.

On December 31, 1971, Pete Duel filmed at the studio all day before returning

ALIAS SMITH AND JONES

home with his girlfriend to watch the episode of *ASJ* being broadcast on television that night. According to his girlfriend, after watching the episode, they both went into the bedroom, where Duel told her he would see her later and returned to the living room.

A few minutes later she heard a gunshot and found Duel lying underneath his Christmas tree with a wound to the head and a gun in his hand. The thirty-one-year-old actor died later that night. Cast members and coworkers insist Duel seemed perfectly fine and healthy on the soundstage that day and couldn't imagine why he would commit suicide. Duel, however, did state in an interview with the *LA Times* shortly before his death that he was struggling a bit with the stress and creative compromises of doing a weekly television show.

With several episodes featuring Duel already in the can, ABC had to move fast to recast the role of Heyes. Roger Davis, who had been doing the program's opening and closing narrations (but whose greatest claim to fame was being Jaclyn Smith's first husband), was chosen.

Although handsome, he didn't possess Duel's shifty demeanor. Then, for the 1972–73 season, ABC scheduled *ASJ* on Saturdays at eight opposite *All in the Family*, which would rule that time slot for the next five years.

Not surprisingly, ABC cancelled *Alias Smith and Jones* in January of 1973.

Pete Duel's real name was Peter Deuel. He co-starred in *Love on a Rooftop* with Judy Carne.

In the '90s, everyone got a talk show.

In the '70s, everyone got a variety show.

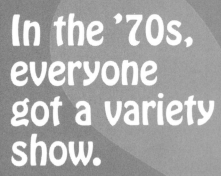

Variety Shows of the
'70s!

A partial list of hosts for these mostly short-lived shows includes:
Tim Conway, Tony Orlando and Dawn, Marilyn McCoo and Billy Davis, Captain and Tennille, Donny and Marie, Melba Moore and Clifton Davis, Burns and Schreiber, the Brady Bunch, Jim Stafford, Julie Andrews, Mac Davis, Glen Campbell, Barbara McNair, Ray Stevens, Ken Berry, David Steinberg, Dick Clark, Dick Cavett, Leslie Uggams, Donna Fargo, Don Knotts, McLean Stevenson, Rich Little, Chuck Barris, Lola Falana, George Kirby, Mary Tyler Moore, Tom Jones, Carol Burnett, Liberace, Sonny and Cher, Cher, Sonny, Dinah Shore, the Hudson Brothers, the Smothers Brothers, the Everly Brothers, the Carpenters, Barbara Mandrell and the Mandrell Sisters, Shields and Yarnell, the Manhattan Transfer, the Starland Vocal Band, Peter Marshall, Kenny Rogers, Pat Paulsen, the Jacksons, John Byner, Johnny Cash, Jerry Reed, Helen Reddy, Andy Williams, Sammy Davis, Jr., Kelly Monteith, Sha Na Na, Bill Cosby, Ben Vereen, Bobby Darin, Bobby Goldsboro, Bobby Vinton, Dolly Parton, Pink Lady, Richard Pryor, Howard Cosell, and, of course, the Muppets.

The Golddiggers!

> *"One show from the 70's that I miss a lot is Dean Martin's Golddiggers. I remember the Golddiggers as a regular on Dean's variety show, and later as a syndicated half-hour variety show sponsored by Chevrolet. These girls did nothing but sing, dance, and strut their stuff. My kind of entertainment! They don't make shows like that anymore—how about some history and pics of the Golddiggers?"*
> *—Roger Henderson*

The Golddiggers started out as regulars on *The Dean Martin Show* in 1965, providing a little T&A for the dry martini crowd. Lee Hale, the group's musical director, put it this way: "The modern recording stars forget audiences have eyes as well as ears. We look for talent, wholesomeness, sex appeal, and vivaciousness, and we prefer amateurs or near-amateurs whose styles we can personally guide."

Dean Martin refused to rehearse at all for his variety show. Instead he showed up for the tapings and winged his way through it, obviously reading off of cue cards. Lots of filler material was needed to ease the star's schedule and young babes parading around in mini-skirts, go-go boots, and bikinis provided plenty of distraction. Cue the Golddiggers.

The Golddiggers were also the stars of Dean's summer replacement series for three years starting in 1968.

There were forty or so Golddiggers over the lifetime of the act, ten or twelve

Former Golddigger Merry Elkins sent us this photo of herself (smiling) with Frank Sinatra, Jr., and other members of the troupe.

My Experience as a Dean Martin Golddigger
by *Francie Mendenhall*
November 1970–
February 1973

Well, there's a lot to say. I could write a book, so highlights will be all for now.

The staff for *The Dean Martin Show* went on a nationwide tour to find new talent for the Golddiggers and they came to Houston. The producer had chosen four of the girls to form another group called "The Ding-a-Ling Sisters" (boy, guess I wasn't thinking too much about my feminist side yet) and there were four open spots. I got one.

Before my life with the Golddiggers, I had literally been brought up in a trunk. My dad ran a legitimate theater in Houston and my brother and I began our careers at an early age. I was seven and my brother was ten when the bug bit us.

By the time we had reached our teen years we had written, acted, danced, sung, stage managed, run a theater in Houston, and in summer stock in upstate New York, props, lights, been on local and national television, and sang in night clubs.

I never dreamed I'd give up theater to giggle and wiggle on national television but I did for a while and I was scared to death. I auditioned in Houston at Patsy Swayzee's Dance Studio (Patrick's mom and my dance teacher and friend) for Jonathan Lucas, Director/Choreographer; Janet Tighe, Producer's Assistant; and Lee Hale, Music Director (Lee's published a book called *Backstage at the Dean Martin Show*).

They asked if I liked to travel and of course instantly I said yes. The thing was, I was to go to LA, film a few *Dean Martin Shows*, go to Vegas, learn the act and perform with the group and Tony Bennett, go to Vietnam with *The Bob Hope Christmas Show*, and then decide if they liked me and I liked them.

Well, I guess we liked each other, 'cause I stayed for over two years. I was flown first class (last time that ever happened!) from Houston to LAX. My mom had sewn new outfits for me so I'd look my best. I was taken to the Starlight Motel on Olive Street down from NBC and my heart sank. Boy, Johnny Carson used to joke about Burbank but I never realized how ugly it really was. The motel was fine, safe, and had a little kitchen. I shared the room with two other new girls: another from Houston, Marilyn, and one from NYC, Janice. We had our call to be at NBC to rehearse in the morning. Don't think I slept much. We were all so excited and nervous. We called family and

at a time. The original Golddiggers roster consisted of: Pamela Beth, Nancy Bonetti, Kathi Brimer, Lezlie Dalton, Dianna Gaye Liekhaus, Debra McFarlain, Lynn Cheryl Steiner, Debbie Thomanson, Mary Kathleen Wright, Peggy Hansen, and Brenda Lynne Powell.

Powell left shortly after the first summer series and the roster changed quite often after that. Basically, as soon as one of the girls wanted more money, producer Greg Garrison would fire her, or a performer would quit to get married. "We can't have married girls," Garrison decided early on. "We're away a lot and they'd have problems with their husbands."

The 1968 summer show (June 20–September 5), *Dean Martin Presents the Golddiggers*, was set in the 1930s and starred Frank Sinatra, Jr., and Joey Heatherton with Paul Lynde, Barbra Heller, Stu Gilliam, the Times Square Two, Skiles and Henderson, and the Les Brown Orchestra rounding out the cast.

One of the Golddiggers that year, Merry Elkins, tells TVparty: "That was an incredible year for me. I stayed just for that first year as my mother wanted me to go back to school. I was the youngest one in the group [shown standing next to Frank Sinatra, Jr., on the previous page] and quite taken with meeting people like Jimmy Stewart, Duke Ellington, and Ella Fitzgerald. I was really pretty young then and star struck (okay, I still am, otherwise I wouldn't have stayed in this business)." Merry is now a successful advertising executive with a major Hollywood firm.

The 1969 summer show (July 17–September 11) starred Lou Rawls, Gail Martin (Dean's Daughter), and Paul Lynde, with supporting players that included Tommy Tune, Darlene Carr, and Albert Brooks.

The 1970 (July 16–September 10) series was set in England and called *The Golddiggers in London*. Producer Garrison explained his master plan to a reporter in 1970: "Our first year we did the 1930s. The second year, the songs of the 1940s. This is our third season so we're moving along to a program of contemporary material—Burt Bacharach and so on—except for the last eight or ten minutes of every week. That will be a big extravaganza of tunes from the early periods."

The last summer romp was filmed before beginning the team's final Bob Hope USO Vietnam tour. The group did these goodwill tours for several years during the '60s, each Christmastime event lasting two weeks with Bob Hope and the Golddiggers doing two shows a day, closing with a version of "Silent Night" that reportedly reduced most of the girls to tears. The battlefields of Vietnam were a long way from the front lines of Hollywood, but those hospital visits meant a lot to the injured troops. These supposed "Golddiggers" were really hard-working gals!

By this point, there were no original Golddiggers left on the show. Hosted by Charles Nelson Reilly, the London-based hour featured Tommy Tune and Marty Feldman in his American debut. Why were they always teaming the Golddiggers with effeminate co-stars, I wonder?

Yes, Dean Martin really was a big drinker.

After the summer programs ran their course, the *Golddiggers* half-hour syndicated weekly series premiered in 1971 and it was an all-star affair. A different male guest-star (like Van Johnson, Rosey Grier, Steve Allen, and Hugh O'Brien) appeared each episode and the show featured comics Alice Ghostley, Charles Nelson Reilly, Jackie Vernon, Barbara Heller, Lonnie Schorr, and Larry Storch.

The syndicated program, produced by Greg Garrison for Chevrolet, ran for two years and was offered to local stations on a barter basis. When it debuted, there were only three holdovers from the previous year's line-up: Liz Kelley (who joined in 1970), Jackie Chidsey, and Susan Lund, who also did double duty as a Dean Martin "Ding-a-Ling" (don't ask).

Other Golddiggers in attendance on the syndicated version included: Michelle Della Fave, Rosetta Cox, Karen Cavenaugh, Lucy Codham, Paula Cinko, Lee Crawford, Jimmie Cannon, Peggy Hansen, Nancy Bonetti, Barbara Sanders, Patricia Mickey, Francie Mendenhall, Lolita Chapel, Lee Crawford, Nancy Reichert, Rebecca Jones, and Janice Whitby.

These relatively low-budget shows were shot on a tight schedule—six weeks for twenty-six episodes. This required the girls to do up to thirteen musical numbers a day, one of the most gruelling schedules anyone has ever endured.

After the Chevrolet syndicated show stopped filming, the Golddiggers toured the country doing car shows and grocery store openings, but they were only receiving about $250 dollars a week for their services and sometimes weren't paid at all.

friends and lay awake trying to sleep.

The morning finally came and we were up and ready and going to "the studio," wow. We walked down the street to NBC and the doorman inside told us where to go. There they all were—the folks that hired me in Houston, the accompanist, and all the girls. They had an earlier starting time. I guess they were prepping the "old girls" to meet the "new girls." They had a few tricks up their sleeves, sort of a mini hazing (messing up the harmonies and making you think you did it!) Sort of naughty on our first day, but we were all soon fast friends.

Everyone had their best best friend, which wasn't necessarily the roommate you had, and everyone was part of a family. After the morning rehearsal for music we broke for lunch, came back and worked on the movement. This was for a segment of *The Dean Martin Show*. As I recall, rehearsals began on Monday. By Thursday we blocked on the set and taped the next day with Mr. Martin. I do recall there wasn't a lot of time. The guest stars came in during the week and, as everyone knows by now, Mr. Martin came in the day of shooting. He liked to be fresh. What a great guy.

We were posed around him while he sat on the couch singing "Welcome to My World," and for my first big taping they placed me right off his right shoulder. I was nervous but, being the professional I'd been all of my life practically, I knew it would be swell. We began the number and when it was time for me to chime in with harmony I gave it all I had (I have an alto voice you really can't miss). Mr. Martin very nicely said, "Cut." When Dean spoke the earth moved around there. I just figured something had gone wrong in the sound booth or something. Mr. Martin asked the producer, pointing his thumb toward me, "New girl?" I died. My God. Was it me!?!

Jonathan, the director, very sweetly came up to me and said, "Don't sing out loud, just move your lips, okay?" Well what did I know? We had already taped our parts in the studio (called a "voiceover") but I thought to make it look "live" I should sing out. Unfortunately, I was singing right in Dean's mic so it sounded like an uneven duet. Boy, what a first day.

Of course, I found out how much money it costs when they "stop tape" and I never did that again (unless it was my solo, of course). Enough! I am writing a novel. I'll give another installment sometime. Bye.

—Francie Mendenhall

Then there was that bad scene in Mexico where the girls were practically held captive; their passports were confiscated and they were forced to perform around the clock. Susan Lund spoke to *Fanfare* magazine about ending her career as a Golddigger in 1972: "That was the end of the line for us. We had a little party. We all put our false eyelashes in a pile and burned them. Then we put all our falsies in a pile and we burned them. Then we all hugged each other and talked about how wonderful it had been."

The girls split up all over the country, some undoubtedly becoming housewives or supermarket clerks, but many of the Golddiggers went on to build strong futures in the Hollywood establishment.

Former Golddigger Jimmie Cannon writes: "Since I was a member of the Golddiggers during the syndicated series (our most successful time) plus a few months before, I was interested in your comments concerning our group.

"I know of none of the girls, with the exception of Karen Yarbrough, whom I believe had five children, who became housewives or supermarket clerks. My career has included a record deal with Warner Brothers, owning my own nightclub, real estate, and at present I own a company, the Cannon Group. My company represents actors for film, TV, commercials, music videos, voiceovers, and industrials. I am also married with a fourteen-year-old son.

"Susan Lund has successfully managed her son's career and continues to do so. Blake won *Junior Star Search* when he was six, had a starring role in the *Little Rascals* movie, and is presently the voice for two animated TV shows.

"The last time I spoke with Liz Kelly, she owned a dance studio. Loyita Chapel is married to Robert Woods, who plays Bo Bucannan on *One Life to Live*, and is raising a son. Francie Mendenhall had a lead in a travelling Broadway show and is presently living in Houston.

"No housewives here!!!"

The Carol Burnett Shows

No question, the most successful variety show of all time was *The Carol Burnett Show* (CBS 1967–1978), but one variety show failure almost derailed Carol Burnett's amazing career before it really got going.

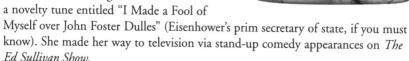

Carol Burnett got her start in off-Broadway theatre, first achieving national attention with a novelty tune entitled "I Made a Fool of Myself over John Foster Dulles" (Eisenhower's prim secretary of state, if you must know). She made her way to television via stand-up comedy appearances on *The Ed Sullivan Show*.

Burnett's first regular series role was on a live sitcom called *Stanley* (September 1956–March 1957), one of those early TV shows with a high-quality pedigree that failed to catch on. In *Stanley*, Buddy Hackett starred as the lackadaisical manager of a New York City hotel lobby newstand/ticket agency with Carol playing his loopy girlfriend Celia. The creators of Sid Caesar's *Your Show of Shows* were behind this program, produced, and directed by Max Liebman, with playwright Neil Simon on the writing staff. This NBC entry barely lasted one season.

During the run of *Stanley*, Burnett did a guest shot on *The Garry Moore Show* (1950–1958), a popular daytime variety program on CBS. This led to Burnett's next big break, as a regular player on the prime-time *Garry Moore Show* (1958–1964), one of the most prestigious television productions of the early '60s.

The producer of the *Moore* show was Bob Banner along with Joe Hamilton. Hamilton and Burnett eventually married and had three children. This caused a minor scandal and almost cost wholesome Burnett her career since he was already married with children when they began dating.

With a pliable face and a circus contortionist's body (*TV Guide* called her "the girl in the rubber mask"), Carol Burnett won the hearts of TV viewers playing the nervous klutz in dozens of preposterous skits. She was an instant hit with the home audience, one of the emerging medium's first prime-time breakout stars.

Each week, gawky Carol would find herself in the most outrageous predicaments. No matter how sketchy the script, the comedienne turned each performance into a farcical romp with her wondrous, spasmodic interpretations. She rapidly became the de-facto star of the program.

In 1962, Burnett left *The Garry Moore Show* to tour with an ambitious stage revue and in 1964 turned up as one of three rotating hosts on *The Entertainers,* a variety series that also featured Bob Newhart and Caterina Valente. This series was a huge, unanticipated bomb, lasting less than a year. Almost nothing has been written about *The Entertainers* and everyone involved seems to have blotted the series from their résumés.

Despite this blunder, CBS gave Carol Burnett a ten-year, million-dollar contract to make one special a season and do two guest shots for the network. She resisted CBS's strong suggestions that she star in another traditional sitcom, reasoning, "They would probably name me Gertrude or Agnes and that's all I'd be forever."

Over the next three years, Burnett hosted some of the finest musical-comedy specials ever broadcast, including the Emmy Award–winning *Julie and Carol at Lincoln Center.* In 1967, CBS finally talked her into hosting a weekly, hour-long variety show of her own.

Carol Burnett's last special before starting her own series was the closest thing she had done to a straight-ahead variety show format since leaving *The Garry Moore Show.* Produced by Bob Banner, the result was *Carol + 2* with guests Lucille Ball and Zero Mostel, an uneven mix of lukewarm skits and overwrought performances, very unusual for a Burnett special, which were all highly acclaimed.

She must have learned something from this experience. Her own series began filming a few weeks later with husband Joe Hamilton producing, yielding much better results. On September 11, 1967, *The Carol Burnett Show* debuted, joining

Burnett Show writer Dick Clair had himself cryogenically frozen moments before his death, to hopefully be revived and cured.

CBS's winning Monday-night schedule that included *Gunsmoke*, *The Lucy Show*, *The Andy Griffith Show*, and *Family Affair*. The series proved a perfect fit. Because of the telecast's initial success, Burnett had her first guest Jim Nabors (*Gomer Pyle*) back for every season opener thereafter as a good-luck charm.

The Carol Burnett Show featured TV bit player Harvey Korman, Lyle Waggoner, and a young high school girl who contacted Burnett because of her remarkable resemblance to the star. In one of those great, true Hollywood discoveries, Vicki Lawrence actually got hired as a regular on a network television series by writing a letter to a star. That could never happen now. Celebrities are instructed not to read or respond to their fan mail because of stalkers.

Characters and skits made famous over the run of the series included Eunice and her bickering family, the disaster-prone Queen of England, Mr. Tudball with his vacuous secretary Mrs. Wiggins, and aged-out movie star Nora Desmond, along with broad satires of classic movies and TV shows. Writers on the staff included veterans of early television and *MAD* magazine.

There were very few changes during the eleven-year run of the program. In 1974, Lyle Waggoner quit the series to co-star in *Wonder Woman*, a move he later regretted. It never occurred to him that he would be upstaged by Linda Carter's breasts—that's not exactly progress. Frequent guest Tim Conway officially joined the regular cast in 1975. His fluid improvisations and attempts to break up the cast led to some of the show's best outings. Burnett wanted Tim Conway to replace Lyle Waggoner right away instead of waiting a year, but Conway had been involved with so many recent flops he was considered by some (even himself) to be a jinx.

Harvey Korman signed an exclusive deal with ABC and left in the spring of 1977 (his ABC sitcom failed in 1978), so Dick Van Dyke was hired as his replacement for the fall. Van Dyke had just lost his own brilliant, Emmy-winning (but short-lived) variety series on NBC and it seemed like a perfect match, but he became dissatisfied with his second-banana status on *The Carol Burnett Show* and abruptly quit in December 1977.

After Van Dyke left, Steve Lawrence and Ken Berry made frequent stopovers to provide a male lead, but this was to be the last season for the series. Burnett decided to walk away in 1978 before the show could be cancelled by the network. An

"One year there were twenty-five different variety shows and a lot of specials, and it was fun!" —*George Schlatter*

exceptional two-hour special was aired as a series finale, with highlights from past years combined with new material.

During the mid-'70s, Carol Burnett began a second career as a film actor, garnering excellent reviews in a remake of *Front Page* and in Robert Altman's comedy/drama classic *The Wedding*. CBS signed Carol to do specials and made-for-TV movies but she was restless to do a series again. During the summer of 1979, she put together *Carol Burnett and Company* for ABC (after CBS passed on the project). The four-episode series featured Vicki Lawrence and Tim Conway with new regulars Craig Richard Nelson and Kenneth Mars. With the variety show format burned out, ratings weren't so great. The series was passed over for fall placement.

That Carol Burnett found any success at all in the '80s is a testament to her good taste and abilities. Burnett's dramatic TV movies of the late '70s were very popular, tackling a number of controversial issues. For instance, *Friendly Fire* (1979) told the story of a couple that lost their child due to military accident; another telefilm chronicled a family's anguish over having a gay son.

In 1980, *The Tim Conway Show* from producer Joe Hamilton debuted on CBS. Harvey Korman, Carol Burnett, and Vicki Lawrence all made several guest appearances on this enjoyable variety hour; the guests even reprised characters and skits from *The Carol Burnett Show*. Harvey Korman joined the regular cast during the second season when the show was trimmed to a half-hour. *The Tim Conway Show* ran from March 1980 until August, 1981, a long run for a variety show in the '80s.

Four years after *The Carol Burnett Show* left the air, the Burnett team put together a wonderful special called *Eunice*, featuring the bickering Harper family. The four-act, ninety-minute production was filmed like a play and featured Carol Burnett as Eunice, Vicki Lawrence as Mama Harper, Betty White as sister Ellen, Harvey Korman as Ed, and Ken Berry as brother Phillip as they raged and aged through the years. Based on the best scripts from the CBS series, this production molded the contentious Harper family into three-dimensional people without eradicating the way-out, farcical nature that made them funny in the first place. The result was perhaps Carol Burnett's finest television work. Building like a low-rent Tennessee Williams' play, events only alluded to in earlier scenes came crashing down around the characters by the fourth act, when the family congregates following Mother Harper's funeral.

Because of the success of the special (broadcast Monday, March 15, 1982), NBC picked up the half-hour sitcom *Mama's Family* as a midseason replacement in January, 1983. The production was headed by Joe Hamilton and Carol Burnett made several guest appearances during the show's first season as Eunice. These

Carol tugged on her ear at the end of every show to let her grandmother back home know that she was doing fine.

episodes stand as some of the funniest sitcoms of the decade, believe it or not.

Regulars included Ken Berry as dullard
brother Vint, Rue McClanahan (*Maude*) as
Thelma's sister Fran, and Dorothy Lyman
(Opal from *All My Children*) as slutty neigh-
bor Naomi Oates. Back occasionally were
Betty White as sister Ellen and Harvey
Korman, who directed several episodes and
served as the show's narrator. When the program returned for a second (and last
network) season, Carol Burnett was nowhere to be seen. She and her husband Joe
Hamilton were splitting up.

Burnett also returned for a few episodes of her favorite daytime soap *All My
Children* in 1983 as Verla Grubbs, something she first did for fun in 1976.

Throughout the rest of the '80s, Carol Burnett could be seen sporadically in specials like *Julie and Carol: Together Again* in 1989, but there was no regular series
for the comedienne until March 31, 1990, when *Carol and Company* debuted on
NBC. This half-hour was part variety show, part movie-of-the-week, with Carol
once again greeting the audience at the opening of each episode but without taking questions. The remainder of the show had her playing a different character in
an unusual but relatively realistic situation, like attending a high school reunion.
There would be no reprising old characters from her long-running '70s series;
these mini-plays were less broad, with more down-to-earth portrayals.

Carol and Company was highly acclaimed but ratings were lukewarm. That a
bold show like this lasted two seasons qualifies it as a success. It must have
impressed CBS, because they launched a brand new *Carol Burnett Show* in 1991,
just weeks after the NBC series left the air. Back in the familiar one-hour variety
show format with a brand new cast of regulars, Burnett was in her element once
again, but America wasn't ready for the return of variety shows, even one hosted
by the first lady of the genre. This series, which I never saw and you probably did-
n't either, lasted only seven weeks.

Today Carol Burnett can be seen occasionally as a sitcom guest star, on the stage
in New York, and on retrospectives of her former CBS series. In November 2001,
her reunion special *Showstoppers* garnered 29.8 million viewers to deliver the best
performance in its time slot that CBS had
seen in over a decade.

Almost fifty years after beginning her
television journey, Carol Burnett has
hopefully found a home on our television
screens forever.

Sonny Cher

It was a 1971 guest spot on the *The Merv Griffin Show* that convinced CBS programming head Fred Silverman that Sonny and Cher, one of the top touring acts of the '60s (but whose hits dried up in 1967), would make vibrant hosts for a five-week summer replacement variety show. The couple's bright musical arrangements interspersed with humorous on-stage bickering scored big in the tacky nightclub lounges they were reduced to performing in. Theirs was an act that many say was largely inspired by Louis Prima and Keely Smith's long-running Las Vegas routine.

When *The Sonny and Cher Comedy Hour* debuted on CBS the first night in August 1971, it was an immediate hit. CBS was hoping to regain the young audience they had lost when they cancelled the popular but controversial *Smothers Brothers Comedy Hour* two years earlier, and Sonny and Cher proved to be just what the network was looking for.

With good reason. The show's producers (Allan Blye and Chris Bearde) and the writers were all *Smothers Brothers* alumni. Tommy Smothers once remarked, "I turned on the TV one night and there was our show. Only it starred Sonny and Cher!" Based on the runaway success of the trial run, *The Sonny and Cher Comedy*

"Before television, nobody even knew what a headache looked like." —*D. Fields*

Hour was back on the air in December of 1971, replacing *The Chicago Teddy Bears*, Friday nights at eight.

"This is an explosion," Fred Silverman gushed about the couple's summer splash. "You could count on one hand the number of times this has happened in the history of television. And it didn't cost us $10 million and two floors of the CBS building to get them." The program featured regulars Terri Garr, Freeman King, Peter Cullen, Billy Van, Murray Langston (later the "Unknown Comic"), Ted Zeigler, and Chastity Bono, the couple's toddler. The series was famous for the catchy musical numbers scored by Billy Barnes and the outlandish outfits designed by Bob Mackie, who did the costumes for Cher only as he was under contract to Carol Burnett for her entire show.

The highlight of the hour was the couple's opening dialogue, during which they flung insults at one another:

SONNY: "Before we go on I just want to remind you of what day this is. It's a very unlucky day."

CHER: "You mean Tuesday the fourth?"

SONNY: "No, it's Friday the thirteenth. What's Tuesday the fourth?"

CHER: "The day we got married."

SONNY: "C'mon Cher, don't make jokes on Friday the thirteenth. Haven't you ever heard of black cats crossing your path and breaking a mirror and then seven years of bad luck?"

CHER: "It'll be eight Tuesday the fourth."

Thanks to massive TV exposure, a string of hit records and concert tours followed that raked in big bucks for the duo and drove ratings even higher. By the fall of 1972, the show was a consistent top-ten winner.

Still, all was not happy in Sonny and Cher land. By 1973, the tabloids were ripe with stories of their public shouting matches, cancelled gigs (including a last-minute cancellation in Vegas, filled by Johnny Carson), and even reports of Cher

sporting a black eye. Cher began scoring solo records just as the couple's recording career was winding down and tensions increased when she moved out of their home. What the public didn't know was that the couple had been living their lives apart with different lovers in separate wings of their Bel Air mansion for some time. Ultimately, Cher wanted a solo career and no longer required a prefix. With the TV program finishing eighth overall for the 1973–74 season, Sonny Bono filed for divorce and fifty-eight hours later on February 22, 1974, the final episode of *The Sonny and Cher Comedy Hour* was taped. CBS was left with no choice but to cancel one of their top shows when it became apparent the talent couldn't work together any longer.

The Sonny and Cher Comedy Hour left the air May 29, 1974. CBS immediately signed Cher to star in her own variety series for winter 1975, but Sonny signed a deal with ABC that would put him on the air in the fall of 1974 with the same producers, writing staff, and all of the regular cast and familiar comedy bits from the earlier series. "We'll have all the same players," Bono said at the time, adding, "We'll be missing one, actually." Network watchers geared up to see what would happen in February when the *Cher* show, scheduled for Sunday nights at seven-thirty on CBS, went up against *The Sonny Comedy Review,* which was scheduled for Sunday nights at eight on ABC. As it turned out, February was a long way off.

Each episode of *The Sonny Comedy Review* began with a different female guest star (like Loretta Swit or Raquel Welch) ribbing Sonny about how short and untalented he was, like in this opening exchange:

Series regular BILLY VAN: "Tell me, Loretta, what's the difference between doing your show and Sonny's show?"

LORETTA SWIT: "Well, in one I'm doing *M.A.S.H.* and in one I'm doing mush."

BILLY VAN: "It's Smokey Robinson! Tell me, how do you feel about doing the show, Smokey?"

SMOKEY ROBINSON: "Well, I used to be surrounded by Miracles and now I need one."

The audience didn't need to be reminded. The effort was a dismal failure, partly because the *Sonny* show started at eight, halfway into the running time of the other network telecasts that started at seven-thirty—and partly because it became painfully obvious Cher was the glue that held this act together.

Many of the comedy skits from the *Comedy Hour* were carried over effectively to the Bono show, including "Sonny's Pizza" and "The Convict," which featured Sonny as a lifer being visited by his footloose wife, now played by Terri Garr instead of Cher. New bits like a mime routine with Sonny and the regulars as the French Foreign Legion were pure dreck. Scripts for the Bono show were uneven at best, good guest stars were scarce, and Cher fought tenaciously to keep little Chastity from appearing on her father's program, relenting only in the series' final few weeks after the lawyers got involved. *The Sonny Comedy Review* was mercifully cancelled with the December 29 episode. The head to head on-air battle of the former team only came about when Sonny guest-starred a few months later on the show that replaced his, *The Six Million Dollar Man*. Cher lost that one.

Cher debuted on Sunday, February 16, 1975, six weeks after Sonny's show was swept away on another network. "I'm scared to death," she admitted at the time. "I'm so afraid of that first walk-out. Here I am—alone, naked to the world. What do you think, world? Do you forgive me?"

The production was headed by *Laugh-In* vet George Schlatter and always opened with Cher draped and silhouetted in the dark, singing low over a lone piano, slowly beginning the opening song. Then, throwing off her wrap as the music picked up tempo, she would strut to the front of the stage, revealing her latest navel-exposing Bob Mackie outfit. A lot of press was generated in 1975 about Cher's exposed belly-button; it had never been done on television before. Even "Jeannie" obscured hers with scarves.

After a spectacular, star-studded premiere with guests Elton John, Bette Midler, and Flip Wilson, *Cher* settled into comfortable but less than spectacular ratings. Renewed for a second season, ratings remained flat. In January of 1976, Cher called it quits as a solo TV act and announced that she and Sonny Bono were re-teaming for a brand new Sonny and Cher program.

"I made the decision after I'd done four *Cher* shows last fall. Nothing to do with the ratings," Cher admitted years later. "Doing a show alone was more than I

SONNY: "I've actually increased my I.Q. twenty-seven points."   CHER "That's fantastic, that makes an even thirty."

could handle. I had to be into everything, from helping on scripts to picking the music. And they had me doing a monologue. That's not like me, to be out there alone making with the jokes."

Sunday night, February 1, 1976, just a month after the *Cher* show left the air, with Cher visibly pregnant by her estranged new husband (drug-addicted rock star Greg Allman), *The Sonny and Cher Show* debuted to top-ten ratings and high expectations. "When we go out there in front of our first audience tonight," Sonny Bono commented before the first taping, "we'll be telling them everything they already knew about Sonny and Cher but were afraid to ask."

The new show started out well enough; the couple got through the familiar opening dialogue and musical number without much trouble.

SONNY: "Well, folks, I don't know if any of you heard about it, but Cher and I aren't married anymore. (Audience gasps.) You mean you haven't heard? No, it's true. Now for the good news. We're back!"

CHER: "And they said it wouldn't last."

SONNY: "You're kidding and I like that. In fact, I love it, Cher. Because, to tell you the truth, working alone really wasn't many laughs."

CHER: "I know, I saw your show."

This production was headed by Nick Vanoff (*The Hollywood Palace*) and featured regulars Ted Zeigler, Billy Van, mime act Shields and Yarnell, and Galaird Sartain (the *Cher* show's only regular). Of course, daughter Chastity Bono was on hand to help mom and dad say goodnight. At least by now she could talk.

CBS censors took a stronger look at this new incarnation, now on an hour earlier than the original to attract younger viewers. The network complained that Cher's clothes and image were not appropriate for a recent divorcée. "Suddenly I should start coming off like Julie Andrews," was Cher's fiery reply. "Hell, Sonny didn't die."

Cher is the only artist to have number one hits in the '60s, '70s, '80s, and the '90s.

The program's audience eroded steadily over time, as did the quality of the comedy skits. For legal reasons, it was decided that none of the characters from previous Sonny and/or Cher formats could be reprised on this new hour. Features the creative staff came up with, like "Sonnytone News," were uninspired to say the least. Still, based on the early strong numbers, the show was brought back for a second term.

The 1976–77 season tried to recapture the spark of the original series with the return of the "LaVern" and "Vamp" sketches, and former regular Terri Garr was brought on as a guest more often. Even seven-year-old Chastity started appearing in more of the musical-comedy segments. It didn't help the couple's image any that the second season started out with Cher now officially divorced from her new husband, the father of her three-month-old baby.

Mid-season, the series was moved to Friday nights at nine, then to Monday nights at ten as the program attempted to appeal to a more adult audience. The opening dialogues were better than ever as they sparred over their separately dysfunctional lives.

The show even reran the very popular animated musical films (like "Big Yellow Taxi" and "Bad, Bad Leroy Brown") from the original *Comedy Hour,* and CBS used the same print ads they had run for the original show, complete with six-year-old pictures. All of this proved to be too little, too late.

The Sonny and Cher Show hovered near the bottom of the ratings for most of the second season before limping off the air August 29, 1977. Sonny and Cher were cancelled for good after hosting four different variety series between them in just six years.

"Commercial television makes so much money doing its worst, it can't afford to do its best." —Fred Friendly

SUMMER REPLACEMENT SHOWS OF THE 70S

[A photo of Joey Heatherton, star of *Joey and Dad*]

During the first three decades of television, there was a crowded slate of network variety shows and they would all go on hiatus for the summer. As an alternative to reruns (which began in spring), original programs showcasing other talents were produced for the off months. This practice ended with the '70s, when the entire musical-comedy genre was laid to rest. Still, the bell-bottom decade began with great promise.

Hit records ran out for the musical duo years earlier, and their movies flopped as well, but Sonny and Cher scored on CBS in 1971 as the summer replacement for *The Ed Sullivan Show*. Ratings were so high, they reappeared with their own regular series that December. Top-ten ratings, number-one records, and sold-out concert dates followed.

After the Sonny and Cher phenomenon, all three networks stopped developing variety shows primarily around comedians and started looking to the top-forty charts for the next wave of musical-variety stars. Every summer season for the next six years, the nets mounted shows starring established pop groups and one-hit wonders, hoping that lightning would strike again. Here is a look at just a few of them:

The Carpenters were riding high on the pop charts in 1971 and they took their act to NBC with *Make Your Own Kind of Music*, a sunny hour with a star-studded regular cast that included trumpeter Al Hirt, comics (and future hit TV producers) Tom Patchett and Jay Tarses, Mark Lindsay, and the New Doodletown Pipers. Special guests during the eight-week run included the Fifth Dimension, Dusty Springfield, Helen Reddy, Jack Jones, and Jose Feliciano.

Audience numbers were good but, unfortunately for NBC, the duo didn't need a regular series. They already had lucrative concert dates and peaking record sales filling their coffers. In 1971 alone, the Carpenters received two Grammy awards and scored four top-ten hits (*For All We Know, Rainy Days and Mondays, Superstar,* and *Bless the Beasts and the Children*).

When *Sanford and Son* debuted on NBC in January of 1972, suddenly shows with blacks in prominent roles were hot. CBS naturally went shopping for a black Sonny and Cher and found them. *The Melba Moore–Clifton Davis Show* was a superlative five-week replacement for *The Carol Burnett Show* in 1972, starring real-life couple Melba Moore (Tony Award–winning star of *Purlie*) and Clifton Davis, (he wrote the song *Never Can Say Goodbye*). The set resembled a ghetto apartment building (think *Sesame Street,* only grittier) with the skits and musical numbers taking place in various exposed units, on the steps, and up on the roof. Guests "checking into" the building included Moms Mabley, Jean Stapleton, and Arte Johnson.

Of course, there was lots of *Sonny and Cher*–style squabbling between the couple, and old-school nightclub comedian Timmie Rogers ("Oh Yeeaaah!") gained a forum for his hilarious bits. Also featured were regulars Liz Torres, Ron Carrey, and Dick

Timmie Rogers on politics: "I want to have the seven party system. Party *every* night!"

Libertini. It was widely reported that CBS was going to bring this show back as a mid-season replacement in 1973, but it was not to be. The couple split soon after, but Clifton Davis turned up in a sitcom called *That's My Mama* in 1974. Melba Moore went on to star in *Melba*, a sitcom that was cancelled after the first episode in 1986 while her ex began a long run with *Amen* that same year.

Ken Berry (*F Troop*) was shocked when his series *Mayberry RFD* was cancelled on CBS in 1971—it was still in the top twenty! *The Ken Berry WOW Show* was a four-week series in July and August of 1972 that attempted to give the likable performer another shot and provide ABC with an idea of Berry's star pull. Produced by Alan Blye

and Chris Bearde (*Sonny and Cher Comedy Hour*) and featuring many of the Sonny and Cher regular players like Terri Garr, Ted Zeigler, Steve Martin, Billy Van, and a young Cheryl Ladd, this variety hour was filled with old-fashioned song-and-dance numbers, the kind Ken Berry was famous for in his Kinney Shoes commercials and his yearly *Carol Burnett Show* appearances. It didn't fly. Ken Berry was unable to find regular series work again until *Mama's Family* rescued his TV career in 1983, if you want to call that a rescue.

If television revived supposed has-beens Sonny and Cher, could it do the same for former teen idol **Bobby Darin**? NBC hoped so. A triumphant Las Vegas comeback had made Bobby Darin a hot property again and a natural to replace Dean Martin during his 1972 summer hiatus. *The Bobby Darin Amusement Company* was produced by Saul Illson and Ernest Chambers (original producers of *The Smothers Brothers Comedy Hour*), with regulars Steve Landesburg, Dick Bakalyan, and Rip Taylor. George Burns, Bobbie Gentry, and Burt Reynolds appeared as special guests on the first episode. The emphasis was on both comedy and music, with Bobby playing characters like "Dusty John the hippie" and "the Godmother" in comedy skits. "Angie and Carmine" was another regular feature with Bobby and comic Dick Bakalyan portraying two regular guys from the Bronx talking on their front stoop, the dialogue partly improvisational. One bizarre (but original) semi-regular feature had Bobby explaining tricky chess moves.

The program was a top-notch production and was brought back in 1973, but the star was gravely ill by that time so the revival only lasted a few short months. Tragically, Bobby Darin died later that same year.

The networks were shooting blanks in an effort to clone Sonny and Cher, the eighth most watched show on the tube by 1974. Then the unthinkable happened—Sonny and Cher called it quits. *Tony Orlando and Dawn* was the first summer show shoved into the Wednesday-night timeslot left unexpectedly empty by the couple's divorce and subsequent cancellation of television's top-rated variety show.

Produced by Illson and Chambers, the opening of each episode mimicked exactly the *S&C Comedy Hour* formula: a musical number, followed by put-downs all around, then back into the musical number. It lacked originality but was a hit with viewers, a show carefully crafted to fill the void left by the battling Bonos.

The series was so successful it was brought back in December, 1974 (in the same

Jerry Reed was a regular on several shows, including *Dean Martin Presents* in 1973 and *Concrete Cowboys* in 1981.

time slot) to replace the low-rated teen drama *Sons and Daughters*. Ratings were high the first season, but the overall quality of the show was not so great and viewership dropped steadily against *Little House on the Prairie* and *That's My Mama* on the other networks.

The emphasis of *Tony Orlando and Dawn* was on getting guest-stars like Carroll O'Connor, Jack Albertson, and Art Carney to sing and dance. The results were decidedly mixed and the novelty wore off quickly. In the fall of 1976, producers shifted the focus to comedy. George Carlin, Edie McClurg, and others were brought on as regulars but the retitled *Tony Orlando and Dawn Rainbow Hour* was scuttled three months later.

After *Tony Orlando and Dawn* ended their initial summer run in 1974, the **Hudson Brothers** also had a successful (but short) stint subbing for *Sonny and Cher*, with the advantage of having the *S&C* producers and writers on board. Featured on *The Hudson Brothers Show* were Gary Owens, Ronnie Graham, Stephanie Edwards, and Australian Rod Hull and his Amazing Emu. That "emu" was actually a hand puppet that would attack poor Rod and throw him (or anyone else) to the floor at the slightest provocation. A remarkable, world-renowned, one-joke comic, Hull was killed in 1999 when he fell from his roof trying to fix his TV antennae.

The Hudson Brothers Show clicked with youngsters, which led to the *Hudson Brothers Razzle Dazzle Show*, an unusual half-hour Saturday-morning CBS variety program that debuted in the fall.

With country music going mainstream, **Mac Davis** attracted huge ratings for his summer of '74 NBC entry. Brought back in December as a mid-season replacement, Davis started strong but was all tuckered out by March. Because those initial summer numbers were so high, NBC made another failed attempt in 1976. They just couldn't believe Mac Davis wasn't able to recapture that audience.

Joey and Dad from July 1975 was an unusual concept, showing just how far CBS was willing to go to get another variety show duo off the ground—but it worked very well thanks in part to the obvious affection the co-stars had for one another. Produced by Allan Blye and Bob Einstein, *Joey and Dad* starred Las Vegas showgirl Joey Heatherton and her father Ray Heatherton, who was known to 1950s juvenile audiences as "The Merry Mailman." The opening dialogues were along familiar lines, but with a generation-gap twist:

DAD: "What's wrong with this tie? I think it's very nice."

JOEY: "Well, uh, I don't want to hurt your feelings, but it would look better on Bozo the Clown."

DAD: "Does that mean you don't like it?"

JOEY: "Daddy, it just doesn't suit you. It's a bad color, it's too loud and it really looks cheap."

DAD: "But it has a sentimental value."

JOEY: "What kind of sentimental value could that ugly, loud, tasteless tie have?"

DAD: "You gave it to me for Father's Day."

Mark Hudson was the bandleader for Joan Rivers's talk show debacle on FOX.

193

Joey and Dad regularly featured comedians Henny Youngman, Pat Proft, and Pat Paulsen, and employed many of the writers from previous Blye and Einstein shows. *Joey and Dad* ran for four weeks in July 1975 as the summer substitute for *Cher*, and guest stars included Captain and Tennille, Frankie Valli, and Sherman Hemsley. One bizarre low point was the "dead parrot" routine lifted from *Monty Python* and performed almost verbatim by Pat Paulsen and Sherman Hemsley.

The Manhattan Transfer took over the *Cher* timeslot for four weeks in August, 1975. This nostalgically musical program concentrated on elaborate production numbers hearkening back to various time periods in order to showcase the vocal versatility of the four hosts. A regular comedy feature was Archie Hahn as "Doughie Duck." Cher blamed these two lightweight replacement shows for eroding her audience that summer, diminishing the return for her show in the fall which in turn forced a Sonny and Cher reunion a few months later.

By 1976, the half-hour variety show was becoming the norm on CBS. Network execs hoped that perhaps the *length* of the show was the reason musical-variety programs were no longer in favor with viewers.

Looking for a pop act with youth appeal (that desperately needed TV exposure), CBS casts its eye toward the Jacksons in 1976. The group had fallen on hard times; this was after the Jackson Five's big hits ended in 1974 and before Michael Jackson's *Off the Wall* album changed the face of music five years later.

The entire Jackson family was present for the TV production except Jermaine, who had a solo record contract. Even little sister Janet was in full force and Michael was a lot more open and friendly back then, too—even though he was totally against the idea of a TV show from the very start. "We shouldn't do it," he argued with his siblings, to no avail. "Look at Tony Orlando. Look at Cher. It's going to really hurt our sales." He claimed to hate doing dumb comedy skits with canned laughter and dressing in silly outfits but was ultimately talked into going along because the family needed the money CBS was offering.

"We're the Jacksons!" Michael chirped to open the first episode. "All of you who were expecting the Osmonds, do not adjust the color on your set." The series scored some impressive ratings despite the fact that the variety show genre was becoming passé by the mid-'70s. Guests for the four-week run included Ed McMahon, who played W.C. Fields to Janet Jackson's Mae West, and Sonny Bono, who appeared in a comedy sketch about the tabloids. This was one of Bono's last network guest-shots—just three years earlier he had the biggest show on television, and now his career was grinding to a dead stop.

Much to Michael's chagrin, *The Jacksons* was brought back in January of 1977, but it failed to catch on as a regular series and was cancelled due to abysmal ratings in March of that same year. Michael accepted some of the blame, saying in part, "I'm not a comedian. Is it really entertaining for me to get up there and crack a few weak jokes and force people to laugh because I'm Michael Jackson, when I know in my heart I'm

The Jacksons left Motown Records in the summer of 1975.

not funny?"

In spite of Michael's dire predictions, mere weeks after *The Jacksons* left the air, the brothers were back on the charts with the hit tune *Enjoy Yourself* and sister Janet Jackson, the TV show's breakout star, was well on her way establishing a solo career. She was discovered by producer Norman Lear on the variety show and, after auditioning, joined the cast of *Good Times* a few months later.

With more misses than hits over the last decade, CBS went out on a limb during the summer of '77 and signed **Shields and Yarnell**, who were known for their San Francisco sidewalk mime routines. They brought their street improv sensibilities to television, proving to be popular guest stars on various variety shows.

Given their own half-hour in July 1977, CBS wanted the usual glitzy, big-name guests but the couple preferred instead to host the street performers they formerly worked with. They developed several popular characters for TV, most notably portraying an off-the-beat robotic couple. *Shields and Yarnell* was the hit CBS was looking for and the show was renewed for mid-season. Brought back in January up against *Laverne and Shirley*, it sank like a stone and the couple broke up shortly thereafter, both awkwardly attempting solo careers.

In keeping with the smaller stars—smaller shows thinking, CBS launched **The Keane Brothers** in August 1977. The fresh-faced, talented (but not terribly well-known) Keane brothers were the Hanson of the '70s—but without the hit albums and millions of fans.

John and Tom Keane (age twelve and thirteen) hosted this thirty-minute variety show on Friday nights at eight-thirty, hoping to capture some of the *Donny and Marie* viewers. Regulars were impressionist Jimmy Caesar, the Anita Mann Dancers, and the Alan Copeland Orchestra. This production was mostly an excuse to show off the musical talents of the boys and to prepare them for fleeting teen idol fame.

Also that summer, **The Starland Vocal Band** headed one of the oddest (but considered by many to be one of the best) replacement shows, taped on location around the country. Regulars included David Letterman, Jeff Altman (*Pink Lady and Jeff*), and political satirists Mark Russell, Peter Bergman, and Phil Proctor.

Mark Russell did basically the same act on this CBS show that he does now in his PBS specials. Bergman and Proctor were revolutionary '60s underground comedians (*Firesign Theatre*) who provided more bite than would be expected in a program hosted by the one-hit wonders who gave us the God-awful "Afternoon Delight" single in 1976.

That was the last summer replacement variety show until the summer of 1988, when the Smothers Brothers hosted a four-week run on CBS, and that was the last until *The Wayne Brady Show* premiered in the summer of 2001. The *Brady* program won its time period easily and was a shoo-in for a midseason slot but ultimately wasn't renewed. History repeats.

Shields and Yarnell were once arrested as a public nuisance for doing their street performances.

The Smothers Brothers Comedy Hour wasn't expected to be a hit when it debuted in February 1967. Scheduled on CBS against the unbeatable number-one rated *Bonanza* on NBC, this was a Hail Mary play on the part of the network.

The Smothers were the latest in a long line of well-known performers who were thrown up against *Bonanza*, all quickly going down in flames. In the previous six years, Jack Benny, Judy Garland, Joey Bishop, Bob Cummings, Perry Mason, and Garry Moore (who was unceremoniously dumped mid-season to make way for the Smothers) all failed to make a dent in the horse opera's ratings.

Unlike previous contenders, the Smothers didn't have strong TV series credibility. The duo began their career in bohemian clubs during the beat era, wandering into television through the back door, performing their musical comedy act on *The Ed Sullivan Show, The Bing Crosby Show, The New Steve Allen Show, The Andy Williams Show,* and folk music programs like *Hootenanny.*

A CBS sitcom called *The Smothers Brothers Show* (in which Tommy played an angel and Dick his playboy brother) hardly made a dent with audiences or critics in 1965. No matter; the brothers had several hit musical/comedy albums under their belt and their own popular catchphrase: "Mom always liked you best."

Why did CBS give the Smothers their own Sunday-night variety hour mere months after cancelling their sitcom? In one of the first examples of demographics shaping network programming, CBS figured a variety program with a youthful appeal might counter *Bonanza's* predominantly

The Smothers Brothers sitcom was headed by Fred DeCordova, the guy who produced *Mr. Adams and Eve.*

THE SMOTHERS BROTHERS

Tommy (left) and Dick (right).

older viewers. The Smothers Brothers, being musical-comedy performers, had the talent and wholesome appeal the network was looking for.

CBS packaged the Smothers's slightly off-beat style with the standard network variety show trappings: rows of dancers, big-name guests, Nelson Riddle as musical director. Failure seemed assured—at least that was the industry buzz. Tommy Smothers shrewdly negotiated a twenty-six-week guarantee going in. If they were going to flop, he reasoned, they may as well get paid.

The gamble worked and the brothers came in sixteenth overall for the season. When the *Comedy Hour* returned for a second year, Tom Smothers exerted more control over the program's content and the show began to develop more of an edge, spoofing topics other television shows wouldn't dare—religion, recreational drugs, the sexual revolution, and political unrest were all comic fodder for this hip new show.

A lot has been written about the *Comedy Hour* and its unique place in television history. Deft satire, brilliant stand-up humor, references to marijuana and the counterculture, innovative video special effects, cutting-edge rock bands, blacklisted performers—as a result of this volatile mixture, the Smothers Brothers grew in popularity and *Bonanza* was no longer number one by 1968.

Still, CBS wasn't all that happy. Outspoken liberal Tommy Smothers was now firmly in control of an hour of network prime-time television, cultivating writers and producers to suit his taste. Asked why he assumed the creative reins, Tom told TVparty: "I'm a meddler. During the *Comedy Hour*, I think we had four different directors. I was in the directing booth. I got my DGA card and I was sitting there telling them how to direct and what pictures to take. Some people choose to do that. Carol Burnett and those people, they didn't really want to develop other projects beside themselves. They worked very hard on their sketches and I think that's why they were so good at it. I was just a pain in the ass. I never did learn my lines."

Tom offered an example of the kind of general resistance to change he encountered from the production staff and network: "We'd have a dress rehearsal and then go to these meetings and they would say, 'That didn't work, this worked, that didn't work and change this.' And I couldn't tell because I was in it. So we'd take the tape and transfer it down and in between shows I'd look at it, going fast-forward to where the problems were.

"They said, 'you're emasculating the directors and producers and you can't do this.' And CBS said, 'you have to bring a union guy in to run the machine.' And

The Smothers Brothers attended San Jose State College.

Bette Davis, who was going through it with us, said, 'Don't you give up but make sure you know what you're doing. You're the one who has to make the taste because you're up there.' She was that kind of person herself and I loved that about her. And that was true of Sinatra. And Roseanne, too. The series that make it are the ones that had strong stars with strong opinions, who were doing it their way. Even Seinfeld, they did it their way."

It wasn't long before Tom discovered that he may have had artistic control contractually but the network had absolute control. "We were the first show that said, 'Hey, man, the war is bad,' and criticized [President] Johnson from a public platform." Popular slang, controversial songs, and entire comedy segments were excised by strict network censors. It was okay in 1967 to make fun of a president's golf game on TV, but not his war.

Because of these censorship battles, Tommy Smothers had been submitting the finished programs too late to be edited before broadcast. Near the end of the third season, CBS demanded that the *Comedy Hour* be completed and ready for network review by Wednesday of each week.

Two weeks after firmly renewing the show for another year, CBS claimed the last show of the season was turned in late and cried breach of contract. They effectively fired the Smothers Brothers, sending all parties into court and squelching Tommy Smothers's idea of filming season four from counterculture ground zero—San Francisco.

It was later proved that the network *did* have the tape in their possession after all. No matter; CBS ultimately refused to run the disputed episode anyway, saying it "would be considered irreverent and offensive by a large segment of our audience." Viewing the show today, it's hard to imagine why.

"In our case, seventy-five percent of the twenty-six shows we've done this season were censored," Tom Smothers told *Look* magazine in June 1969. "And we're mild. Now, if we're thrown off that easily, what will happen to someone who has something really important to say?"

The Smothers offered the censored episode on a syndicated basis, hoping that stations would sign on for a ninety-minute special with new segments added. "No one would take it." Tom Smothers recalls, "We were going to sue CBS, ABC, and NBC on a first amendment cause and the head of William Morris said 'You know, Tommy, you're violating the rights of kings, you can't do that.' And, of course, none of the affiliates would touch us because Nixon was coming down through the FCC on everybody."

Their first national appearance was on the Jack Paar *Tonight Show*.

Indeed, rumor had it that Richard Nixon pressured CBS to cancel the *Comedy Hour* because the newly elected president didn't want a weekly comedy show ridiculing his administration and its aggressive Vietnam war policy the way the Smothers had done throughout the Johnson administration. "I just keep hoping that one of those Nixon tapes will be about us because I know he hated us." Tom told TVparty.

A year later, the brothers were back on the air with *The Smothers Summer Show*, albeit on another network, ABC. Hoping the brothers could pick up where they left off, eleven new episodes were ordered and they aired from July to September 1970. Ratings were light from the beginning. When asked about this series, Tom Smothers admits, "It was a struggle. We had some funny things there. We had a poet's corner where songwriter-performers were on. We did four shows without an audience and a live myna bird that every-body talked to, saying the words 'Heavy, far out.'" One series highlight was a short film by Academy Award–winning designer Saul Bass. The last episode featured guests the Edwin Hawkins Singers ("Oh Happy Day") and John Denver. For the finale, Pat Paulsen sang "There's No Business Like Show Business" as the cast members said their goodbyes.

It was hoped that the Wednesday-night series might catch on and ABC would exercise its option to renew in January, but it was no match for *Hawaii Five-O* on CBS. It didn't help that the Smothers show followed another variety hour, one hosted by the Everly Brothers. The audience was brothered out by the time the Smothers came on at ten.

Tommy Smothers had this to say about the *Smothers Brothers Summer Show* in the *Saturday Review*: "We compromised. Everybody knew the situation. The network wanted the same kind of stand-up variety show—but without the satire. The budget was low, the network's concept was singers and dancers. There was no fun in it anymore; our momentum was broken. I was embarrassed to see the early shows, but the network liked them."

In 1971, the syndicated half-hour *Tom Smothers Organic Prime-Time Space Ride* came and went, unable to get enough stations signed up to be financially viable. The Smothers won their lawsuit against CBS that year but were rarely seen on television for the next few seasons. In fact, the duo was broken up for a time. Tommy Smothers appeared as a solo guest on other variety shows, while Dick Smothers concentrated on his passion, stock car racing.

In 1974, NBC went to Carol Burnett's producer, Joe Hamilton, and offered him a time slot for any star he wanted to build a variety series around. Hamilton chose the Smothers Brothers. After all, the brothers were a solid top-twenty hit when the plug was pulled just five years earlier and the highly-rated *Sonny and Cher Comedy Hour* was created almost entirely by the Smothers's former writers and producers.

Hamilton promised NBC there would be no controversy this time, that the new

Pat Paulsen wrote the Smother's tune "I Fell into a Vat of Chocolate."

series would have more in common with *The Carol Burnett Show* than with the original *Comedy Hour*.

Tom Smothers recalls that frustrating period: "Before we started the show I was told by William Morris that 'You guys are just dead in the water, it's very important, take the show, it's Joe Hamilton, producer of the *Carol Burnett Show*, blah, blah.' The conditions were unbearable but they said things could change. It could be a big hit. So I did a guest spot on *Carol Burnett* and I saw how the writers worked and the stuff they were putting together. Eight weeks before the show, we weren't even in full production or anything, I begged him [Hamilton], 'Please, let's don't do this thing, let's just abort it' and he said, 'Nope, you're doing it and you're going to do what you're told.' So that was it."

Obviously, the match of producer and stars was not a good one from the start. "I couldn't ask for a reshoot or they would take it out of my pay." Tom remembers. "I couldn't have a writer's meeting without an okay from him. I was a little rude to him, quietly, but then I finally said, 'Fuck it.'"

At 8 PM on Monday, January 13, 1975 (in the newly designated family hour) *The Smothers Brothers Show* debuted, stripped of controversy and spontaneity. Because of high anticipation, the series bowed at number four, proving the audience was ready for the return of the comedy duo. "It was huge. He [Hamilton] said, 'See!' But I knew it was going to go down. I said, 'Man, they're not going to buy it next week.' And each week the ratings just dropped and dropped because it was vacuous crap."

Joe Hamilton had succeeded miserably in his quest. The NBC Smothers hour was standard *Carol Burnett Show* fare, circa 1975 (Burnett's show ended in 1978). With worn-out comedy sketches and lame guests like gossip columnist Rona Barrett singing "That Old Feeling," it's not hard to guess why ratings quickly slid into the mid-forties.

With little to lose, NBC let Tommy Smothers take over as producer of the last four shows left in their thirteen-week contract and these programs stand out as truly excellent entertainment, maybe the finest variety hours produced during the '70s. Comedy writers/performers Don Novello, Steve Martin, Bob Einstein, and Pat Paulsen signed on for those last four episodes.

Asked how he ended up producing those shows, Tom Smothers relates, "I slowly broke Joe Hamilton's spirit. When the numbers went down, he saw it was a hit and then he had a flop. He left and said, 'You can have the show.' We had a great network liaison at NBC. He was a big fan and he was the one who made sure that we could shut it down and start again. We stopped on the third of March and started again on April 28. We did four shows and they were just incredible.

Steve Martin got his start writing for the Smothers, as did Rob Reiner and a host of other talented creators and performers.

"Only four writers stayed. Don Novello came in. We brought in a different director, Peter Calabrese out of Philadelphia. God, he was talented. The shows had a nice edge to them. We were placed in a new time slot and the first show featured Linda Rondstat, Hoyt Axton, and Don Novello (Father Guido Sarducci). And it was almost picked up."

The other three episodes produced by Tommy Smothers included an all-music show with Arlo Guthrie, Don McLean, Kris Kristofferson, and Rita Coolidge; a reunion of original series regulars Mason Williams, John Hartford, and Leigh French (with "Share a little more tea with Goldie"); and, on the last show, a psychedelic trip guest-starring Lily Tomlin, Ringo Starr, and Pat Paulsen.

The reunion episode caused a bit of controversy with numerous references to pot-smoking and religion. In fact, one of the punchlines in the "Tea with Goldie" sketch was censored because of a marijuana reference. Also seen were skits where Bob Einstein reprised his Officer Judy character, this time meeting biblical figures played by Tommy. None of the controversy helped the ratings significantly.

Despite the critical praise heaped on those last four productions, the May 26 episode was the last on NBC. If the Smothers had been allowed to continue, they might have done what no other prime-time variety show was able to; appeal to the growing young, hip, jaded twenty-something audience that would discover *Saturday Night Live* just a few months (and a few hours) later on the same network.

"We didn't have another show until we did four one-hour adventure shows for Universal, *Fitz and Bones* (in 1981). That was kind of bad."

In 1988, the Smothers Brothers got another shot at a variety series when their twentieth anniversary reunion special scored big ratings on CBS. Unlike most retrospectives, this one focused on new material by the Smothers regulars. "We just had little clips to put John Hartford and Glen Campbell in perspective. There were not a whole lot of old clips." The familiar gang was back, including Leigh French and Pat Paulsen. "Every time we did a show we brought him back; here he is running for president again. We always had really good writers writing stuff for him. It was smart stuff."

In a surprise move, *The Smothers Brothers Comedy Hour* was brought back into production in March of 1988 when a writers strike shut down every television show in Hollywood. As writers, producers, and performers, the Smothers were allowed to work as such and guests did their own material as well so there were no labor conflicts. It was the only prime-time television show in pro-

"Red meat is NOT bad for you. Now blue-green meat, THAT'S bad for you!" —*Tommy Smothers*

duction during that long, bitter dispute.

This effort had Tom Smothers again at the helm. Regulars included Pat Paulsen (running for president yet again) and Jim Stafford, along with many of the '60s' supporting players like Bob Einstein, Leigh French, and Jennifer Warnes making guest appearances. Other guest stars included Harry Belafonte, Billy ("You doesn't have to call me Johnson") Saluga, Toni Basil, Gallagher, Billy Vera, K.D. Lang, and Dianne Shure. The focus of this series was on the outstanding roster of guests, many of whom were relatively or completely unknown to television audiences. One of the most refreshing aspects of this revival was seeing how Dick Smothers had matured as a performer, exuding a warm confidence that smoothed over the new, unnaturally faster pace of the '80s shows.

The sets were minimal and reminiscent of the old series. Thankfully gone were the bombastic musical numbers that were forced on most variety shows of the '60s and '70s. This entertaining series only lasted a few months, but, then, audiences rejected every attempt to launch a variety show in the '80s.

The *Smothers Brothers Comedy Hour* was brought back yet again in January of 1989. The show took on an almost circus-like feel, complete with clever seamless transitions from one segment to the next. Gallagher and Bill ("Jose Jiminez") Dana were signed as regulars and former Smothers alumni Glen Campbell and Jennifer Warnes (who had a hit song in 1989) returned as guests. The series was seen irregularly for several months, finally ending with four weeks of shows in August of 1989.

With the success of the *Carol Burnett Show* reunion on CBS in 2001, a Smothers revival seems like a natural. "It was just about a done deal and it just went away," Tom explains. "Jeff Margolis, the director/producer said they're going and William Morris said they're going and the word was out that it was a set deal and it just went away. And I don't know if it's the political climate or what.

"Somebody said, 'Don't you wish you were on television today when you can say anything you want?' Well, nothing's being said. The last show that was ever in prime-time that did political satire was the Smothers Brothers thirty-five years ago. And people just do not see that. That have a delusion that everything is really free, but everybody's self-censoring, basically."

Besides performing, Tom Smothers also runs the Smothers/Remick Ridge Winery in Northern California's Sonoma Valley and Dick Smothers is a corporate motivational speaker.

You can catch the Smothers Brothers live in Las Vegas every year. They gave 103 concerts around the country in 2001.

203

The Richard Pryor Show

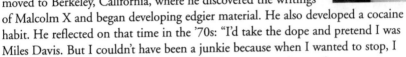

In 1970, after several successful years as a nightclub comedian and frequent *Ed Sullivan Show* guest, Richard Pryor grew tired of doing what he called "white bread humor" and walked off the stage during a show at the Aladin Hotel in Las Vegas and away from a career that had been building for several years. The comic moved to Berkeley, California, where he discovered the writings of Malcolm X and began developing edgier material. He also developed a cocaine habit. He reflected on that time in the '70s: "I'd take the dope and pretend I was Miles Davis. But I couldn't have been a junkie because when I wanted to stop, I stopped on a dime." (We all know that didn't turn out to be true!)

A string of hit movies (*Silver Streak, Greased Lightning*) and comedy albums in the mid-'70s made Richard Pryor a superstar. On May 5, 1977, Pryor hosted a brilliant special on NBC featuring guests LaWanda Page, John Belushi, the Pips (who performed a medley of their hits without any lead vocals), and a powerful dramatic performance by poet Maya Angelou. Pryor played his drunk "Willie" character, "Idi Amin Dada," and money-grubbing television evangelist "Reverend James L. White," who gets donation phones ringing off the hook when he announces they're collecting money for a "Back to Africa" campaign.

The segment with Maya Angelou may be one of the most profound moments in television history. Starting out as a very funny comedy skit with "Willie" getting into a drunken brawl in a bar, the piece suddenly takes a harrowing (and enlightening) turn when Willie stumbles home to his anguished wife (Angelou). This is something you have to see for yourself, truly one of those moments that remind you of the power television can have.

The special was a critical and ratings smash. Pryor's appearances on *Saturday Night Live* had been numeric gold for the network as well, so NBC programmers pondered the unthinkable—giving the most militant and sexually suggestive comedian of the decade his own weekly television series.

NBC only gave the star a ten-week contract, in part because there hadn't been a successful variety show launched in over five years. For reasons only a network executive could divine, *The Richard Pryor Show* was scheduled on Tuesday nights at 8 PM, opposite *Happy Days* and *Laverne and Shirley*. Why would NBC put their most controversial and adult star on during the "family hour" when they specifically promised the comic during negotiations that his show wouldn't start before 9 PM? You tell me.

This unexpected move caused Richard Pryor to have second thoughts about doing a series at all. He reportedly broke down in an early writer's meeting, confessing, "I bit off more than I can chew." Reduced to tears, the comedian told his new staff, "I don't want to be on TV. I'm in a trap. I can't do this." The dumbstruck writers tried to convince him that he could do something special on television and labored for days trying to convince him to change his mind and go forward. Pryor eventually agreed to do four shows but not the ten that he originally signed for. A unique roster of supporting players was assembled for the variety

Richard Pryor returned to series TV in 1984 with a Saturday morning show, *Pryor's Place*, produced by Sid and Marty Krofft.

hour: Sandra Bernhardt, Robin Williams, Marsha Warfield, Victor DeLapp, Jimmy Martinez, Tim Reid, Paul Mooney, Argus Hamilton, and "Detroit" John Witherspoon. The show was produced by John Moffitt and Rocco Urbisci for Burt Sugarman Productions, and there would be no major guest-stars.

Battles with the network censors began as soon as production started. Pryor was unnerved to find out, after signing his lucrative contract with the network, that he wouldn't be given free rein to do whatever he wanted. "It's bullshit, there's no other word for it—and lots of it. I think they hire people, about six thousand of them, to do nothing but mess with people." The frustrated star told *Ebony* magazine in 1977, "The problem with censors is that they don't like for people to communicate. I think it is on purpose and very political. A lot of silly stuff went down about anything I tried to do. It was just frustrating."

To spoof the situation he found himself in, Richard Pryor appeared at the beginning of his first show stating firmly that he will never be compromised. When the camera pulled back, you saw he was naked (actually wearing a bodystocking) and his dick was missing. NBC ordered the "offensive" scene removed, so it ran instead on the evening news on all three networks. More people saw that "censored" clip on the news than ever saw *The Richard Pryor Show* itself. Another skit on the first episode that caused some flack had Pryor playing a flamboyant rock singer who machine guns his all-white audience to death.

The controversy didn't stop there. The second episode featured a long, slow sequence with a woman describing a lesbian experience in the park. One of the most revealing moments of the series came during the final show. Part of that episode was done like a "roast," only there were no guest celebrities to fling insults at the host, just the supporting cast. It was a long, tense television moment as the regulars either kissed Pryor's ass or burnt their bridges behind them. The pained host just gazed downward much of the time, rarely looking up or sincerely laughing. This did not appear to be a happy group.

After the four episodes were in the can, neither star nor network was willing to continue. *The Richard Pryor Show* was one of the lowest-rated shows of that year— *Happy Days* and *Laverne and Shirley*, on the other hand, were the number-one and -two rated shows in 1977. NBC and Richard Pryor announced that the remainder of the contract would be made up of six specials to be broadcast over the next three years. Pryor promised, "I'm going to do them the way I want and then they can kiss my behind." The specials were never filmed.

Was Richard Pryor bitter about his television experience? No, not at all. He had this to say: "One week of truth on TV could just straighten out everything. One hundred and twenty-seven million people watch television every night; that's why they use it to sell stuff. They've misused it a long time so now it's just a business, that's all. They're not going to write shows about how to revolutionize America. The top-rated shows are for retarded people."

Television is a device that enables people who haven't anything to do to watch people who can't do anything.

205

TOTIE VS KISS

Important events can take place in the most unlikely places. In 1974, glam-rockers KISS made their very first national TV appearance on the Mike Douglas afternoon musical variety talk show.

Important, because KISS changed the face of music with their outrageous outfits, makeup, and frightening stage persona. Initially, they were treated like freaks by the television establishment; that changed when the band became

Whatever happened to that KISS amusement park Gene Simmons was always talking about?

a runaway cash magnet over the next thirty years.

How strange it must have seemed on that Tuesday afternoon, June 11, 1974, when Gene Simmons first came out to talk to Mike Douglas and his guests, which included comics Totie Fields and Robert Klein. So strange that supposedly hip comedian Robert Klein wouldn't even shake Simmon's hand.

The guests on the panel treated the lead singer of KISS like a bad joke, but few people today could even identify one of the other 'celebrities' on the stage that afternoon, so what does that tell you?

Host Mike Douglas was simply flabbergasted at Gene's statement that he represents "evil incarnate." Mike's questions were all in the "how-many-in-your-band" vein, but Totie Fields got in a few funny shots:

Totie asked, "Wouldn't it be funny if, under this, he's just a nice Jewish boy?" Gene Simmons replied, "You should only know." To which Totie zinged, "I do, you can't hide the hook!"

Ms. Fields was a genuinely sharp and witty but caustic comedian who had a massive cancer growing in her legs that summer. They were amputated shortly after this appearance. She returned to performing on the *Mike Douglas Show* in a wheelchair, incorporating her health problems into her comedy act very effectively, but her comeback was a short one. The cancer won out a short time later.

In a taped segment, the band did a rocking version of "Firehouse" and teenagers all over the country beat a path to their record stores for KISS vinyl. Before long, churches were burning KISS albums as fast as parents could snatch them up, a true sign of success in '70s rock 'n' roll.

Until KISS came along in the early '70s, teenyboppers ruled the charts and minds of TV viewers.

Cher and Diana Ross both dated Gene Simmons.

What Happened to
Paul Lynde?

Paul Lynde had a strong career in television all throughout the '60s and '70s. He appeared in a handful of memorable *Bewitched* episodes as a semi-regular character (Uncle Arthur). He was the center square and comedy star of the long-running daytime game show *Hollywood Squares* and had a one-year stint as the lead in his own sitcom, *The Paul Lynde Show* in 1972.

Lynde had come to prominence on Broadway and in motion pictures; his big successes were *Bye, Bye Birdie* (both play and film) and *Under the Yum Yum Tree*. He became a popular guest star on dozens of sitcoms in the early '60s, landing his recurring role on the hit show *Bewitched* in 1965.

Lynde's career almost hit the skids at that point. He was a *big* drinker and, one evening in 1965, a young actor he was partying with in San Francisco fell from the comedian's hotel room to his death eight floors below. The story would have been live on CNN today, but at that time you could still hush things up in the press.

When *Bewitched* was cancelled in 1972, most of the writers and crew moved over to producer William Asher's next project for ABC, *The Paul Lynde Show*. Like *Bewitched*, the *Lynde* show had an unbelievable fantasy concept: Paul Lynde playing a straight guy living in the suburbs with a wife and two kids and dealing with the everyday frustrations of life. This preposterous premise proved to be too much of a stretch even for people who watched TV on a regular basis. The series was axed after only one season. The next

Lynde and Laughter!

Premiere In Paul's delightful new series, he has a great job, nice wife, two daughters and a new son-in-law. Boy is Paul miserable!

8:00 The Paul Lynde Show
ABC ③ ⑤ ⑧ ⑫

Peter Marshall: "What are 'dual-purpose cattle' good for that other cattle aren't?"
Paul Lynde: "They give milk . . . and cookies, but I don't recommend the cookies."

fall, Lynde was wedged into the cast of *The New Temperature's Rising* and that sitcom failed, too.

Fortunately, Paul Lynde didn't quit his day job. Occupying the center square on *The Hollywood Squares* brought him into American living rooms five mornings a week beginning in 1966. Housewives delighted in his witty repartee:

PETER MARSHALL: "In television, who lived in Doodyville?"

PAUL LYNDE: "Oh, the Ty-De-Bowl Man."

By the mid '70s Paul Lynde was feeling boxed in, so to speak, and frustrated. He was still a hot property, voted America's favorite comedian in a 1974 poll and highly sought out for every manner of TV game and variety show.

That was no longer the case when Lynde was fired from *Hollywood Squares* in 1979 for being drunk and belligerent on the set once too often. On several occasions he had to be forcibly removed from the studio because of his outrageous tirades, lashing out angrily at his fellow celebs, audience members, and contestants.

Can you imagine being so drunk you couldn't answer three questions in a half-hour show? By that point they gave him all the jokes and answers anyway, all he had to do was show up for work one day a week. He was replaced on *Squares* by Henny Youngman.

With game shows falling out of favor and variety shows practically nonexistent by 1980, no one wanted Paul Lynde for television roles anymore and the spotlight faded.

In 1982, I was doing trade ads for minor celebrities and one of our clients was an up-and-coming male model. This was a time when (let's face it) male model meant male prostitute. Anyway, this guy came in to look at the ad I'd done for him and he showed me a check he'd received the previous night made out for a thousand dollars—signed by Paul Lynde.

It was pretty clear to me what the money was for; in fact he came right out and told me it was for having sex with the comedian! He was really proud of himself.

A week later, on Monday, January 11, 1982, Paul Lynde was found dead in his West Hollywood home, in bed naked with a bottle of amyl nitrate (an inhalant used to enhance sex—I looked it up!) by his side.

I was told he had had a heart attack the previous Saturday night while having sex with someone who just walked out of the Beverly Hills home when the seizure happened, without even bothering to call an ambulance. Was Lynde's guest that night the male prostitute I talked with earlier in the week? I suspect it was. That guy eventually went on to become a very well-known GQ fashion model of the early '90s.

For some reason, no one in the '70s could tell Paul Lynde was a big queen!?!

SHAZAM!

CBS Saturday mornings 1974–1977

Exciting but preachy live-action Filmation show about a boy, Billy Batson (Michael Gray), who screams "Shazam!" and turns into the super-powered Captain Marvel (Jackson Bostwick, later replaced by John Davey). Also along for the ride: Mentor (Les Tremayne), assigned by the animated Elders to look after Billy as they travel the country in a fully equipped RV.

CBS couldn't call the program Captain Marvel because of possible trademark infringement with Marvel Comics, even though Captain Marvel was created decades before Marvel Comics ever came along. *Shazam!* stressed "cooperation, using reasoned judgements, and the importance of wholesome relationships between child and adult."

The Captain was joined by *The Mighty Isis* (Joanna Cameron) in 1975. Isis was the '70s version of Xena, except no violence of any kind was allowed on Saturday mornings, so these two heroes just flew around dispensing advice.

Former teen idol Michael Gray now owns a flower shop in LA with his wife.

"*Shazam!* was revived several years ago. They eliminated the Billy Batson/Captain Marvel character, kept the Winnebago, and renamed it *MTV's Road Rules.*" —Rodney

Gene Roddenberry:
WHAT MIGHT HAVE BEEN...

ABOVE: Planet Earth with John Saxon

The decade between the cancellation of the original *Star Trek* series in 1969 and the debut of *Star Trek: The Motion Picture* in 1979 was a lean one for television producer, writer, and *Trek* creator Gene Roddenberry. Though he made valiant efforts, he only got one series off the ground during that time, the Saturday-morning cartoon version of *Star Trek* in 1973.

A massive letter-writing campaign organized by fans (but secretly instigated by Roddenberry himself) got *Star Trek* renewed after NBC cancelled it in 1968. When the network moved the show to the Friday-night-at-ten death-slot, Roddenberry issued an ultimatum: restore the program to an appropriate timeslot or he would quit. Having just proven there was a vocal audience for his work, Roddenberry was surprised when the network didn't back down and he was forced to walk away from the show he had created and nurtured for two years. This resulted in a dreadful last season for *Star Trek*.

For the 1968–69 season, Roddenberry hoped to move from the stars to the vines with a new version of *Tarzan*. The last TV Tarzan (Ron Ely) didn't make much of an impression cavorting around NBC's jungle just two years earlier, so Roddenberry hoped instead to concentrate on the Lord Greystoke side of the ape-man's personality. This project made it to script but not to film

A pilot for another possible series, *Assignment: Earth* starring Robert Lansing and Terri Garr, was shot and incorporated into a third-season episode of *Star Trek*. The series would have followed Gary Seven, a human raised and trained by aliens to prevent Earth from destroying itself, a common theme in Roddenberry's work. NBC passed on *Assignment: Earth*, espionage and sci-fi angles weren't drawing audiences like they used to. So Roddenberry released a book written with Stephen E. Whitfield in 1968. *The Making of Star Trek* was one of the most thorough and insightful books that had been written about the television industry, but this did little to satiate *Star Trek* fans who searched the cathode-blue horizons for any sign of a new Roddenberry sci-fi project, a wait that stretched into years. Meanwhile, Roddenberry produced the motion picture bomb *Pretty Maids All in a Row*, starring Rock Hudson, Angie Dickinson, and Telly Savalas, and wrote scripts for *Alias Smith and Jones*.

Gene Roddenberry was entitled to half the profits from *Star Trek*, but this amounted to very little in the early '70s because the show had yet to fully catch on in syndication. The struggling producer confessed to an interviewer, "For a couple of years our only income was lecture fees I got from colleges where kids still loved *Star Trek*, even though it was not a commercial success."

Every TV show that was dropped by the networks in the '60s had millions of faithful viewers, but no one had ever organized those fans before. In 1972, the first major *Star Trek* convention was held in New York City with Roddenberry and Majel Barrett (Nurse Chapel on *Star Trek* and Roddenberry's wife) as special guests. Organizers expected six hundred attendees; instead three thousand "trekkies" showed up to worship the man they dubbed the "Great Bird of the Galaxy." The *LA Times* soon dubbed *Star Trek* "the show that won't die," beginning a slow and quiet resurrection. Roddenberry started a mail-order firm called Lincoln Enterprises to provide hungry fanatics with *Star Trek* prop and costume recreations, script reproductions, keychains, and Tribbles.

NBC floated the idea of a *Star Trek* TV movie in 1972, but it would be 1973 before Roddenberry got busy on his own projects again. That summer the animated *Star Trek* got underway (page 217) and *Genesis II* was put into production for fall 1974 weekly prime-time placement on CBS.

Broadcast as a TV-movie in March of 1973, *Genesis II* told the story of Dylan Hunt (Alex Cord), an adventurous twentieth century research scientist who awakens from suspended animation to a post-apocalyptic world. Dylan joins a band of twenty-second century peacekeepers who utilize an underground tube system that rockets them to the far reaches of the planet to seek out strange new life forms, to boldly go where . . . (you get the idea). "It had one thing in common with *Star Trek,*" Roddenberry confided, "and that was you could bring in a good writer and say to him, 'What bothers you about the world,' and go and invent a place in this new world and have it happen there." The pilot film co-starred Mariette Hartley and Ted Cassidy (Lurch from the *Addams Family*), and also featured Majel Barrett in a supporting role. She would appear in all of Roddenberry's pilots during the 1970s.

A season's worth of scripts written primarily by Gene Roddenberry had Dylan and his travelling PAX Council encountering all manner of social mutations: leaders of a poor village are drugging their people into subservience; Dylan falls through a portal into 1974 Manhattan and tries in vain to communicate with his past self through the girl he's fallen in love with; inhabitants of the Nevada desert are living life as presented in old TV western reruns; the PAX Council battles Company B, highly-trained commandos, awakened from the twentieth century, who were raised with no free will of their own.

One of the better scripts, "Robot's Return," was loosely adapted for the first *Star Trek* motion picture. It concerned a group of twentieth century astronauts returned from the stars, having evolved into robotic hybrids searching for the "gods" that created them. Confronting instead the primitive nature of their creator and realizing that earthlings may reach out again to the stars, the mandroids question whether it would be wise to help man's progress.

In the end, CBS chose to go with a TV version of *Planet of the Apes* and not *Genesis II* for the fall of '74. "[CBS programmer Fred Silverman] thought the monkeys were so cute he cancelled *Genesis II,*" Roddenberry lamented to an interviewer, "Several of us tried to warn him that it was a one-time joke. He didn't listen and it was a disaster that cost them many millions of dollars." With the stench of *Planet of the Apes* still fresh on the CBS lawn, Roddenberry's project was shelved—for the time being.

ABC was interested in the concept. Roddenberry took *Genesis II* and reworked it slightly as *Planet Earth,* brought to life in a tele-film directed by *Trek*'s Marc

Daniels, starring John Saxon in the Dylan Hunt role (Alex Cord wasn't available). The story, based on one of Roddenberry's *Genesis II* scripts, focused on a society dominated by women where men are kept as pets. Vastly inferior to the original, ABC aired *Planet Earth* to a hungry audience of Trekkies and was considering a regular slot for the series when creative conflicts left Roddenberry and ABC at odds. *Tribune*, a bleak future-world cop series for Warner Bros was another no-go that year.

The tendency in Hollywood is to replicate success. With that in mind, Roddenberry and writer Gene L. Coon took all of the best elements from *Star Trek* and jammed them into one character: Questor.

Produced for Universal, Questor was basically Mr. Spock in a buddy show format. Cast in the lead role was none other than Leonard Nimoy, who posed in makeup for production photos and agreed to do the weekly series if *Questor* was picked up. Between script and shooting, Roddenberry inexplicably dumped Nimoy without bothering to tell the actor. In fact, Leonard Nimoy thought he was still attached to the project even after Robert Foxworth was hired for the role.

The pilot film aired on NBC in 1974 as *The Questor Tapes* and told the tale of an emotionless, super-powered, synthetic man who is paired with one of the scientists who assembled him to search for his mysterious programmer.

Instead of a spaceship, Questor and Dr. Jerry Robinson (played by Mike Farrell) could look out over the entire world from their high-tech "Information Center," spying on just about anybody in the world while videotaping their comings and goings. A private jet could get them to hotspots fast, but as with the "Prime Directive" from *Trek*, the artificial man could not interfere in the lives of humans in any significant way.

The android's brainwaves are activated by tapes (just like the TRS-80) that come from a suspicious source, so the series would trace Questor's efforts to find out more about his creator. Scripts were ordered that had Questor walking underwater to disable a boat; delving into the world of ESP; eerily assuming the identity of a surgeon; and flying to Switzerland to investigate a scientist being held captive for his nuclear waste formula.

Like Mr. Spock, humor would come from the android's inability to understand slang and a tendency to take things too literally. He had the ability to change his face to resemble others, but "lying will always be difficult for Questor since the logical answer to any question is the truth." Roddenberry's concept further detailed that "information is converted by Questor's computer mind into probabilities, not certainties. He can only estimate the odds on whether certain events will occur or not. His powers of observation are substantially better than human and his computer memory is that of total recall. Since love, empathy, and hate cannot be computed, Questor is totally and completely dependent on Jerry Robinson to help guide him in such areas."

Roddenberry actually began work on *Questor* in 1972 but passed it over to writer/producer Gene L. Coon (who was responsible for some of *Star Trek*'s best scripts) so he could concentrate on *Genesis II*. Coon died in 1973 before the *Questor* script could be filmed.

The series was green-lighted and slated for Friday nights at ten. That's right, the "timeslot of death," the same night and time that did in the original *Star Trek*. Once again Roddenberry was forced to battle NBC over changes large and small. For one, the network demanded that the Jerry Robinson character be dropped. They liked the show's overall concept, they insisted, they just wanted to tweak it a bit. Instead of being a two lead show, *Questor* should be centered around one character.

The network took control of the show and rewrote the writer's guide to make it more like *The Fugitive*, with the robot not only looking for his creator, but also on the run from "a five nation combine" of secret agents. "Questor is on the move," the new NBC format dictated, "He has no contacts with the human world. Questor cannot stand by and let a human be injured. The fact that he may give himself away by doing so becomes less important than the fact that he can't delay while a human dies." Basically, the complete opposite of the original idea. Farrell asked for and was granted a release from *Questor* to wisely take another series that was offered to him—*M.A.S.H.* Not wanting to work on what amounted to a tiresome chase series, Roddenberry reluctantly let the project languish. Ultimately unsatisfying, *Questor* is still considered by many to be Roddenberry's best effort after *Star Trek*.

In May, 1975 Roddenberry was brought in by Paramount to develop a possible *Star Trek* movie, but his script was rejected and the project shelved. Gene worked on a pilot that year called *The Nine*, a bizarre, semiautobiographical concoction that combined a screwed-up TV producer with a commune of telepathic creatures. This was another no-sale, as were *Magna One*, about a race of future people who live undersea and *Battlefield Earth*, which had humans living in "fat and happy" slavery under alien control. None of these storylines were fully realized, and it would be two years before another Roddenberry concept made it to the screen.

Preaching to the choir and passing the plate, Roddenberry recorded a record album in 1976, *Inside Star Trek*, where he expounded on *Trek* philosophy and history. He also talked about his battles with the NBC censors and his frustrating efforts to launch *Questor* and *Genesis II*.

Further afield from his previous work, *Spectre* was created, written, and produced by Gene Roddenberry for airing on NBC May 21, 1977. This supernatural thriller starred Gig Young and Robert Culp as two paranormalists battling a great and powerful force plaguing a wealthy London financier. Directed by Clive Donner, *Spectre* had little in common with *Star Trek* or any previous Roddenberry project. The concept promised "horrors unimaginable, a descent into a corner of hell" but rattled off as an anemic, talky '70s melodrama.

After *Spectre*, Gene Roddenberry gave up on getting another TV series off the ground. *Star Wars* hit the movie houses in 1977 and suddenly science-fiction was

Battlefield Earth (not to be confused with the John Travolta movie) was revived for syndication in 1997 as *Earth: Final Conflict*.

hot again. *Star Trek* fandom was a far-reaching, big business on its own and a revival of the series in some form was already in the works. At one point, it was announced that *Star Trek* would return in syndication with the original cast, but all of the sets would be miniatures, even the Enterprise interiors. To save production costs, the actors would be working entirely against a blue screen. This awful idea never came about but in mid-'70s convention appearances, James Doohan and others talked about a new series in development at Paramount called *Star Trek II*. Story elements from *ST II* scripts by Roddenberry and others were used in the first *Star Trek* movie that was released to record-breaking box office in 1979. The *Star Trek* film series is still a huge success almost twenty-five years later.

Subsequent television spin-offs and aggressive merchandising over the years have combined to make Roddenberry's creation one of the most valuable franchises in the world, more popular than it ever was in the '60s and '70s, securing his place in history as the Ray Kroc of outer space.

Gene Roddenberry, the visionary who kept his dream alive against all odds (with a little help from uncredited contributors, pills, pot, cocaine, alcohol, a massive ego, and the adulation of thousands) died on October 24, 1991, just a few days before Irwin Allen took his last flight to the stars.

STAR TREK [ANIMATED]
September 1973–August 1975 / 22 episodes

This was more enjoyable to me than the first *Star Trek* series; somehow the aliens are more believable when everyone is a cartoon.

Produced at Filmation, who were churning out the highly popular *Archie* cartoons in 1973, the refreshing series was headed by D.C. Fontana, story editor and script supervisor on the original *Star Trek*. The first episode was written by Samuel A. Peeples, who had written the second pilot for the live-action series. Several plotlines were continued over from the original series, including the return of Harry Mudd and those troublesome Tribbles, who reappeared in an episode by original script-writer David Gerrold. Science fiction author Larry Niven also contributed an excellent script; other stories were provided by *Star Trek* scribes David P. Harmon, Paul Schneider, Stephen Kandel, and Walter Koenig, who played Ensign Chekov during live-action *Trek*'s third season. Limited animation was a hindrance at times, but the cartoon version allowed writers to expand on ideas that would have been too expensive to film for a live-action program.

The animated *Star Trek* cost quite a bit more than other Saturday-morning shows, so NBC ordered only sixteen episodes for the first season. The entire original cast was brought back. Basically, no one was doing anything of real importance and most needed the work. To cut down on production costs there were lots of narration sequences over stock animation of the Enterprise floating in space.

There were some conflicts. Nichelle Nichols's and George Takei's cartoon likenesses were being used but they weren't originally hired to provide the character's voices (Paramount owns their younger faces, apparently). Hoping to save money, Roddenberry decided to have Majel Barrett voice Uhura and James Doohan do his best Sulu imitation. Only a promised work stoppage by Leonard Nimoy got the original actors on board. *Star Trek* won the Emmy in 1974 as "Outstanding Children's Series" and before long there was a flood of prime-time shows converted to cartoon format starring the original cast members on Saturday mornings.

Renewed for a second season, only six new episodes were produced.

The show the stars couldn't control!

Good Times
(they weren't!)

Good Times was a rare breed of television show, a spinoff of a spinoff (*All in The Family* begat *Maude* and *Maude* begat *Good Times*). Still, as it was conceived, *Good Times* was one of the most original shows on the tube when it premiered—and one of the funniest.

Debuting on February 1, 1974, the series starred Esther Rolle in the part she originated on the smash hit *Maude*, sardonic maid Florida Evans. Dramatic actor John Amos (*Roots*) was again cast as Florida's other half; he had been seen on *Maude* occasionally as husband Henry, now re-named James. In the role of the youngest son Michael (the militant in the family) was Ralph Carter—he was appearing in the hit Broadway musical *Raisin* before (and right after) *Good Times* hit the airwaves.

Sister Thelma was played by BerNadette Stanis with Ja'net DuBois (*Love of Life*) acting the part of sassy neighbor Willona Woods.

Good Times replaced *Planet of the Apes* on Friday nights.

Cast as older brother JJ, aspiring comic strip artist and painter, was Jimmie Walker, a little-known stand-up comic who got his big break on *The Jack Paar Show* in 1972.

Good Times was a hit right out of the box, the seventeenth most popular show of the 1973–74 season. The concept was daring—relevant, controversial topics tackled with humor, but from an African-American perspective. Forget that all of the first season writers were white and Jewish, close enough. During the first season, busing, bullies, guns, gangs, prejudice, and black-on-black crime provided fodder for thoughtful and genuinely funny episodes. These were topics previously unexplored on sitcoms. John Amos was particularly strong as the head of the household and the exchanges between JJ and sister Thelma are some of television's silliest moments.

The reaction that Jimmie Walker got was overwhelming—and unexpected. The studio audience went into convulsions on his first entrance, before he even opened his mouth. On the second episode, he uttered the phrase that paid. From then on he was "Kid Dyn-o-mite!" and the series was his.

Television critics had a field day describing Jimmie Walker to their readers. *Newsweek* said: "His beanpole body suggests a vitamin deficiency, his Silly Putty face flaps around a set of buck teeth that could have come from a joke store." *TV Guide* wrote: "He has the neck movement of an automatic sprinkler and the bulb-eyed glare of an aggravated emu, all supported by a physique that resembles an inverted six-foot tuning fork."

Walker's popularity led to a six-week engagement in Las Vegas, a hit motion picture (*Let's Do It Again*), a best-selling comedy album (*Dyn-o-mite!*), t-shirts, belts, socks, pajamas, and even a talking doll. (I'll let you guess what the doll said when you pulled its string.)

When the series was moved to Tuesday nights in the fall of 1974, it did even better in the Nielsen ratings, landing solidly in the top ten as the writers relied more and more on JJ's antics to carry the show—often deferring dialogue to a simple notation in the scripts: "JJ reacts."

Jimmie Walker starred in the series *At Ease* on ABC in the summer of 1983.

Esther Rolle and John Amos were furious that the direction of their series veered to what they believed was offensive comedy. They had been led to think that the program would be more uplifting in nature, that the characters on *Good Times* could provide positive role models for young people in similar surroundings. For that very reason, it was Rolle's insistence at the beginning that the Evans be a two-parent family despite CBS's desire for a sitcom about a single mom.

Rolle complained about the JJ character to *Ebony* magazine in 1975: "He's eighteen and he doesn't work. He can't read or write. He doesn't think. The show didn't start out to be that. Michael's role of a bright, thinking child, has been reduced. Little by little—with the help of the artist, I suppose, because they couldn't do that to me—they have made J.J. more stupid and enlarged the role. Negative images have been slipped in on us through the character of the oldest child."

For his part, Jimmie Walker stayed above the fray, concentrating on his nightclub act instead. "I'm no actor," he told *TV Guide*. "I'm a comic who lucked into a good thing. What the show has done for me, with all that exposure, is get me where I'm goin' a lot quicker."

When the 1975–76 season rolled around, both Amos and Rolle threatened to quit if something wasn't done about the show's shifting focus. Both actors were given fat raises to stay, but Amos held out until the eleventh hour before returning to work. Writers were prepared to do away with his character in case he chose not to return.

Plots during the 1975–76 season: the family throws a rent party for a neighbor, a hood wants to exhibit JJ's paintings, and James brings home a gun for his family's protection even though Florida's dead set against it.

Ratings began to dip as the show competed with the monster hit *Happy Days* on ABC. Johnny Brown (*Laugh-In*) joined the cast as Bookman, the lazy, useless building superintendent, providing another comic foil (and undesirable stereotype) to play off of the Evans family.

In the fall of 1976, John Amos left the series. "I did not quit the show but was in fact fired," the acclaimed stage and screen actor tells TVparty. "I was informed by phone that I was considered a disruptive factor and that my option would not be picked up for that season or any other episodes." His character James was written out with the explanation that he was going to work in another state, but he was killed in a car accident before the family could join him. With no strong male role model left in the series, acclaimed dramatic actor Moses Gunn signed on to be Florida's new love interest, Carl Dixon. JJ became even more of a focus for the series

John Amos has a one-man show on tour, *Halley's Comet*.

after Amos' departure and this (may have) led to Esther Rolle's abrupt departure in 1977. The official explanation was that the actor was ill and unable to return. A new storyline was created that had Florida marrying Carl over the summer. While on their honeymoon, it was explained, the couple decided to stay down south for Carl's health.

The Evans family went from a two-parent family to a no-parent family, with good neighbor Willona looking in on the kids every once in a while. A new character was introduced for the 1977–78 season—Janet Jackson (yes, that Janet Jackson) as a sassy tyke named Penny, Willona's newly adopted daughter. JJ got a job as an artist for an ad agency so he could finally support the family. Ironically, it was the departure of the lead actors that ultimately forced the JJ character to grow up.

With audience numbers falling rapidly, Esther Rolle returned to *Good Times* in the fall of 1978, with a promise from the network that the JJ character would be toned down. She didn't want his antics totally eliminated, she told a reporter: "But they can be real. I think there's a happy medium here somewhere." Nothing was made of the supposed wedding or of Florida's new husband. She simply came back alone.

If Rolle's return was supposed to improve things for the Evans family, it didn't. The first plotline for the 1978 season had JJ losing his job at the ad agency and getting involved with drug dealers to help out the family.

It was too late to save the Evans family anyway; the show had irrevocably lost its balance and was shelved in December 1978, returning in April 1979. In a rare move, a final episode of the series was filmed with everyone getting what they wanted—including JJ, who finally sold his comic strip.

Esther Rolle was already used to controversy before *Good Times* aired.

When *Maude* debuted in 1972, there was an uproar because executive producer Norman Lear cast a black woman in the role of the maid. It was time to bury these stereotypes, not create a new generation of them, critics complained. But Lear was looking for a character that could provide a credible counterpoint to Bea Arthur's "loveable" liberal, someone of color that could comment on timely racial conflicts.

When Rolle moved over to *Good Times,* Lear didn't dare cast another black woman (at least not immediately) as Maude's maid, so the part went to acclaimed British actress Hermione Baddeley.

Esther Rolle won an Emmy for her role in the TV movie *The Summer of My German Soldier* in 1978 and much acclaim in 1979 for her dramatic turn in the television adaptation of Maya Angelou's classic *I Know Why the Caged Bird Sings.*

Rolle passed away in 1999, leaving her career memorabilia (including an Emmy and her *Good Times* scripts) to the African-American Research Library in Ft. Lauderdale, Florida.

Esther Rolle was a regular on *Singer and Sons* in 1990.

TVparty's Billy Ingram interviews Lucy's Official Number-One Fan, Michael Stern, about his unique friendship with the queen of television comedy.

BI: How did you meet Lucille Ball?

MS: I met her when I was twelve. I went to a filming of one of her shows, *Here's Lucy*. That's the way I knew her, not as Lucy Ricardo but as Lucy Carter. That's what she looked most like when she wasn't playing Lucy.

BI: Did you get to meet her the first time you went to a taping?

MS: The very first time no, but the next time I went with my scrapbook and pictures. I went to her mom, who went to every single show, because I knew what she looked like. She said, "How would you like to meet Lucy after the show?"

I got to backstage to a place called "Lucy Lane" which Universal Studios built for her behind the set. There was a boutique shop and a hair-and-makeup place, it looked like a street. No one really saw it but the cast and crew. When I met her, she was standing in front of her dressing room, three steps up, and I remember looking up at her and she was like twelve feet tall! She was really nice to me, she signed an autograph, looked through my scrap book, gave me a kiss, and off I went. And then I happened to go over and over again and we became buddies.

BI: What was a taping of *Here's Lucy* like?

MS: I can remember it like it was yesterday. It was on Thursday afternoons. When they filmed it at Universal Studios, they got most of their audience from the Universal Tour. So if you were on a tour bus at one o'clock on a Thursday afternoon, they'd say, "Congratulations everybody, you're going to a taping of *Here's Lucy* with Lucille Ball" and everyone would get excited.

Gary Morton (Lucy's husband and a stand-up comedian) would do the warm up for fifteen or twenty minutes, then Lucy came out and answered questions. When they would introduce Lucy, she would literally run from one end of the stage to the other, waving. And the audience went crazy. She would introduce the cast and then they would film the show from start to finish, almost without stopping. They might do half a scene over or pick up a line, but that's it.

BI: Was she sorry that *Here's Lucy* ended?

MS: I think she was tired of the weekly grind and television was changing. That's when *All in the Family* was starting, *Good Times* and all these Norman Lear shows were on, and she wasn't that type of person.

It was time for her to relax. The kids were grown and she was going to do yearly specials. She probably thought she was going to do more than she did; she only did a handful of them, like five or six.

Once she retired from her weekly series she needed new friends. She happened to see me over and over again and she said, "Get a life! There's more to me than just Lucy."

Gary Morton was a guest on *Playboy's Penthouse*.

Life with Lucy

I got a job at a department store and she came by one day to see if I was really working. She bought six hundred dollars worth of linens from me. She gave me her home phone number and said, "Do you play backgammon?" and I said "No," and she said, "You'll learn." She taught me how to play backgammon and I still play to this day.

BI: Why did she do *Life with Lucy?* It was a terrible show.
MS: Well, not while you were there. The show was sold out to the general public before they filmed one shot of footage. It was like going to *Friends*, which is sold out forever. When you were there you had a great time.

When she did her last series, *Life with Lucy*, she couldn't believe that twelve years had passed between the two shows. She was having so much fun. She had more energy than I had and I was twenty-five. She wanted to do everything. She wasn't like a star. She was happy to be coming back; she even said she was bringing two hundred people back to work. She was happy that some of the same people that worked on *I Love Lucy* were with her forty years later. The sound man, who was hard of hearing, which she always thought was funny; the director; Gale Gordon; her stand-in; they were all there. Oh, and her writers. She was able to get other writers, who wrote for *M.A.S.H.* or whatever, but she wanted her writers.

BI: Looking back that may have been a mistake.
MS: There were lot of mistakes. She was missing an Ethel. One of the best episodes they had was with Audrey Meadows who played her sister. Lucy had more fun with John Ritter than with anybody. On that week, Lucy called it "Ritter-itis" because he kept making her laugh. During the actual filming he broke her up. She had to say "Cut!" She said that was only the third time in her life while filming a show that she actually had to say "Cut" because she was laughing so hard. It was not like her.

BI: She had a reputation for being very demanding to work with.
MS: When she did *Life with Lucy*, she was tough. She was doing everybody's job. She did the cameraman's job, the lighting, the stagehands. She couldn't just be an actress. She had to be wearing all these hats.

If Lucy said something, she was tough about it, like "Hey, you're off your mark." Was she nasty? Absolutely not. She was firm, but twenty seconds later when she had a break, she was playing Password or backgammon. She was having a lot of fun, like a little schoolgirl.

They had three or four directors. There was a director named Bruce Bilson and he wanted more of a quiet set. After lunch everybody was talking about what they had for lunch. "I had this, I had that" and finally the director yelled, "I don't care what anybody had for lunch. I don't care what you had for lunch, I don't care what you had for lunch, I want this place quiet!" And about twenty seconds later, Lucille Ball said, "I got tuna" and broke everyone up laughing. From then on it was a happy set. People could come by and watch rehearsals; it was a free set.

Her biggest competition was herself. *I Love Lucy* was on another channel at the same time; *The Lucy Show* was on another channel at the same time. Would you rather watch a forty year-old Lucille Ball or a seventy-five-year-old Lucille Ball? Most people chose the forty year-old Lucy.

BI: When *Life with Lucy* was cancelled, is it true that she felt like people didn't like her anymore?

MS: Absolutely. She was devastated. She said she had never been fired before and she really thought nobody liked her anymore. She was really hurt. I think she was more upset with ABC because they didn't give her a chance, seven episodes then out. All the reviews were bad. And she said, "You know what, it wouldn't have been so bad if the reviews said, 'Lucille Ball's new series had no pizzazz' or whatever, but they kept knocking me." They said: "Lucille Ball is old," "She should be in a retirement home," "She should be dead." Literally, they were saying the nastiest things about her. That she could not understand.

BI: You were at the Academy Awards with Lucille Ball?

MS: I was going to be a seat filler. The second she walked through the door she grabbed me and said, "Michael, come with me." Even at the Academy Awards fifteen years ago there were a lot of credentials. You can't go here, you can't go there without credentials. And, believe me, I was at the bottom of the totem pole in terms of credentials. She grabs me and I go everywhere with her. It didn't matter, credentials or not, I was with the president, I was with the queen. I was going everywhere with her. I was in the Green Room and meeting all her friends, "You know Jimmy Stewart, this is Cyd Charisse." These were major stars. She gave me her ticket to the audience, so I literally sat in the second row the entire time. I was no longer a seat filler.

BI: How was she feeling at that time? She died just a few weeks later.

MS: She had been ill but when I was with her she looked great. When I saw her on tape years later, yeah, I could see she was ill. When you were with her you couldn't tell.

BI: The day Lucy died, the world changed forever in a small way. I just couldn't imagine that Lucille Ball would no longer be there.

MS: She died like at 6:11 in the morning. By 6:15, *Entertainment Tonight* was calling me, USA Today and Dan Rather's office in New York and *Good Morning America.* It was the biggest news story.

Lucie Arnaz said something on a talk show a few months later. She said, "Lucille Ball is dead but Lucy Ricardo is still alive." And that's true, Lucy Ricardo *is* alive and she'll always be alive with Ricky and Fred and Ethel and Little Ricky. And that's true.

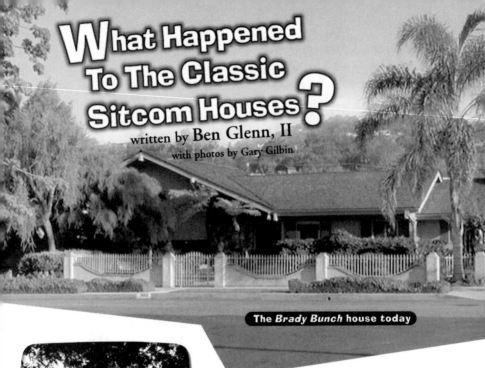

What Happened To The Classic Sitcom Houses?

written by **Ben Glenn, II**

with photos by Gary Gilbin

The *Brady Bunch* house today

As a child, I always dreamed of magically entering Television Land and visiting the homes of my favorite sitcom families. This would be familiar territory—after all, having watched rerun upon endless rerun, I knew my way around their houses as well as they did.

Nothing would have given me more pleasure than to lounge in the Bradys' sunken living room, enter the Munsters' trap-door staircase by pulling the griffin-shaped newel post, or park my blue Chevrolet convertible in the driveway of Samantha and Darrin's Cape Cod on Morning Glory Circle. Indeed, in many cases, the houses that TV sitcom families lived in are as distinctive as the shows themselves. This makes sense, given that a comedy centered on home life should, by definition, establish a strong sense of place for the viewer.

Today, as an adult, I am constantly struck by the fact that many people I talk to still believe that these houses were real, and that the shows were actually filmed

A newel post supports the handrail at either the top or bottom of a flight of stairs.

inside them. And so, in true TVparty fashion, I thought I would "demystify" our television heritage a bit by leading us through a "where are they now?" of classic TV sitcom homes.

Most of the famous TV sitcom houses we know and love were located on movie-studio backlots. Beginning in the mid-1950s, when television proved itself to be a profitable venture, movie studios established television production units and began generating series. Columbia and Universal appear to have been the most active in this arena, largely because they could use their existing facilities, rather than build new ones, to handle the production load. Among these facilities were outdoor sets on the backlot, built years earlier for motion pictures and still sitting there, ready to use.

Therefore, unlike earlier sitcoms such as *The Honeymooners* and *I Love Lucy*, which were filmed before a studio audience in a theater-like setting with the action taking place largely indoors, movie-studio-produced shows such as *Leave It to Beaver* were free to use backlot exteriors, allowing the action to take place out-of-doors and within a town or neighborhood. The studio audience was replaced with a laugh track, and interior scenes were filmed on nearby studio soundstages.

Outdoor sets such as the *Bewitched* home are known in the industry as "shells"—that is, they generally are constructed of three sides and a roof, and often are missing the back wall and/or one of the side walls.

Inside, the interior is one big raw, unfinished space (no rooms!), with the structure's matrix of scaffolding, pipes, electrical wires, and beams fully exposed. Usually ladders are built into the structure, allowing actors to climb to the second floor to do

The *Bewitched* house today

a scene from an upper-story window or the roof.

When in use, the homes are "dressed" by adding front doors, window treatments, and landscaping, and an L-shaped temporary wall is placed inside the front door to give the illusion of an interior. When not in use, however, the shells are usually stripped of their doors, curtains, and landscaping, and in many cases appear neglected and poorly maintained.

Not all studio backlot houses are façades. For example, several newer homes on the Warner Bros lot are complete, with four sides and a roof. During inactive periods these structures are used to store lighting and other production equipment. It can be disheartening to see these old sets in person. They always seem surprisingly small and, as I mentioned, poorly maintained—studios fix them up only when they're about to be used.

A number of classic houses have been structurally altered over the years for use in other productions. Remember, Hollywood studios are not museums. In general, they maintain very little regard for history, and often have no qualms about altering or even destroying vintage sets for a project as fleeting as a network pilot.

One need only watch the upsetting *60 Minutes* segment documenting the demolition of the legendary MGM backlot—to make way for a housing development—to understand. Therefore, you will be disappointed if, for example, you expect *The Partridge Family* house to look now just as it did in when the series was in production in the early 1970s.

UNIVERSAL STUDIOS
(California):

The Munsters, the Cleavers, and more. Universal Studios boasts what is today the largest backlot in Hollywood. It consists of hundreds of outdoor sets, and Universal's famous backlot tour (and now theme park) attracts an astonishing thirty-five thousands visitors each day. The tour was begun in 1964, and at that time visitors could view moviemaking in action and visit the sets of Universal's popular TV series produced by its television production company, Revue.

The heart of Universal's TV Land is Colonial Street, situated on the Upper Lot at Universal City. Here can be found the house façades used on *Leave It to Beaver*, *The Munsters*, and the TV series adaptations of *Harper Valley PTA* and *Animal House*. Colonial Street's mix of homes and other buildings is an intentional mishmash, giving the studio a wide range of architectural styles to draw upon.

The Munster house has a particularly interesting history. It was probably constructed in the early '20s as a pleasant Victorian home. Originally, the right side of the house was surmounted by a hexagonal, flat-topped turret, rather than the pointed tower that stands today. (In fact, the hexagonal turret can be seen in the color pilot of *The*

Munsters.) When the house was featured in the 1962 film, *The Second Time Around,* the hexagonal turret was burned as part of the storyline; concurrently, the house must have been selected for *The Munsters* and then rebuilt with the eerie tower portion that TVpartyers know well.

When *The Munsters* entered pre-production, Universal spent a reported one million dollars to transform the nostalgic Victorian façade into a creepy mansion. Features such as a dilapidated stovepipe and weathervane were installed on the roof, and the home's grounds were "dressed" with groupings of arthritic prop trees (real trees that had been "embalmed" for repeated use), hanging moss, tumbleweeds, dead bushes, and strewn leaves. Finally, an imposing stone gate was added, and the finished set was photographed with a wide-angle lens, often from slightly below or above, making it appear massive.

Despite this expense, the majority of scenes were filmed indoors. "We used the house very little," recalled Al Lewis in a recent interview. Universal featured the Munster house on its early studio tours, often allowing children to visit the set and have their photos taken with the cast. When *The Munsters* finished production in 1966, Universal continued to use the house. In keeping with studio practice, the structure was "undressed"—stripped of its gate, landscaping, and architectural adornments—and by the late 1970s was painted a cheery yellow and featured in the short-lived NBC series *Shirley* starring Shirley Jones.

Universal later attempted to convert the house into a Cape Cod–style home for use on *Murder, She Wrote* by removing the center window peak and the gothic-arched porch, replacing it with a homey wraparound veranda. The house stands as

MORE HOMES FOUND:

"Just a couple of little comments about the *Mary Tyler Moore* house. I grew up two blocks away from the house in Minneapolis. If I was just five years older that would have been me holding the flag on the crosswalk, helping Mary and the kids cross the street in the opening credits. That was my corner!

"When I was a youngster out playing, cars of curious Mary fans would always stop and ask where the house was. Tour buses used to come by now and then, an amazing amount of attention for just one house. The woman who lived there hated all the tourists. She used to try to piss people off by hanging signs out of her second story window telling them to go away, and I remember she got political at one point with a big 'Impeach Nixon' sign.

"The woman had no children, so none of us had any real reason to go into the house (we were also told by our parents not to bug her) but the neighborhood legend among the kids was that there was pink fuzz on the walls in the basement, along with a full swimming pool (I think that rumor started after some kid had one too many Pixie Stix).

"The colorful apartment building which was Mary's pad later on in the series is actually low-income housing. It looks groovy from a distance, but I'm afraid it's fallen into some disrepair. In Minneapolis the building made the news a few years ago as the scene of a couple of murders. The elevators were always dangerously broken—the victims, presumably the losers in bad drug deals, were killed by being thrown down the elevator shafts from the upper floors."
—Louise

"In the late 1970s, *Mork and Mindy* was a fairly popular show, as you well know. It launched the careers of Robin Williams and his co-star Pam Dauber. Miss Dauber played Mindy, a college student at the University of Colorado at Boulder.

"Many exterior scenes were indeed shot in and around Boulder, Colorado, primarily for the opening and closing credits, and some stock shots for establishing locale, such as an exterior of Mindy's boarding or apartment house, the downtown Boulder Mall where Mindy's father owned a record store, the campus of "C.U." itself, and so forth.

"The program was largely a set piece, however, shot using primarily interiors built on Southern California soundstages. About this time, I lived in Florida and had a girlfriend who graduated high school and moved to Boulder to begin school at the real University there the same year *Mork and Mindy* debuted on TV. I visited Boulder twice, once on vacation and later to take up a short-lived residence.

"While there, I distinctly remember getting

such today, although it has been painted a weatherworn gray to remind visitors of its spooky past.

Not far from the Munster house on Colonial Street is the Cleaver home from *Leave It to Beaver*. Actually, the Cleavers had two houses, both of which are here. The more famous of the two, a stone and wood rambler, remained intact and in use throughout the 1980s, and was restored somewhat for the short-lived revival series, *The New Leave It to Beaver*.

By the mid-1990s, however, the original façade had fallen into such disrepair that a replica had to be built for the 1997 film version of the series. This replica is located on Colonial Street, too, but appears to be a scaled-down version of the gracious original. The genuine Cleaver rambler can be seen—in color—as it appeared during the making of *Leave It to Beaver* in the 1956 Universal film *Never Say Goodbye* starring Rock Hudson (shown regularly on AMC).

WARNER BROS

The Warner Bros (formerly Columbia) Ranch: A TV Land Goldmine! Along with Universal, Columbia was the other major Hollywood studio that devoted a hefty portion of its production schedule to television series. The studio never grew to the grand scale of MGM, Universal, or Warner Bros.; in fact, its facilities consisted mostly of a series of offices and soundstages on Gower Street in downtown Hollywood, and a small backlot located in southern Burbank.

By the mid-1950s, Columbia's motion picture output was flagging (largely churning out low-budget William Castle films and the like), and so the studio turned to televi-

The *Bewitched* house today

sion, thus creating its Screen Gems production unit.

When we TVpartyers think "Screen Gems," visions of *Bewitched, I Dream of Jeannie,* and *The Partridge Family* are immediately called to mind.

Indeed, Screen Gems produced all of these shows and more, and these families' famous addresses can still be found (for the most part) on the old Columbia backlot in Burbank.

Long referred to as "the Ranch," this property is located between Oak Street and Verdugo Avenue at Hollywood Way, just a short drive from the Warner Bros main lot. Like Universal's Colonial Street, the Ranch comprises an assortment of architectural styles—suburban homes, two gas stations, a church, and nineteenth century–style townhouses—encircling a central park with trees, a fountain, and a swimming pool.

At one end is the famous Stephens house at 1164 Morning Glory Circle from *Bewitched*. This charming Cape Cod must be one of the most appealing of TV homes, for it was used extensively throughout the series and—unlike other TV homes—the interior spaces appeared to match those of the exterior.

In reality, the Stephens house is a shell: the structure has no back or right-side wall, and only a partial left wall. (Pedestrians can see the rear of the shell at the corner of North Kenwood and West Oak Streets in Burbank). Other than that, the structure is satisfying to see because it looks much as it did in the 1960s.

Even after staging a real fire in the house for an episode of *Home Improvement*, studio carpenters repaired the structure and made only minor alterations, such as replacing the original paned windows with casement ones. The

'the nickel tour' of Boulder at one time or another, during which I was driven past the real house used for the exterior shots of Mindy's house on *Mork and Mindy*. I could not possibly give you the address, since then as now I am largely unfamiliar with most of Boulder. But the house I saw was indeed 'Mindy's house.' The residents of the house at the time had already put up a tall 'spite fence'—in the front yard, no less—to diminish the view of so many tourists and TV fans. Yet, the multi-story Victorian (?) style home was still visible above the fence from many angles, enough to make a clear identification of it as 'Mork from Ork's' home on Earth."
—DJQ

"Regarding your section on famous TV show homes and their locations, I would like to add a little tidbit on Colonial Street on the Universal Backlot.

"The location of this street is not where it originally stood when the TV shows *Leave It to Beaver, The Munsters,* and *Marcus Welby, M.D.* were shot. Actually the Colonial Street that exists today can be considered a Bizarro version of the original street. I say this because when the street was in its original condition and original location, the famous façades were in different locations than they are today.

"If you look back at the old Welby series you will notice that the house appeared to be at a "bend" in the street. This was because the house was at the end of a street that continued on the right. The Munster house was located in about the same area of the street it is today except that street did not turn out to the left of its location. The street was basically one long street with homes on both sides that came to bend at the end of it. Sort of an upside-down "L" shape.

"The other thing was the street's location. Colonial Street was originally located in the lower backlot behind Mockingbird Square, commonly referred to as the *Back to the Future* Hill Valley location. The street was behind the clock tower and adjacent to the lake that used to contain the partial replica of a paddle wheel boat for the 1960s TV series *Showboat*.

"It was moved to its current location in the late '70s and early '80s to make room for production facilities. What you may not know is that there is a small 'neighborhood' street located directly behind Colonial Street that is a collection of *real* homes. When I say *real* homes I mean a house with four walls, a roof, living rooms, and bedrooms. Universal bought these homes from the city of Los Angeles in the late 1950s after the city had bought them from their original owners under the eminent domain law so the city and Walter O'Malley could build Dodger Stadium at Chavez Ravine. Before the stadium was built, Chavez Ravine was a

main things which dramatically alter the façade's appearance are the two Burbank sky-scrapers that now rise up behind it.

Unfortunately, the fate of *The Partridge Family* house is not as happy. While the original Mondrian-inspired bus is long destroyed, the Partridge home—which often doubled as Abner and Gladys Kravitz's house in *Bewitched*—remained untouched until something called *Lethal Weapon II* came along. That film's script called for a suburban house to be firebombed, and unfortunately the studio—Warner Bros.—chose the Partridge house.

Today, the charming triangular entryway is gone, and the structure has been rebuilt to resemble a barn-like, contemporary home. Fortunately, the adjacent garage where Shirley, Keith, Laurie, and the gang rehearsed those groovy numbers still stands. The Partridge house is not a façade but a fully enclosed structure which is used to store lighting and other equipment when it's not being blown up.

Directly next door to the Partridge house is Maj. Anthony Nelson's Cocoa Beach home from *I Dream of Jeannie*. This house, with its recognizable ivy-covered porch trellis, also served as the Anderson family's residence on the benchmark sitcom *Father*

The *Happy Days* house 1975

Knows Best. Today the house is, happily, still intact, with only minor changes to the front porch area.

As with the Partridge house, this structure is fully enclosed (the back exterior wall is simply white concrete) and is used for equipment storage. The Ranch is full of more familiar TV Land sites: the houses from *Dennis the Menace* and *Hazel*; a red-brick church, hilariously chopped off on the back and sides where the camera doesn't reach; and the widely used central park, which can still be seen today in the opening credits of *Friends*.

PARAMOUNT STUDIOS
Nobody's Home!

Paramount boasts itself as the "oldest movie studio in Hollywood." Technically, this is true, because Paramount is located in Hollywood proper, while the other studios have long since relocated to the Los Angeles suburbs of Burbank, Century City, Culver City, and so forth.

However, with its in-town location, Paramount has a relatively small backlot—nothing near the sprawl of Universal or Warner Bros. In fact, it has minimal residential street sets, and therefore the studio used exteriors of real homes around Los Angeles as the homes of several of its TV families. We'll locate two for you here: the Bradys' and the Cunninghams'.

Recognizing the limitations of the Paramount backlot, and perhaps in an effort to imbue their production with a bit more realism, Sherwood Schwartz's team sought out an actual suburban Los Angeles home for *The Brady Bunch*. Of course, the house would be used only for stock exterior shots, with the action filmed almost entirely on Paramount's Stage 5. The house they selected is perhaps the most famous in American television.

favorite place for the studios to shoot plenty of their feature films and television shows.

"Theatrical productions like the *Eastside Kids/Bowery Boys, Laurel and Hardy, Abbott and Costello,* and a host of others shot in and around Chavez Ravine. TV shows like *Highway Patrol* and others also used Chavez Ravine. Some of those old homes have survived and were there behind Colonial Street on the Universal Backlot.

"It seems that in late 1999 the old homes on the backlot, that were saved from Chavez Ravine that would've been destroyed in 1959 to make way for the construction of Dodger Stadium, were themselves "moved out" of their location behind Colonial Street. The guide I spoke with could not tell me if they were in fact destroyed or moved to another location or sold to someone else.

"I happened to catch a broadcast of the 1974 film *Earthquake* and noticed that during the sequence of the main earthquake there is a scene at the end during which a voice off camera yells to an on camera actor to 'turn off the gas.' The actor runs into a house and the home explodes in a ball of fire. The house and the street were in fact the collection of homes I spoke of from Chavez Ravine that sat behind Colonial Street. The street and homes appear again when actress Geneviève Bujold comes home after the quake to look for her son. It's interesting to note that when this film was made, Colonial Street was still located on the lower lot."
—Sal Gomez

"The real reason they had to stop filming the exterior of a real mansion for *The Beverly Hillbillies* was the show became so popular that the owners asked Filmways not to give out the address, because tourists might come. When *TV Guide* found out the address and published it, the house was besieged by hordes of tourists, some of whom would actually walk right in, without even knocking, and ask for Jed and Granny! As a result, the owners had to tell Filmways they couldn't film there anymore.

"Also, you didn't point out that the Munsters house is actually pink, and the Cleavers' house on *Leave It to Beaver* was also used for *Marcus Welby,* and *The Partridge Family* house was also used for *My Three Sons.*"
—A Reader

"I just loved your story about sitcom houses and their current condition. I have gone to California three times and each time I have attempted to get onto the "Ranch."

"My first trip in '86 was the Burbank tour on foot. When I asked, where is the *Bewitched* house, our guide said, 'Oh, we don't take you there!'

"After finding out that day that the Ranch was down the street I went there and tried to

In spring 1969, Schwartz's team identified the now-immortal house. Located at 11222 Dilling Street in North Hollywood (also referred to as Studio City) in the San Fernando Valley, the split-level house was built in 1959 by Luther B. Carson; Carson's widow, Louise Weddington Carson, was living in the house alone when the house was selected for *The Brady Bunch*.

In 1973, Mrs. Carson sold the house to Violet and George McAllister. Mrs. McAllister lives in the house to this day, although it looks quite different now with its landscaping and surrounding white iron fence.

As many TVpartyers know, the window on the home's A-frame section was a prop, and has long been removed. Given the house's changed appearance, a three-sided façade replicating its 1969 look was built for the two Brady Bunch movies.

Garry Marshall encountered a similar problem when his *Love, American Style* segment "Love in the Happy Days" was picked up as a series by Paramount Television.

Again, with little to choose from on the backlot, the production team went into Los Angeles in search of a traditional-style house which would likely be found in 1950s mid-America. They found it at 565 North Cahuenga Boulevard, just a few blocks from Paramount's lot on Melrose Avenue. The Cunningham house is still there—but without Fonzie's motorcycle in the driveway or the swing on the front porch.

The 'Happy Days' house today

QUICK HITS: The Clampetts' mansion; Mary's boarding house; and the Addams Family mystery

The exterior of the Clampett mansion seen on *The Beverly Hillbillies* was a real house. The show's production studio, Filmways, had no backlot from which to draw upon. So, they selected a home in the grandest section of Bel Air.

For many years, the property was hidden by a high hedge that deterred sightseers. In the 1980s, however, the mansion was torn down and another residence was built on the site.

Mary Richards' charming bachelorette pad in *The Mary Tyler Moore Show* (before she moved to her highrise apartment) supposedly was located on the upper floor of Phyllis Lindstrom's house. The series was filmed at CBS's Studio Center facility in Los Angeles, but the house used for exterior shots can be found at 2104 Kenwood Parkway in Minneapolis, Minnesota.

Finally, *The Addams Family* house remains an industry mystery. While the house shown in the familiar opening credits was certainly a matte painting, there are several episodes which use an actual house. Did one exist? Even the most knowledgeable *Addams Family* fans don't know, although one authority swears that the Addams house can be seen in the movie *Willard.*

There you have it, TVpartyers—a directory to many beloved sitcom houses.

So next time you're in Los Angeles (or Minneapolis!), take map in hand and set out to see these landmarks of popular culture. You may be slightly dismayed by the way a favorite old set looks today, but at least you can say that you were right there, where all the laughs started.

get a look through the ivy fence. On my second trip, the guard was gone. I was determined to get there in 1996. I told the young man at the gate my life's dream to see the Ranch and that this was my third trip from Florida. He let us drive in!! I was told to stay in my car.

"I passed the Boston row townhouses; there was Dennis the Menace next to the Wilson's house—Halloo, Mr. Wilson. Thanks to David of the Dennis the Menace site I can visit there often. David is just as nice as can be.

"I knew the Partridge Family house was quite different but, as you said, there was the famous garage. The Partridge house could be viewed in its early time by watching *Dennis the Menace.* I think there was a church on that corner across from the Bewitched house, but it has been torn down for another home. We sat outside the *Bewitched* house and I really wanted ed to get out and knock on the door and explore the whole Ranch.

"Then we drove next door to see Hazel; it was her day off. More houses came along, and a gas station as you made the left-hand turn. I remember Samantha repairing Johnny's dad's car there so he could watch Johnny race his soap box.

"Next was the fancy two-story brick used in *Hazel* when she went to work for Mr. B's brother. This was also in *Bewitched* for the home of Darrin's old girlfriend, Sheila, and Mr. Crinky, news reporter on Dennis, and so many more.

"I have fun just making the connections on all the different homes used. It has been reported that the *Bewitched* house has now been enclosed on all three sides and now houses lawn mowers for the upkeep of the Ranch. This house is a favorite of the employees and they fought to repair it after *Home Improvement* blew it up.

"In looking at shows in the early '60s, the garage for *Bewitched* looks to be there without the house? I hope that the Ranch is left alone as far as tearing down façades. They would be tearing down our childhood memories of great and wonderful times gone by."
—Sincerely, Cathy M

"Regarding the *Addams Family* house: The house used for some of the exteriors (the front door opening shot) and as well as being the base for the drawing at the opening credits was located at Twenty-one Chester Place. It was originally owned by Estelle Doheny and her husband E.L. Doheny (of Teapot Dome fame).

"My grandparents (Paul and Helen Grafe) rented the house from 1935 to about 1969 when it was torn down for a parking lot.

"In addition, the house was used for some interior shots in *Seven Days in May.*"
—Joe Nesbitt

I accidently drove onto the set of *Eight Is Enough* when they were shooting exteriors. No one cared, so I ate lunch from catering!

fabulous brett somers

When *Match Game '79* left the CBS daytime schedule after a six-year run, and after the nightly syndicated version played out in 1981, celebrities that had been on the air daily were rarely seen on TV again. Particularly missed was *Match Game*'s true star (in my opinion), Brett Somers.

Just as demand for *The Sonny and Cher Comedy Hour* almost singlehandedly launched the *TV Land* network in the early '90s, *Match Game* reruns have become a linchpin for the up-and-coming Game Show Network, creating a whole new audience for the program that came to define '70s daytime TV.

The Game Show Network exposure has also created a new audience for the regular panelists, especially for little-known (outside of *Match Game*) Brett Somers. Very little has been written about the lady, whose career in television began in the mid-'50s with guest turns on dramatic shows like *Kraft Television Theater*, continuing into the early '60s with roles on *Ben Casey*, *Naked City*, *The Defenders*, and *The FBI*. In 1971, she began a memorable recurring role on *The Odd Couple* as Oscar's wacky, acerbic ex-wife Blanche (in real life, Brett was *Odd Couple* star Jack Klugman's wife). In addition, Somers had a supporting role as Perry Mason's secretary Gertie on the 1973 CBS drama *The New Perry Mason*.

The daily game show format started coming back into vogue in 1972, thanks to the success of Goodson/Todman's *The New Price Is Right* on CBS. In 1973, *TNPIR* producers were launching an updated version of their '60s hit *Match Game* with host Gene Rayburn. They wanted Jack Klugman so badly for the first week's episodes, they reluctantly agreed to his demand that his wife be booked on the show for a later week.

Brett clicked with the audience that first week and stayed for the next nine years. Her smoky responses and the good-natured way she interacted with host Rayburn and the other panelists gave this new *Match Game* the edge it needed to become the top-rated daytime program of the mid-'70s.

By 1975, Klugman and Somers's messy separation smeared the tabloid headlines just as Brett was gaining her own fame. Any sordid revelations that came out in the press about her "Hollywood marriage" only solidified Brett's image as a liberated, thoroughly modern kind of gal.

During the run of *Match Game* (there were two, the daytime version, 1973–1979, and the syndicated *Match Game PM*, 1975–1981), Brett Somers turned up in TV movies and on comedy programs like *Love American Style, The Bob Crane Show, Barney Miller*, and, of course, *The Love Boat.*

When the *Match Game* was revived on NBC as *The Match Game–Hollywood Squares Hour* in 1983, two venerable game shows were mashed unsatisfactory into one star-packed debacle. Gene Rayburn was back as the host of the *Match Game* half of the program, and John Bauman (*Sha Na Na*) was the host for the *Hollywood Squares* half. Charles Nelson Reilly appeared as a regular panelist, but Brett Somers was nowhere to be seen during the show's mercifully short eight-month run.

In 1990, ABC and Mark Goodson Productions revived the *Match Game* again, this time with comic Ross Shafer as host. There was a concerted effort to recreate the feel of '70s show–Charles Nelson Reilly was back as a regular panelist and Brett Somers was even brought in as a guest a few weeks after the series debuted. Her carefree wit remained intact.

The set was updated for the '90s, with what looked like the Time Tunnel in the background. The magic of the '70s show was effectively recaptured in this entertaining half-hour, but, by 1990, game shows had fallen seriously out of favor. This version of *Match Game* lasted just two years.

Match Game was revived yet again in 1998 (in syndication) with a new host but with no appearances by Brett Somers or Charles Nelson Reilly. Hasta la vista, *Match Game.*

Where is Brett today? She lives a quiet life, away from the public eye. One TVpartyer tells us of a recent encounter: "I am a student from Manhattanville College and just wanted to tell you that Brett was a guest in one our classes. She is doing very well and is currently living in Connecticut. She's a great acting coach and helped our class very much."

We get more mail on Brett Somers than any other star—she's huge but no one knows it!

237

HOLMES & YO YO

Nineteen seventy-six was a very good year for the big three networks. Prime-time commercials were selling at prices 50 percent higher than the year before and were sold out well into 1977. "This season we could sell a test pattern" was the way one network executive put it. And sell test patterns they did.

One of the misguided series foisted on unsuspecting viewers in 1976 was *Holmes and YoYo*. "To an eight-year-old kid it was cool stuff," one former viewer observed. "It was about a guy with a computer in his chest." *Holmes and YoYo* (Saturday nights from eight to eight-thirty) followed the misadventures of two New York City police detectives. Unknown to almost everyone, one of the partners happens to be a super-sophisticated robot.

Never was there a more miscast robot in television history. John Shuck (*McMillan and Wife*) played Gregory "YoYo" Yoyonovich, 427 pounds of police department relay circuits and body armor. He *looked* more like 220 pounds of doughnut-eating actor. Richard B. Schull played his partner on the force,

Detective Alexander Holmes, Bruce Kirby played Capt. Harry Sedford, and Andrea Howard was Officer Maxine Moon, the girl who swoons after YoYo, never suspecting his secret.

YoYo has the power to eat anything, he possesses a built-in trash compactor that can absorb the shock of a bomb, a photographic memory, an independent power source, and he can print out full-color proofs. Just what

you might look for in an assistant today, but YoYo is constantly malfunctioning. A bullet causes him to break out dancing, magnets fly out at him, he picks up radio signals from Sweden, and when his circuits blow he repeats, "Bunco Squad, Bunco Squad, Bunco Squad" over and over.

Holmes and YoYo was conceived as a comedy version of the highly successful 'Six Million Dollar Man/Woman/Boy/Dog' franchise that ABC was exploiting at the time. If the show reminded one of *Get Smart*, it's because they shared the same producers. Leonard Stern was executive producer and Arne Sultan producer.

Most of the jokes on *Holmes and YoYo* were *Get Smart* throwaways: "Whyn'tcha try a bite of my blue plate?" Holmes asks YoYo. YoYo eats the plate. Punch the laugh track machine all the way to ten.

To contrast the stupid jokes and add an air of danger, the crimes were treated more realistically than usual for a sitcom. The real danger proved to be on the other channels—*Holmes and YoYo* lasted only three months opposite *The Jeffersons* and *Emergency*, two gigantic hits in '76.

ABC had high hopes for another 'robot that looked like a man' series—a drama called *Futurecop*.

The pilot was shown as a special two-hour movie on March 25, 1977, starring John Amos and Ernest Borgnine as two big-city cops who team up with a mechanical partner (Michael Shannon).

The producers of that program were sued for plagiarism by noted science-fiction author Harlan Ellison. Ellison contended that the *Futurecop* screenplay was stolen from one of his teleplays, *Brillo*.

Brillo, which was written for ABC, was shown to an NBC executive. That guy then went over to Paramount and put together the *Futurecop* project and sold it back to the same guys at ABC who rejected *Brillo*. Ellison prevailed in court.

239

TOUGH
GUY

Is there a curse on former *Our Gang* and *Little Rascal* stars?

"Scotty" Beckett's pathetic life of drug addiction (and arrest for assaulting his stepdaughter with a crutch), Stymie's decent into an alcoholic hell, Alfalfa's brutal killing in an argument over a few dollars, "Weezer" Robert Hutchins's abusive childhood and early death, and Robert Blake's rocky television career / personal problems are just a few examples of the supposed *Our Gang* curse.

In 2001, things took a turn for the worse for sixty-eight-year-old Robert Blake with the shocking murder of his new bride. The finger of blame has been pointed straight at him since then.

How did it come to this?

Blake began his career in 1939 at age six playing Mickey in MGM's *Our Gang* comedies (credited on screen as Mickey Gubitosi), rounding out the '40s portraying the plucky Indian boy "Little Beaver" in another popular movie series, *Red Ryder*. Young Robert Blake made seven to twelve films a year for eight years

straight, but, all during that time, the youngster led a desperate life—the victim of a drunken, violent stepfather who would beat him and his brother, sister, and mother mercilessly at night.

As he grew into his teens, movie roles came much less frequently. In his twenties, Robert Blake moved into television where he could pick up supporting roles on shows like *Fireside Theater*. He became a frequent guest on the many western series of the '60s, just as his *Red Ryder* theatrical shorts and *Our Gang* comedies were finding new life in TV syndication.

In 1963, Robert Blake was cast as a regular on *The Richard Boone Show*, a one-hour anthology. Boone had just come off a very successful run on CBS with *Have Gun—Will Travel* and Blake was a guest star during the last season. The *Boone* show lasted only one year, so Blake went back to western guest shots and small movie roles, finally gaining the respect of the

acting community with his rivoting performance as the
psychotic killer in the motion picture *In Cold Blood* in
1967 and with a strong part in *Tell Them Willie Boy Is
Here* in 1969.

As the '70s unfolded, so did the actor's addictions.
"I was strung out on heroin for two years, stole,
smashed motorcycles into trees, boozed, ate pills by
the handful," Robert Blake once confessed. "Self
destruction? I could write a book."

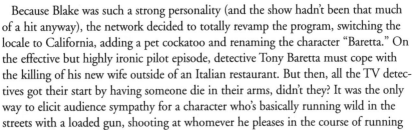

Robert Blake is high-tension undercover cop
Tony Baretta. He'll use any trick in the book, including
disguises, to blast the underworld

BARETTA
ⒶⒷ 9:00PM ③⑤⑧⑫

TV STARDOM

In 1974, Tony Musante made the decision not
to return for a second season of his ABC cop
series *Toma*. He didn't care for the weekly series
grind, so producer Jo Swerling, Jr., signed Robert
Blake to take over the role. The series was to be retitled *Toma, Starring
Robert Blake*.

Because Blake was such a strong personality (and the show hadn't been that much
of a hit anyway), the network decided to totally revamp the program, switching the
locale to California, adding a pet cockatoo and renaming the character "Baretta." On
the effective but highly ironic pilot episode, detective Tony Baretta must cope with
the killing of his new wife outside of an Italian restaurant. But then, all the TV detectives got their start by having someone die in their arms, didn't they? It was the only
way to elicit audience sympathy for a character who's basically running wild in the
streets with a loaded gun, shooting at whomever he pleases in the course of running

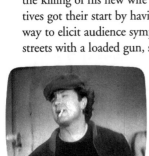

his "private detective" business.

Baretta debuted mid-season in January, 1975 and was
an immediate winner, at least by '75 ABC standards. A
subsequent Emmy win that year for the actor put
Robert Blake on top of the world. He took full advantage of the situation and started demanding more intel-
ligent scripts, and battling on the set and in court for
primary control over the production. He had his wife

Sondra brought in as a frequent guest-star and began completely ignoring directors he
didn't like, effectively directing the show himself. "The guild says you gotta have a
director, so you stick a director in the chair," Blake arrogantly stated in 1976. "It's like
sticking a broomstick in the chair. The show directs itself, anyway."

Blake was further quoted in *Esquire* magazine as saying this about his employers:
"Here at Universal, nobody listens and nobody cares. As far as most people are concerned, they just as soon turn out *Perry Mason* or Donald Duck, it don't make no difference. 'Cause once you sell the hour, as long as it's on the air, it don't matter. You're
on the air or you ain't on the air."

Intense battles on the set ultimately led to original producer Swerling's ouster, and
there were many other production personnel firings. Blake had legitimate complaints—he wanted a quality production he could be proud of—but he later had to

The Bionic Woman and *Charlie's Angels* were teamed with *Baretta* on Wednesday nights for the 1976–77 season.

admit that excessive drug use was clouding his daily judgment. When asked to describe himself at this time in his life, Blake used words like "crazy," "hostile," and "full of hate," and he sought therapy to control those intense feelings.

Solidly in the top ten for the 1976–77 season, Robert Blake announced he would not return for a fourth year of *Baretta* because of a contract dispute with Universal. The studio, faced with losing one of its top productions, acquiesced. With an offer of more money and control over every aspect of the program, Blake decided to return.

Blake was finally handed what he battled so long and hard for, but ratings went south as soon as the 1977–78 season got underway. When ABC moved the show from its Wednesday-night lineup to Thursdays, numbers continued to dip. Less than a year after his victory over Universal, *Baretta* was canceled in 1978. Robert Blake's marriage dissolved soon after.

To many observers, Robert Blake's confrontational nature and admitted substance abuse led to the early demise of the series. Because of his erratic behavior, Blake found subsequent TV work difficult to find. "Don't do the crime, if you can't do the time," the industry seemed to be saying as the doors slammed shut.

In 1981, Robert Blake roared back with five TV movies in one year, three in the role of detective Joe Dancer. He hosted *Saturday Night Live* in 1982, starred as Joe Dancer in another TV movie, and was seen as Jimmy Hoffa in the telefilm *Blood Feud* in 1983.

Because of his reputation, in order to get the Hoffa role, Blake was forced to put his salary in escrow, collectable only if he stayed drug- and trouble-free on the set. This was necessary because the production's insurance company refused to cover him otherwise. Blake insisted this was no problem; he was drug-free and ready to move forward. He collected the check and won critical acclaim for his performance.

In March 1985, a TV movie pilot starring Robert Blake as a tough inner-city priest scored impressive ratings against powerhouse *Dynasty* on ABC. *Hell Town* the series joined the NBC lineup on September 4, 1985.

Hell Town was *Baretta* in a priest's collar, right down to the tough talk, gritty streets (shot on location in East LA) and, for good measure, a Sammy Davis, Jr., theme song (he had scored a top-forty hit with *Baretta*'s theme). Typical episode plot: Father Noah "Hardstep" Rivers (Robert Blake) tries to convert a prostitute by helping her homeless little brother.

Despite heavy promotion and a natural times-lot after *Highway to Heaven*, *Hell Town* tanked against *Dynasty* on a weekly basis. The show was canceled after a few short months, broadcasting the last episode on Christmas night 1985. There were few roles for Robert Blake on television after 1986, although he resurfaced to play the title role in *Judgment Day: The John List Story* in 1993. His most notable part in the nineties was a supporting role in the 1995 theatrical release *Money Train*.

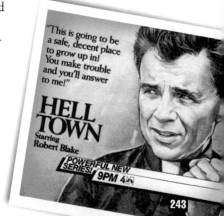

"This is going to be a safe, decent place to grow up in! You make trouble and you'll answer to me!"

HELL TOWN

Starring Robert Blake

POWERFUL NEW SERIES! 9PM 4📺

Michael D. Roberts played Baretta's informant "Rooster."

LIFE IMITATES ART

(Why is that never a good thing?)

Robert Blake was living in relative obscurity after only a few scattered acting jobs in the nineties, his rarified existence as a weekly TV celebrity far behind him. On the evening of Friday, May 4, 2001, Robert Blake made headlines when his new wife, forty-four-year-old Bonny Lee Bakley, was shot once in the head and once in the shoulder while sitting in their car on a Sherman Oaks side street. She was pronounced dead at the hospital a short time later.

Bakley, the mother of Blake's eleven-month-old child, had a checkered past, including run-ins with the law and a supposed child by Jerry Lee Lewis (or so she claimed, but it wasn't true). She'd recently been on probation in Arkansas for carrying a false ID, and she had dozens of them. Because of her past, Blake and Bakley reportedly signed an unusual prenuptial agreement, stating that she couldn't engage in any sort of criminal activity during the marriage.

The fatal shooting happened near Vitello's Italian restaurant in a quiet San Fernando Valley neighborhood. The couple left the place together, strolling a block and a half to the car. Blake told police that his wife stayed behind while he went back into the eatery to retrieve a gun that had slipped from his waistband, a gun he said he was carrying for his wife's protection (he had a valid concealed weapon permit). This was disputed somewhat by people in the restaurant who observed the actor when he walked back in the door. The restaurant owner, who was well known to the actor, claimed Blake reentered the establishment to nervously drink two glasses of water, but saw him retrieve nothing. It was reported that others in the restaurant remembered him asking, calmly, if anyone knew CPR. Why he needed someone who knew CPR (before he discovered his wife was shot) remains unknown.

According to Blake, when he returned to the car he discovered his wife had been shot. What no one disputes is, while his wife hemorrhaged and lay dying in the car, Robert Blake ran in a panic to the nearby home of Sean Stanek, a total stranger, for help. "He was falling apart." Stanek told the press. "He was sick, he was throwing up, he was shaking, he was crying. He was really messed up." Blake entered the hospital for high blood pressure that night and was released early the next day.

Suspicions were raised almost immediately. Could Robert Blake have done the unthinkable and killed his wife? Did he hire someone to do it? Why did he park so far from the restaurant when there were spaces closer to the eatery? If Blake says he walked into the restaurant with a gun, then lost it, what happened to it? Is it relevant that Bonny Bakley told her half-brother Peter Carlyon that she lived in fear for her life? Carlyon claims that Blake told Bakley flat out, "There's a bullet with your name on it."

"I'm 99.9% sure it's him," Carlyon told the press days after the murder, "He [Blake] was making a lot of verbal threats. She didn't want him carrying the gun because he had been making threats against her. She told the entire family that if anything happened to her, he was behind it." Ironically, Peter Carlyon also claimed that he felt his

The theme for *Baretta* was *Keep Your Eye On The Sparrow* by Sammy Davis, Jr., Robert Blake better keep his eye on the soap.

sister would have died happy, knowing she was the wife of a star. It was her life-long dream. "She was just a harmless scam artist. I don't think she had any true to life enemies that would kill her." Bonny's mother believes Blake killed her for control over the baby.

DAMAGE CONTROL

"Apparently she's had some criminal history," Blake's attorney told the AP hours after the murder, hoping to shift the focus from his client to the victim, "So it could be any number of people that had it in for her." Braun released a tape recording of a conversation between Bakley and a friend: "I thought, well, when I met Blake I kinda wanted him but I kinda didn't because he wasn't, like, up to par with the looks," Bonny Bakley is heard casually saying. "I thought, well, I don't know if I really would want him the rest of my life because he's going to get even older and worse looking and I'm already in love with Christian [Brando, son of Marlon]."

How romantic . . .

Police found documents in Bakley's apartment (she had been banished to a service house behind her husband's home) indicating she was running a lonely hearts service targeting old men and prison inmates, even mailing out nude pictures of herself in exchange for a donation. She was allegedly planning to swindle Oscar-nominated actor Gary Busey and may have even contacted Busey's mother. Bakley may have been a "harmless scam artist," but you have to give her credit for opening up new markets, though I question just how lucrative they may have been.

Christian Brando, who served almost five years in prison for the shooting death of his half-sister's boyfriend, warned Bonny to be careful. "You better get a handle on that and really think what you're doing," Brando admonished her in a phone conversation. "Running around sending letters to guys, embezzling money from all these idiots. You're lucky—not on my behalf—but you're lucky somebody ain't out there to put a bullet in your head."

A private investigator (hired by Blake's lawyers) claimed that a few weeks before the murder, a stranger was showing up in front of the actor's Studio City home. Described as being in his early twenties with a crew cut, the stranger would watch the property from a black four-door pickup. Was Bakley being stalked? Why didn't someone go outside and say, "Hey, pickup drivin' man, why are you staring at my house?"

NOT ANOTHER O.J.

With a high-profile celebrity murder case on their hands, the LAPD moved methodically, not wanting another O.J. Simpson–style fiasco. In a search of Blake's house the weekend after the murder, police recovered two 9mm handguns, along with paperwork and phone records. Police interviewed Robert Blake twice about the killing, immediately after the shoot-

Whitman Mayo (Grady from *Sanford and Son*) was known on *Hell Town* as "One Ball."

ing and again a day later. His home was in disarray according to ABC News, with scrawling on the wall reading, "I am not going down for this."

A third search of Blake's home was conducted a few days later. Police were looking for financial records and a second diary kept by Bakley. Friends and family members of the victim swore the diary contained evidence of the blatant threats made by her husband.

Meanwhile, police found the murder weapon in a trash dump near the crime scene. The gun could not be traced to Robert Blake at that time and *The New York Post* reported that police determined brass bullet casings found near the body did not match the bullets taken from a search of Blake's home.

In the days that followed, a media assault began and the nation's most prestigeous news organizations snapped into action. *The National Enquirer* announced they were giving the police a tape that reportedly depicted the actor pressuring Bonny Lee Bakley to get an abortion, accusing his future wife of trapping him into marriage by lying about using birth control. The murder was so shocking that model citizen O.J. Simpson took a break from the exhaustive search for the killer of his own wife to tell the TV show *Extra*, "I know that watching TV is only going to frustrate him. As far as I'm concerned, this man is innocent until a jury comes back and calls him guilty."

When Blake's ex-wife Sondra was confronted with the news of the murder, she reluctantly recalled her rocky 1982 breakup, when her husband grew violent and threatened to kill her—with his gun planted in her mouth! She would say little more about the split in the few TV interviews she consented to, refusing to discuss anything that wasn't already on the public record. Was she afraid to say more? She wouldn't say.

Curiously, Blake has admitted in past interviews to almost killing two people, the father of a girl he dated and a therapist. "I felt like a killer and I liked it. It was an exciting feeling . . ." he stated in a frank 1976 interview.

Days after the shooting, the LAPD announced that they were confident of a swift arrest in the Bakley case and that Robert Blake was definitely considered a suspect. Still, months drifted by with no apparent movement on the case.

Pathetically, the first funeral service for Bakley had to be called off because the morbid crowd of tabloid reporters and curiosity-seekers frenzied by nonstop TV news coverage made any sort of dignified ceremony impossible.

SAY IT AIN'T SO, LITTLE BEAVER!

In February 2002, almost a year after the murder, Robert Blake's lawyer Harland Braun announced to the world that he might have found Bakley's killer—a man currently under arrest for armed robbery who Braun felt "would be a prime suspect in this type of killing," a man allegedly humiliated by

Hell Town was seen in the same Wednesday-night-at-nine timeslot that *Baretta* had nine years earlier.

one of Bakley's lonely hearts schemes. With police turning up the heat on his client, some saw this announcement as a cynical diversionary tactic. Indeed, just a month later, the tables turned when Blake and his bodyguard Earl Caldwell were arrested in connection with the murder. April 18, 2002, attorney Braun was on the scene at Blake's sister's home in the Hidden Hills area of Los Angeles to advise the actor "to come outside peacefully" and surrender to authorities.

Bakley attorney Cary W. Goldstein told CNN after the arrest, "I think that after thousands and thousands of hours of investigation by the LAPD, they have concluded that Robert Blake and Earl Caldwell are responsible for the death of Bonny Bakley." The eleven-month investigation led detectives to twenty states and yielded over nine hundred pieces of evidence.

Braun stated on the day after the arrest that Blake was innocent and in good spirits while being held in a medical unit where high-profile inmates are assigned to keep them away from the general inmate population. By that Monday, the Los Angeles District Attorney had charged Blake with murder and two counts of solicitation of murder and conspiracy. Blake's bodyguard, Earle Caldwell, forty-six, was charged with conspiracy to commit murder. Prosecutors alleged the actor instructed Caldwell to keep a list "of items for use in the murder of Bonny Lee Bakley." That list, the complaint charged, included, "two shovels, small sledge, crowbar, twenty-five auto, 'get blank gun ready,' old rugs, duct tape, Draino, pool acid, lye, plant."

Police offered a motive at a news conference after the arrest—Blake was unhappy in his short marriage and allegedly tried to hire several unidentified individuals to kill Bakley. Having failed at that, the theory goes, Blake shot her himself in cold blood as she sat in his car near Vitello's restaurant. And the murder weapon found in the dumpster? The serial number on the .38-caliber Walther PPK handgun had been filed off, but using new forensic techniques (not available back in the *Baretta* days), LA sleuths were able to read the number and trace the gun right back to Robert Blake.

Blake, almost seventy years old, was charged with a special circumstance ("lying in wait") in connection with the murder. As a result he could face the death penalty. Bakley's understandably bitter sibling Joel said on hearing the news, "He deserves to get it."

TVpow!

A self-indulgent artist rendering of what the game may have looked like . . .

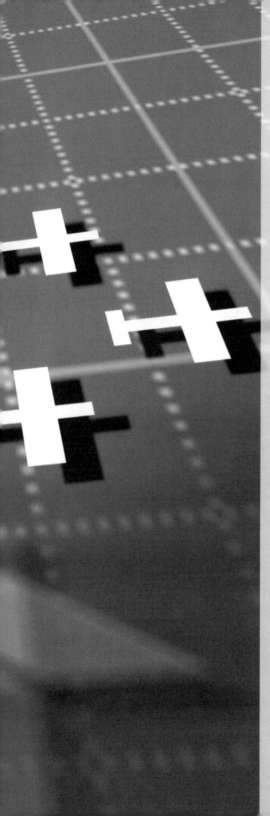

TV Pow was a phenomenon seen on local stations around the country, a last ditch effort to lure kids to local programming via their love of a new technology—video games like Pong, Pac-Man, and Donkey Kong.

Viewers could play at home if they were lucky enough to get their call on the air. All they had to do was yell "POW!" through the telephone to play.

"KTVU enlisted Pat McCormick to host what would be their last live kids' show, called *TV Pow*. It was a game show for kids; a giant version of Mattel Intellivision was put on the screen and kids called in to play the giant video game over the phone. The game was voice-activated by the kids going "Pow! Pow! Pow!" All too often, McCormick would have to stop the kids from overmodulating and going too fast. This concept lasted about a year."
—Jim

"Unfortunately, I don't have any video, but I can tell you that the system used was not an Intellivision—it was a semi-obscure system made by Fairchild. I know this because my best friend had one and we used to practice the 'pow game' while mocking the kids who pointlessly yelled 'powpowpow-powpowpow' in a futile blur."
—Regards, Paul

"At first, *TV Pow* used a Fairchild Channel F video game, then later on they replaced it with an Intellivision with a space war–type game for it.

"*The Barney Show* was a replacement for *TV Pow*, it was another live-action show where the viewers would talk to a semi-animated cartoon character while playing *TV Pow*. Well, Barney wasn't really an animated character; it looked like a transparency that was overlaid on the video monitor.

"The show pretty much was just the camera pointing at the TV set where Barney was animated. it was being controlled like a puppet. The person who did Barney could move his left and right hands (and I think his head) up and down and his mouth moved. Then they would chromakey a background for him. When Barney called a viewer, I think they showed him holding a phone. When it was time to play the videogame, they would put Barney towards the left part of the screen, superimposed on the background of the video game."
—Matt Fox, SJ, CA

249

Remembering
Read All
About It!

by Zachary Houle

Three kids in a coach house. An alien with a floating head. A teleporter to another world. Two robots named Otto and Theta.

If that brings back any memories, then you probably watched an '80s children's TV show about writing called *Read All about It!* It lasted just two seasons, and has been off the air since the mid-'90s, but it's fondly remembered by some wistful Gen-Xers as one of the best educational shows aimed at the eight- to twelve-year-olds.

It might be a cliché, but this definitely was a show ahead of its time. And that's notwithstanding the fact that time travel was a major plot point.

Read All about It! was a fifteen-minute show shot to videotape by Canadian educational TV broadcaster TV Ontario from 1979 to 1982. All but the last episode of both seasons (twenty shows each) were cliffhangers in the best matinee serial tradition. It took two years to shoot a batch of twenty episodes, which explains why the kids suddenly jump a few inches at certain points. Part of the cheese, perhaps, but also part of the charm.

Season one saw ten-year-old Chris Anderson (David Collard) inheriting a small coach house in small, sleepy Herbertville, Ontario, from his missing uncle. The uncle was an inventor, so the building was home to two sentient robots, Otto and Theta. Otto was a typewriter who could

print his thoughts out, while Theta was a talking computer at a time when the home PC was still in its infancy.

Joined by two schoolgirls—the cute, sunshine-y Lynne and the bossy, nerdy Samantha—the trio discovers that Chris's uncle is being held captive on another planet, Trialveron, in a galaxy far, far away. And, whaddyaknow, there's a handy little desk lamp in the coach house that acts as a teleportation device to that planet. The kids soon learn that Trialveron's leader is a floating head called Duneedon who also just so happens to be Herbertville's mayor, Don Eden, in full-body form. Confused? Yeah, the kids think the adults wouldn't get what was going on, so they start their own newspaper with the help of Otto and Theta as a means of striking back at the floating head.

Naturally, all hell breaks loose. Also not helping is the fact that the desk lamp . . . er, transporter . . . somehow allows storybook characters like Captain Hook and the Queen of Hearts to come to life. (As if fighting aliens wasn't enough!)

Season two saw the series take a radical left turn into more mature subject matter, like racial prejudice. The teleporter becomes a time machine and the *Chronicle* staff soon discover that a black child, Alex, was trapped in the War of 1812. The kids dive in to save him from a live of slavery, and, well, on it goes. Duneedon only guest stars in this season as the baddie—he got less screen time because actor Sean Hewitt had other gigs come up, including a role in a long-forgotten Hollywood horror movie called *The Sender*. Plus, Sam wound up moving away from Herbertville with her family halfway through. But more on that in a few moments.

Soon after its debut, *Read* started picking up industry broadcasting awards. It was later sold to PBS in the States, and shown in eighty other countries, primarily for use teaching English as a second language. There was even a novelization written in 1981 by Clive Endersby, the show's screenwriter.

Its influence can be still felt today. I know of an editor in New York who was a fan of the show growing up, and this was probably one of the first shows that encouraged desktop publishing as a means of self-expression. *Read All about It!* just might have had a small, yet significant, part in creating the 'zine and Web blogging phenoms of today.

Some of the show's child actors got caught in the magic web of creativity that *Read* encouraged, too. David Collard (Chris) started his own film production company, Fieldview, in Toronto. After working as a self-employed commercial video producer since 1989, he has written, and now hopes to shoot, an independent feature film called *How Beautiful the Sunset*. Lydia Zajc (Lynne) went on to become a reporter with Reuters, and spent some time working as a senior technology editor with the *South China Morning Post* in Hong Kong.

That said, not everyone involved in Read went onto greener pastures. Sean Hewitt had a role in the John Travolta howler *Battlefield Earth*. The other two main actors, Stacey Arnold (Samantha) and Michael Dwyer (Alex), have gone AWOL, just like the show itself.

"Television: A medium. So called because it is neither rare nor well done." —Ernie Kovacs

251

Read is only available by hunting down old videos in school libraries or by contacting International Tele-film (*www.itf.ca*), who now owns the distribution rights. Getting tapes of all forty episodes from the last source will currently cost you about thirteen hundred dollars Canadian, so you're almost better off dealing with any bootleggers you run into who have tapes of the show.

But memories are almost always free—or, at least, the cost of a phone bill—and I managed to track down Jeremy Pollock, the show's producer/director. We talked for about ninety minutes, and the interview was the type of gig that made the ten-year-old inside me do summersaults. If anything, his remarks are a telling account of what it was like to work in educational kid's TV at the dawn of the '80s. And they might shed a little light on whatever the hell happened to Sam.

ZH: The series seems to have taken its cues from a lot of different places. I see a little *Dr. Who* in the program, along with some elements of what PBS was trying to do in *The Letter People*.

JP: Well, yes, there was all that. The research that went into the project before we got underway was quite extensive. We did a lot of interviewing with the intended audience, and this was just after the first *Star Wars* came out. So there was a tremendous interest in space travel and aliens . . . and it was something kids wanted to see in a show. That was a very strong impetus for us to involve space, some kind of time travel.

ZH: I was surprised to find out there was a novelization. It seems to me there was a little cottage industry built around the show.

JP: Well, [the novelization] was about the extent of it. The one thing TVO [a government-run TV station] never got into, for political reasons, was getting into a cottage industry of spinoff merchandise. Certainly, PBS and their production affiliates have done remarkably well. The whole aspect of toys coming out of TV shows was also still new at that point, but the interest here was to create a whole new level of reading. So by creating a book around the series, we presented an audience with another type of reading. And that was the main impetus behind that book.

Reading is necessary within the series itself . . . [through] the two robot characters, Otto and Theta. Theta spoke, but Otto didn't speak. So he had to be read in order to understand what was going on.

ZH: That really worked effectively. The one episode I remember well is where the kids are all in the coach house, and Otto prints out some sort of garbled message. One of the characters goes "Ah, this is some kind of code" and goes to work on it, then figures out the message is "Duneedon was here." But then Sam crossed out a letter, adds another, and it becomes "Duneedon is here." And that's when the floating head pops up, and traps the kids.

JP: Yeah, it was the end of the first twenty shows when that happened.

ZH: So what was it sort of like to work on this weird little show?

JP: Terrific. It was during the halcyon days at TV Ontario, where budgets were certainly healthy. It was quite a big project by our standards, so we had an opportunity to experiment and play and stretch technically. [Note: Each episode cost tens of thousands of dollars, varying with the episode, not taking inflation into account. Since 1996, the Ontario government has all but eliminated in-house production at the station, save for current event–type programming.]

The kids kept growing, though, as they often do. So there's a big difference between the Chris and Lynne you see at the beginning of the series, and the kids you see at the end. In a four-year period, they went from approximately 11 to 15, and it's clearly one of the times when kids grow and change. So there was that element that was a factor for us to try and work around.

ZH: How was the show cast?

JP: We initially saw the kids separately and began pairing them up, and having them work off each other. I remember David [Collard] and Lydia [Zajc] were the first two who connected, so we locked them in pretty fast. And then Stacey [Arnold] worked awfully well as part of the group. She and Lydia connected. They were both born in March only ten days apart, so they connected very quickly.

Sean Hewitt had a great face, which was part of the reason we hired him. He has a terrific face for villainous types. (Laughs.)

ZH: The show was really quite groundbreaking in the second season, in that the issue of one of the latter character's race was raised as a significant plot point. How did that issue, the issue of Alex being black in 1812, come about?

JP: I think the issue of Alex being black back in the early 1800s was something that just evolved. We didn't create that kind of situation for any specific reason; the two things just ended up meeting once we had determined the War of 1812 was a significant historical hook for this project. We wanted one and that's the one we selected. From that, the choice of Alex in the second block of shows . . . [coming] from a colored background [became] a conscious decision. We wanted to show a type of minority as part of this group [of children] and to that extent we auditioned a number of different representatives, if you will, from different ethnic communities. Michael was just terrific. He auditioned and worked so well, so it wasn't a difficult decision.

The War of 1812 was one of the most rewarding and challenging block of shows that we did in the entire series, simply because a great deal of it was shot on location at the battlefield out at Queenston Heights, Ontario. The uniform for General Brock—one of the historical characters brought into the show—was rebuilt basically from the skin out. We ended up contributing it to Brock University in St. Catherines, Ontario, after the show was finished.

ZH: Working with kids must have been a challenge. Did you have to resort to any tricks to kind of prod them to do what you wanted them to?

JP: I didn't resort to the tricks that are well known in the industry. I didn't yell or berate them in any way, but the one instance that does come to mind is . . . Sam's departure [in the second season]. There was a sequence between her and Lynne, and I remember sitting down with Stacy [Arnold, who played Sam] and saying, "It would really work awfully well if you think you can shed some tears in this sequence. It would make it totally believable if you were able to cry. Do you think you can do that?" We discussed it, we had a private one-on-one discussion—everyone else faded [into the background] on request—and we basically talked and worked our way up to a point where she said, "Okay, I'm pretty sure I can do this now."

I'd made an arrangement with the studio director that I would give him a little hand signal and we'd just go into it, period. It's a very delicate line to reach that point and then start doing all the yelling and stuff that goes on in a studio as you're getting ready for a shot or take. It would completely ruin the thing. So I had planned this with the studio director, and everybody else knew what needed to be done. I just basically gave a little hand signal, moved out of the shot, and we tried it several times. She was never able to cry, but the delivery ended up being quite believable because of the effort that had gone into it. I was not disappointed that she hadn't been able to shed tears, and I did not resort to onions or any of the other little tricks often used, because—as I said to her at the time—"I don't want fake tears for the picture. If there are tears, it's because you feel it, and it's coming from the heart. And that's how it will happen. If it happens, terrific. If it doesn't happen, there's no problem at all." That was the basis in which we both understood and we worked, just the two of us, to bring her to a point where she'd able to cry. But she never did. (Laughs.)

ZH: So why did she leave the show anyhow? I know she came back . . .

JP: Yes, towards the end of the second season.

ZH: But was it working around her schedule or a matter of her growing too old for the part?

JP: Partly that, and some of it was scheduling, as I recall. But, certainly the content of the show did change, and now we can get into the finer elements of tight budgets. When the fourth character, Alex, came in, it reflected in our budgets and it became evident that we were not going to be able to afford four kids in all shows. And so the decision was to use Sam less frequently.

ZH: But why did you cut her loose over, say, Lynne or Chris?

JP: [Her character] had always been, right from the start, a bit more critical, a bit more difficult. Some of our audience testing in the first season brought up some comments about Sam being, in some respects, the least favorite of the three because she was bossy. Her demeanor was seen by the kids [watching the show] as being a little too aggressive. We made subtle changes [to her character], but it became evident that we wanted another character, Alex. We didn't think the three of them [Chris, Lynne, and Sam] could carry all four years and we needed fresh blood for story; we couldn't keep all four running simultaneously in all the shows. So some of that viewer feedback was factored into the decision.

We didn't ignore some of the early feedback we got, either. If one has the opportunity to see the very first three shows [in season one] of the series, you're going to see a completely different Sam. Thinking back to those first few episodes, I have to reflect that, God, we really did miss the mark a little. Sam was quite bookish, if you will, not only in her wardrobe but her presentation. She was wearing glasses, and they were book-y glasses. In a sense, she had a strike against her in those first three shows, and the response was essentially to those kinds of elements, and we [the crew] immediately sat down and said to ourselves, "Okay, we've got to be subtle about this, but we've got to swing her out of that little box." And they softened up the wardrobe, and got rid of the glasses.

ZH: I remember overalls. It was such a late '70s thing, but I remember her wearing the overalls.

JP: Yes, [Stacey] loved the overalls. And, a little bit later, the tight jeans. (Laughs.) She was totally uncomfortable in the early wardrobe, and that showed in the end result. When we sat down and asked her how she wanted to change, only then did we find a sort of nice transition into something she felt better being in. And it made a difference in her performance.

Now when you're speaking of true actors, kids aren't. (Laughs.) Kids don't act, they react to what you're giving them. They don't act in the truest sense of actors themselves. Professional and experienced actors could care less what they're wearing. But when you are dealing with kids, who have very limited or no experience, these are the kinds of things that make a huge difference. If they like what they're wearing, they're going to be more comfortable and more confident.

ZH: As I mentioned earlier, getting her off the show really changed the dynamic. Did you ever get feedback about that?

JP: We got feedback with Sam's departure, which was particularly an emotional show. She went to move out west with her family, and moving is one of the critical issues for children. It's a difficult challenge for them, especially if they haven't moved before. We got positive feedback on it. People liked the way it'd been handled, and understood why Sam had to move. They didn't necessarily like the fact she had to go, but it was presented in a completely believable way.

As far as the dynamic of the characters go, we didn't get feedback on that. I'd always felt that, personally speaking as a director, Alex didn't quite fit in to the group as well. The first three really did lock, and Lydia and David locked—in fact, they're still pals. Stacey worked well as well, but sometimes her character was not perhaps as appealing to the age range.

ZH: I guess, coming only a few years after *Star Wars*, that some of the special effects must have been tough to pull off. Was there any problems during shooting?

JP: When we had our miniature storybook characters standing on a desk looking at three kids, we literally had to put them in a blue-screen studio, find marks—sometimes up in the lighting grid—to replicate the placement of where a kid's face was. The actors basically had to swing from one mark to another, from one kid to another. They couldn't see anything. It was a huge element of trust. When the shots were married, that's when we found out whether or not it worked, but it was great fun.

ZH: The show obviously had two successful seasons—it now has a little cult following. Was there ever plans for a third season?

JP: It had always been planned from the outset as two seasons. We found out at the end of the second season that popularity wasn't a particularly valuable asset for us. (Laughs.) There was tremendous angst and just a huge outcry when teachers and classes across Canada and the U.S. found out that *Read All about It!* was finishing. They wanted a third season. We had tremendous support: classes and teachers wrote letters from all across North America, telling us how important it was in the classroom.

I think it's worth noting that we're looking at a completely different era. You have to go back and realize that cable didn't exist and these shows were delivered through standard broadcast. The teaching community had to come to us in order to be able to present the show. One of the huge benefits of small-format tape, Beta and VHS, when it arrived was that, now, this kind of material was legitimately a teaching aid because it could be taken off the shelf and used whenever the teacher found it convenient. It wasn't until the availability of small-format tape and the ability to deliver hard copies of programs to schools and libraries . . . that [educational TV for older grades] began to take off. It was a really tough sell in the '70s.

"Television! Teacher, mother, secret lover." —*Homer Simpson*

ZH: So you heard from a lot of classes about the show, then?

JP: Well, there were two types of rewarding feedback we'd get. One would be the letters we'd receive from classrooms. In particular, I remember a large brown manila envelope arriving from somewhere in the southern U.S. We opened it, and out fell all these little letters from a classroom on second and third grade foolscap. It was almost like newsprint—very poor quality paper—and it was written in very stubby pencil. And the grammar was atrocious. Not to stereotype, but there was a sense that these were poor kids, yet they were making an effort. I'm telling you, when all of us in the office looked at this, we all looked at each other—about four or five of us—and said "Oh my God. These kids actually took the time and effort to write to us because of this show." We suspected that many of these children had never written a letter in their life. That was very touching.

I also remember one instance where I personally went to a classroom situation and was introduced to the class as a "surprise." As soon as the show came on air and the lights went down, myself and a few other people from TVO sort of slipped into the back of this school library—unbeknownst to the kids. And when the show was finished, the lights came up and we were introduced. I was just amazed. They could not stop asking questions. I found out after the fact that some of these kids were challenged in some way . . .

There was one little guy whose hand just kept coming up at every opportunity and we had a little chat. After the session was completed, the teacher came over to us and said, "I just wanted to tell you that that little fellow who kept putting his hand up at the front used to stay under a table in the classroom. He would not come out [before watching the show]."

So these are the kind of things that came back that really counted. It did win awards and it was very successful. But these are the kinds of stories that made it so worthwhile. At the end of the day, that's what was really satisfying.

THE IRONIC DEATH OF REDD FOXX

A Harlem nightclub comedian since the '40s, Redd Foxx found television success late in life with two hit series and three failures during a twenty-year period.

Foxx became relatively well-known in 1955 with his hilarious party album *Laff of the Party*, wall to wall raunchy stories recorded before a live audience. *Laff* and Redd's subsequent dirty joke LPs sold over fifteen million copies, but the comic saw little of the money. "I got robbed so bad," Foxx complained, "I just didn't want to make anymore."

It was in the rowdy, late-night dives that Redd Foxx defined the 'Fred Sanford' character he would make famous on TV in the '70s—in fact, many of the show's character actors came from Redd's club days, including Slappy White and LaWanda Page (who had a particularly filthy act).

A *Tonight Show* appearance in the '60s led to a few guest roles on TV and a part as the Junkman in the 1970 blaxploitation film *Cotton Goes to Harlem*. Producer Norman Lear saw the movie and cast Redd Foxx in his new sitcom for NBC.

Sanford and Son debuted in 1972. Centering around junk dealer Fred Sanford and his adult son living in Watts, the show immediately became one of the biggest hits on NBC during the dacron-polyester decade, and the second smash for Norman Lear and Bud Yorkin after *All in the Family* scored big on CBS. *Sanford and Son* landed in the top ten every week it was on the air, becoming the lynchpin of NBC's phenomenally successful Friday night schedule. Redd took to his new success by living large, exerting more creative control over the show and indulging his love of Las Vegas casinos and pretty women (he wasn't married to). Cocaine was consumed openly on the set; Redd even wore a gold coke spoon around his neck and was frequently seen waving a gun in rehearsals as paranoia eventually set in.

"Enjoy some of the money. You ever see a Brinks truck following a hearse?" —*Redd Foxx*

Because he was relatively unknown to TV audiences when he got his big break, Foxx's contract didn't take into account what a big star he would become. He engaged in a bitter public dispute with the producers, feeling he was being taken advantage of.

Foxx walked off the production and sat out a half-season in 1975, ostensibly because NBC wouldn't give him a dressing room with a window. The network claimed the star was out of line, that the issue was a smoke screen to get out of his contract and sign a better deal elsewhere.

Foxx gave in and returned to the series when NBC slapped an injunction on him, preventing him from working anywhere else, effectively cutting off his flow of money. Unfortunately for the star's case, ratings stayed high while he was out, hitting a peak in an episode that didn't even feature Redd Foxx.

Sanford and Son was so hot for NBC it was running two nights a week during the summer of 1976, but for whatever reason (and the actor's drug and alcohol consumption was surely a factor), the network that capitulated to everyone from Bob Hope to Johnny Carson over the years refused to (or could not) make Redd Foxx happy.

To bust up NBC's winning schedule, ABC paid Foxx a small fortune to executive produce and star in his own hour-long variety show in the fall of 1977. The strategy worked; NBC's hold on Friday nights was broken. The network attempted to keep the franchise going with *Sanford Arms* starring LaWanda Page, Whitman "Grady" Mayo, Don "Bubba" Bexley, Raymond "Woody" Allen, Theodore Wilson, and all of the *Sanford and Son* regulars except Foxx and Demond Wilson.

Why no Lamont? When Demond Wilson asked NBC for a huge raise to be the solo star of *Sanford and Son* after Redd's departure, NBC passed—remembering Wilson's own unfortunate cocaine habit and considering, no doubt, the story that he once chased Norman Lear down the hall with a gun. *Sanford Arms* was a major disappointment, lasting only a few weeks.

Meanwhile over at ABC, the *The Redd Foxx Comedy Hour* was scheduled for Thursday nights at ten starting September 15, 1977, with guest star LaWanda Page in a racy massage parlor routine that had ABC censors on their toes. Famous for his dirty humor, in the first episode Redd joked, "The only thing I can do from my nightclub act is smoke!" (You can't even do *that* now . . .)

The stellar cast included comedy veterans Slappy White, Billy Barty, Hal Smith (drunk Otis from *The Andy Griffith Show*), Bill Saluga (as Raymond J. "You doesn't have to call me" Johnson), the Gerald Wilson Orchestra, and "Iron Jaw" Wilson, who could pick up tables and chairs with his teeth. 'The Redd Foxx Comedy Hour' marked one of the first appearances of co-producer Bob Einstein's "Super Dave Osborne" character and the return of Andy Kaufman's surrealistic routines to prime-time television.

Most of the early monologues and audience chats revolved around how much money Redd Foxx was making and how rich he was going to be ("Here I am at ABC, which stands for, 'A Big Check.'"). He often took questions from the audience, which led to some hilarious exchanges and gave the comedian a chance to exhibit his razor caustic wit:

QUESTION FROM THE AUDIENCE: "What was the most important moment in your career?"

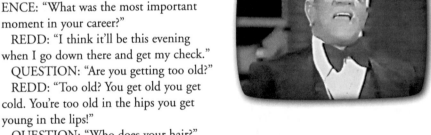

REDD: "I think it'll be this evening when I go down there and get my check."

QUESTION: "Are you getting too old?"

REDD: "Too old? You get old you get cold. You're too old in the hips you get young in the lips!"

QUESTION: "Who does your hair?"

REDD: "Anybody. Who does your lips?"

The sketches were better than the usual variety fare, with Redd "walking off the set" in the middle of routines over differences with the producers and just generally acting the petulant, spoiled superstar role. The entire program was an undisciplined, unbridled affair—brilliant when it worked, odd but interesting when it didn't, coming off like a variety show produced in the Bizarro world. *The Redd*

Redd Foxx on his third wife: "I just opened my wallet and there she was."

Foxx Comedy Hour was an excellent effort overall, with the star at the top of his game, but the production ended up one of the lowest-rated shows of the year.

With *Comedy Hour* cancelled in just six weeks, ABC bought out his contract and Redd bounced around doing his Vegas act and appearing as a guest on what few variety shows were left on television.

Redd's next series, *Sanford* in January, 1980, was an attempt by NBC to revive the Fred Sanford character with new producers and none of the old series regulars except Rollo (Nathaniel Taylor).

Fred is still in the junkyard, but now saddled with an obese, live-in good-ol'-boy named Cal who has invested in the "business."

Fred is also dating a wealthy Beverly Hills socialite with a stereo-typically stuffy family. When initial ratings proved shallow, LaWanda Page was brought in as Aunt Ester, but without strong scripts this lackadaisical misadventure lasted only a few months.

Six years later, ABC tried a new approach. This time, instead of being a cantan-kerous old coot, Redd became nice-guy newstand owner Al Hughes. In *The Redd Foxx Show*, Al lives with his adopted streetwise little white girl Toni (Pamela Segall). Also featured in the cast were Nathaniel "Rollo" Taylor (as Jim-Jam), Barry Van Dyke (*Diagnosis Murder*), Theodore Wilson (*Sanford Arms*), Sinbad, and "Iron Jaw" Wilson, with a theme song by Kool and the Gang. One notable episode featured guest-star Carroll O'Connor (Archie Bunker), a first-time meet-ing of these '70s sitcom icons

After filming just a handful of episodes and seeing disappointing results, *The Redd Foxx Show* was re-tooled. Out went the kid and in came Al's combative ex-wife Felicia (Beverly Todd) to generate tension and get a few insults flying. It was a vain attempt to make the show more *Sanford*-like. *The Redd Foxx Show* lasted only four months and hard times followed for the comedian.

It looked like Redd's luck was finally turning around when Eddie Murphy cast him in *Harlem Nights*. Though the 1989 film was a relative flop, critics agreed that supporting players Redd Foxx and Della Reese stole the movie. But bankruptcy followed for the comedian that same year as the IRS swept down on him for unpaid back taxes. "I was treated like I wasn't human," he lamented to the press after the IRS removed him from his home and took everything he owned.

What happened to all the money Foxx made with his long run on *Sanford and Son* and that big ABC contract? Much of it went up his nose. Three divorces and an otherwise extravagant lifestyle left him with few assets by the end of the '80s.

Redd's real name was John Sanford; his brother was called Fred.

261

Redd's strong showing in *Harlem Nights* led to a new TV series in 1991—*The Royal Family*, co-starring Della Reese and produced by Eddie Murphy as part of his development deal with CBS. Redd and Della had known each other for some twenty years, working together in Vegas and on television several times (including an episode of *Sanford and Son*) and the ease they had with one another showed in the final production. Critics were kind, network promotion was high and ratings respectable for the debut of *The Royal Family* with numbers getting better each week.

Redd Foxx was still bitter. When asked by *Ebony* magazine in 1991 what his thoughts were about returning to television, the comedian moaned, "The IRS will come in and take the money anyway, and have me living like a bum. Whatever comes out of it, comes out. I'm so disillusioned about the last one that I don't have any thoughts, really." Ironically, *The Royal Family* was not the first title for the show. "They had an idea called *Chest Pains*, but that sounded too much like Fred Sanford." It was a sadly prophetic title.

On October 11, 1991 (just a month after the first episode aired), Redd Foxx suffered a massive heart attack during rehearsals. At first the cast and crew laughed at him; they thought he was joking around, doing his "I'm coming, Elizabeth" shtick from *Sanford and Son*. He was always clowning on the set.

This was no joke, but no one on the set was willing to immediately help as Redd Foxx lay dying. No member of the crew wanted to risk his job and be known as the person who injured the star of the show, just in case he was okay later.

Della Reese (the star of CBS's *Touched by an Angel*) ran to his side and prayed over him, pleading, "Don't die, Redd, don't die!" but it was to no avail. Reese performed the funeral service in Las Vegas, attended by most of Foxx's cronies from his nightclub and television years. Notably missing: Demond Wilson.

His death was written into *The Royal Family*, but Redd was playing the sympathetic character with a nagging wife, so it appeared to the audience that Della Reese had yelled at the poor guy until he had a heart attack and died! Redd Foxx was replaced by the acerbic Jackée (*227*) but *The Royal Family* passed quietly after three months.

A Flip Wilson impostor attended Redd Foxx's funeral and was photographed in *People* magazine hugging Della at the service.

The Night Chicago Died
(from embarrassment)

On November 22, 1987, video hackers managed to override the Chicago PBS station's broadcast of *Dr. Who* for ninety seconds and replace it with a signal beamed from their secret location. Drunk with mad power, they also hijacked the WGN-TV signal for a several moments.

With the ability to control one of the world's largest broadcast markets firmly in their grasp, what was their motive? Were they terrorists with a hell-bent message of doom? Or was this a people's uprising, a trial run before they would take back the airwaves from the purveyors of lowest-common-denominator entertainment? Perhaps they would use their newfound platform to present great works of drama reminiscent of the anthology programs of the '50s, or the whimsical but wholesome sitcoms of the '60s? What Chicagoans were treated to instead were a couple of dorks wearing Max Headroom masks dropping their trousers and getting spanked, while the camera panned wildly about, exposing a plain corrugated metal background. It was probably shot in someone's garage, but, then again, Bill Gates started that way . . .

This incident made the national news but the perpetrators were never caught in spite of an investigation. You have to admire the nerve of these guys—true, it wasn't Shakespeare, but the networks had a hard time filling the airwaves when *they* first got started.

Of course, we all know if the ratings had been good for the *Show Me Your Ass and I'll Paddle It* show, it would still be on today in Chicago.

Dusty, Nature Boy, & the Legend of Baby Doll

Crockett Promotion's Worldwide Wrestling

by **Billy Ingram** & **John Hitchcock**

In the mid-1940s, when television was brand-new technology, producers began exploring ways to attract an audience with exciting visual content. Radio was still the dominant medium for home entertainment; television was just beginning to define its identity and needed to create programming that radio couldn't replicate.

Professional (read: theatrical) wrestling was the first sport to become popular on the tube because it was inexpensive to stage and relatively easy to shoot. With those old heavy-duty TV cameras tied to inch-thick cables, broadcasters needed a tightly confined spectacle. Wrestling and boxing were naturals. By the '50s, local stations filled several hours each week with matches featuring famous old-school wrestlers like the Baron and Gorgeous George battling alongside popular local bruisers. In the '80s wrestling went mainstream with national superstars like Hulk Hogan and Andre the Giant raking in millions from pay-per-view matches, books, movies, videos, and dolls.

Pro-wrestling is more than just sport, it's blue collar ballet, a soap opera for guys.

To set up a good match, you have to weave a compelling story with characters people care about. No one did that better than the syndicated NWA Mid-Atlantic Championship Wrestling programs from the '70s and '80s, produced by Crockett Promotions out of Charlotte, North Carolina.

As I write this, one of Crockett's biggest stars, "Nature Boy" Ric Flair, is at the top of his game, just as he was back in 1985 during NWA's golden age. Flair trained in the AWA in Minneapolis, moving to Charlotte in 1974. He survived a horrendous plane crash on October 4, 1975, a tragedy that ended the career of the legendary Johnny Valentine. Six months later, Ric Flair made his comeback and did it with a vengeance; he is considered to be the greatest wrestler of all time.

TIED TO THE STAKE,
AND I MUST STAY THE COURSE

As with any career path, Ric Flair has made more than a few enemies and found himself at the center of some intense feuds and outrageous ambushes over the years. Needless to say, he and his teammates "the Four Horsemen" (Ole and Arn Anderson and Tully Blanchard) were responsible for more than their share of dirty tricks against unsuspecting opponents as well.

Some of Flair's toughest televised battles were against foes like Ivan and Nikita Koloff, Wahoo McDaniel, and Magnum TA. He and Dusty "The American Dream" Rhodes in particular were long-time rivals, carrying on one of the most famous feuds in Mid-Atlantic history. These mice and rats and such small deer had been Nature Boy's food for ten long years.

During one brutal, fenced-in match in 1985, the Russian Nikita Koloff had Flair on the ropes and badly injured when Dusty surprised everyone by bravely entering the ring to stop the slaughter. He quickly vanquished the Russians, giving Ric Flair time to recuperate. In a shocking display of Reagan-era gratitude, Flair's teamates rushed the ring, blindsiding Dusty just as Nature Boy padlocked the cage door and gleefully joined in the ruthless beating. Ingratitude, thou marble-hearted fiend!

For the next few minutes, the Four Horsemen did as much damage as they could to the nearly unconscious Rhodes. Dusty's buddies looked on helplessly, unable to breech the cage as he was pummelled mercilessly by four opponents at once. Dusty was carried out on a stretcher that night, the bones in his leg shattered.

TIME SHALL UNFOLD WHAT PLAITED CUNNING HIDES

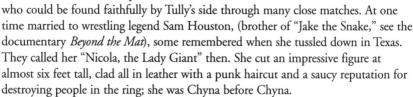

Ric Flair's teamate Tully Blanchard had it all in 1985. He was a former (and future) US Heavyweight Champion, he was rich, and when he searched the world over for the most desirable woman on earth, "the Perfect Ten," he found her.

Her name was Baby Doll (aka Nicole or possibly Nicola Roberts), a statuesque, blond bombshell who could be found faithfully by Tully's side through many close matches. At one time married to wrestling legend Sam Houston, (brother of "Jake the Snake," see the documentary *Beyond the Mat*), some remembered when she tussled down in Texas. They called her "Nicola, the Lady Giant" then. She cut an impressive figure at almost six feet tall, clad all in leather with a punk haircut and a saucy reputation for destroying people in the ring; she was Chyna before Chyna.

In 1984, Nicole turned up down south with a new identity and a brand new dream. She realized if she couldn't be champion herself, she could be the *girlfriend* of the champion. After teaming with Tully Blanchard as his ringside valet, she saw her vision blooming into reality—until one unscheduled sparring in 1985 left tough-guy Tully Blanchard reeling and Baby Doll rethinking her future.

Tully was in the ring one ordinary night, finishing up a journeyman's match (with Baby Doll on the side cheering him to victory) when he suddenly found himself facing one of Dusty Rhodes' fiercest allies, mighty Magnum TA, who surreptitiously entered the ring disguised as a cop. By the time Tully noticed the intruder, poor Baby Doll was handcuffed to the ropes and struggling, forced to watch as Magnum delivered his devastating move—the "Belly-to-Belly"—on her man Tully.

Appearing at a fan appreciation event in Greensboro, North Carolina a few days later, Tully publicly slapped Baby Doll for not helping

These shows were offered to stations on a barter basis—get the show for free, but run our commercials!

him against Magnum. It fell to Dusty Rhodes to gallantly come to her rescue. Upon such sacrifices, the gods themselves throw incense; Baby Doll shocked wrestling insiders by running straight into Dusty's arms. Tully's bitter archrival, "the American Dream," now had his coveted Doll. It was the shot heard 'round the wrestling world, signaling the senses-shattering mayhem that inevitably lay ahead.

OH, THAT WAY
MADNESS LIES

When Television Heavyweight Champion and humble son of a plumber Dusty Rhodes strutted into the ring to face Tully Blanchard one electric night in winter 1986, it was with the knowledge that Tully's beloved protégé was now in his arms. Rhodes was out for blood, especially since Blanchard was one of the men who ambushed him in the ring and maliciously crushed his leg just a few weeks earlier—a leg now protected for this match by a specially made, steel-reinforced boot.

That boot was the subject of a bit of controversy. It was made to protect Dusty's leg and allow him to make the match. Without it, he would be unfairly vulnerable to attack, but his opponents cried foul. They suspected Dusty would use the hardened footwear as a weapon. The American Dream assured his critics that he would fight clean.

Despite his injury (or maybe because of it) Dusty Rhodes was unbeatable that night; he even brought Baby Doll up to dance around the ring to further piss Blanchard off. As Baby Doll led the cheers from the sidelines, Rhodes unleashed a firestorm that laid waste even to the referee, who was rendered unconscious on the cold coliseum floor. Dusty took advantage of that lapse in supervision to use his reinforced boot as a hammer, crushing Tully's ankle in the ring (in a bold move known as irony).

Not merely content with winning a hard-fought match, the American Dream took a moment to attack Blanchard's manager, James J. Dillon, who was ringside. While Dusty was applying the sleeper hold, Dillon managed to surreptitiously toss a pair of brass knuckles into the ring, shifting the balance of power. Blanchard beat Dusty's face to a pulp with those brass knuckles and a free-for-all ensued, when the referee recovered and Tully was judged victorious. Even Baby Doll sprang into the ring to angrily display her outrage, a first hint that perhaps she wasn't quite as dainty as everyone believed.

THAT GLIB AND OILY ART,
TO SPEAK AND PURPOSE NOT

As the outspoken manager of wrestling's young guns the Midnite Express, Jim Cornette was a picture of preppy '80s style in 1986.

Jim Cornette is one of the great TV personalities of all time in my opinion.

Always neatly dressed in *Miami Vice*-style tie, sportcoat, and button-down shirt with his tennis racquet consistently at hand, Cornette exuded a cool confidence that masked an egomaniacal, vicious malcontent. Cornette's ironic prop—the tennis racquet, symbol of leisure—got more use in and around the ring than it ever got on the court—Cornette blitzed his wrestler's opponents with it every chance he got.

As for his attitude toward the fans, Cornette was prone to making comments like, "As for all the people wanting to know about the Midnite Express, writing all the cards, all the letters, all the phone calls. The fact of the matter is it's none of your business so don't you be bothering us with your crummy comments and your stupid questions because we don't have time for ya."

Nor was he known to respect his opponents outside of the ring. In one infamous in-studio confrontation with Baby Doll, Cornette demanded that she deliver his rambling message to Dusty: "He is going to apologize to me and he's going

apologize to Big Bubba and he's going to admit that you're ugly and he's a goof and we were right all along and he is going to look in that camera and he is going to apologize, most importantly, to my mother in Louisville, Kentucky, who has demanded it, and I'm going to get that and I'm going to get that soon. Now you go back, Fatso, and you tell him that!" When Cornette didn't get the response he wanted, he instructed his bodyguard Big Bubba to shove the unsuspecting Baby Doll to the floor.

Today, Jim Cornette is a highly respected businessman working for the WWF where he operates the Mid-Ohio Wrestling "boot camp" for up-and-coming players. I certainly hope he's not responsible for teaching sportsmanship and ethics, because there was an incident in the summer of '86 that Jim Cornette might wish to forget; it's undoubtedly one of the most shameful moments in the entire history of professional sports.

One sweltering summer eve, "the Midnite Express" (Loverboy Dennis and Beautiful Bobby) rushed the ring, tossed everybody out (including the referee) to allow Jim Cornette to step up and take the mic. He called out Dusty Rhodes with insults about his trademark cowboy hats: "That sure is a nice hat, Mr. Dream. Did you get a free cup of soup with that hat?" This was after weeks of rude comments broadcast over the air like, "Let me tell you something, Dusty Rhodes and Magnum TA. You bring Baby Doll, bring her right on down there to ringside, set her big fat rear end right in the chair there, and she is going to open those big wide eyes and she is going to watch her boys, 'Dolly's boys,' get embarrassed, get humiliated, get struck down by the greatest tag team in professional wrestling!"

The taunts had their desired effect. When Dusty could take no more, he flew into the ring only to be overwhelmed by Cornette's posse and brought down hard. He

John Hitchcock (co-author of this article) used to mercilessly harass Magnum TA during the live matches.

watched in horror as his precious Baby Doll was restrained by Beautiful Bobby while Jim Cornette slammed her repeatedly with a tennis racquet to the stomach.

Naturally one would expect Jim Cornette and the Midnight Express to flee the arena in embarrassment. Instead, they triumphantly bragged about the whole thing as announcer David "Whip Him Like a Dog" Crockett threw down his microphone and stormed off the set in disgust.

Microphone in hand, Cornette expressed no remorse over the incident. In fact, he taunted his victims mercilessly from the announcer's booth as Dusty and his teammates carried their broken Doll from the arena: "You call that a man? I call that a piece of garbage! They're going down the aisle right now, to cart the trash out! I can whip you any day of the week, Baby Doll!"

WE'RE VILLAINS BY NECESSITY, FOOLS BY HEAVENLY COMPULSION

Considered by many to be the most creative and effective manager of all time, Jim Cornette's flaws (if he had any) lay in his over-exuberance, his all-out need to win and his obvious unfamiliarity with the concept of good sportsmanship. Still, even forgiving the man's excesses, he had gone too far this time.

As a result of his assault on Baby Doll and numerous other dirty dealings, Cornette found himself at the mercy of two mysterious men in black during an unexpected ring invasion. The James Boys, faces covered in dark masks and clad in black trench coats, rushed the mat during one of Cornette's matches, easily bouncing the Midnite Express from the ring. The James Boys didn't come to wrestle that night, they came for Cornette, wrapping a rope around his neck and carrying him bodily from the arena to a waiting El Camino in the parking lot.

Strung to the back bumper, with the vehicle revved up and ready to tear off, Jim

Cornette was certain to become a bloody smear across the Coliseum asphalt when the Midnite Express rescued him just in the nick of time. Observers noted that Baby Doll could clearly be seen laughing from the back seat of that speeding El Camino.

True fans knew that the James Boys were in fact none other than Dusty Rhodes and Magnum TA in disguise—out for some "western vigilante-style justice." "This is an old

world solution to a new world problem," was their unremorseful take on things.

UNDIVULGED CRIMES, UNWHIPP'D OF JUSTICE
(or Payback's a Bitch!)

"When the mighty fall, the jackals come to call." Shakespeare first wrote those words some four hundred years ago, but Dusty Rhodes came to know all too well what they mean in modern times.

The American Dream had a score to settle in 1986 with Heavyweight Champion Ric Flair. But no card was scheduled between these two bitter enemies the night they rumbled unexpectedly down in Dixie.

Conveniently, Dusty defeated his scheduled foe before the bell was even rung. He called out over the audience for Ric Flair to enter the ring, daring him to come forward and face his fury. The audience was with Dusty all the way, they chanted Flair's name until the champion was forced to respond.

"To be the man," Ric Flair would say, "you've got to beat the man." Flair walked that aisle confidently, dressed in what looked like one of Mae West's beaded nightgowns. He was ready to do battle, agitated and fed up with the relentless taunts from Dusty. Hardly able to contain his excitement as Flair entered the ring, Dusty kissed his true love Baby Doll for luck as Flair passed his championship belt over to the referee. This one would count.

The impromptu match-up didn't go well for the champion from the start. Beaten badly by Dusty, frustrated and desperate, Flair even lunged at Baby Doll to try to get at Rhodes. The Coliseum erupted in turmoil when the Four Horsemen rushed the ring to sabotage Dusty's brief moment of triumph and a general melee ensued as the program abruptly left the air that night.

The next time Dusty was in the same arena with the Four Horsemen, he was fury personified—daring them to come out from the dressing rooms and face him in the ring. Ole and Arne Anderson, along with Tully Blanchard, answered the call together and hammered Dusty to the mat before his teammates could come to his rescue. With so many recent

Today, Tully Blanchard is a man of the cloth—let he who is without sin, indeed!

humiliations and stunning losses for Dusty Rhodes, Baby Doll could see from the sidelines that her goal of being the girlfriend of a World Champion was evaporating from sight. It was a dream she was determined to have come true—but at what cost, she must have asked herself.

As Dusty lay stricken on the mat with his opponents demolishing him (again), Baby Doll's mind was surely racing toward the future. She was born to be the doll of champion, she reasoned, and Dusty was facing his greatest challenge ever, an upcoming match with his arch-rival Nature Boy Ric Flair. It was time to work her special brand of magic and take control of her destiny.

THE GODS ARE JUST,
AND OF OUR PLEASANT VICES
MAKE INSTRUMENTS TO PLAGUE US.

The Charlotte Coliseum was sold out and the audience was rocking the floorboards for the start of the World Championship match in 1986 between Dusty Rhodes and Ric Flair. Way down south in the land of vengeance, Nature Boy was on his home turf, but he would need every advantage against this bull of the woods (if you will). Dusty was still highly irritated over the craven attacks inflicted upon himself and his beloved Baby Doll and couldn't wait to get his hands on Ric Flair again. He entered the ring proudly that night in Carolina, with his loyal lady by his side, as she had been through dozens of matches. After all, behind every man . . .

Flair was in peak form, but Dusty was a force of nature that night, the match was his to win from the beginning. Within moments of the bell, Flair was reeling, nearly passed out from the blows. As Dusty went to make an easy pin (and pick up that championship belt he paid a hellish price for), unexpectedly—seemingly out of nowhere—Baby Doll sneaked along the side of the ring, grabbed Ric Flair's limp foot and placed it on the ropes. As the rules require, the ref stopped the pin count and Dusty recoiled in confusion. "What had just happened?," he seemed to say. He knew he had Flair pinned! The audience couldn't believe their eyes as shock and anger pierced the arena.

Momentary confusion gave Nature Boy the advantage he needed, knocking the injured legs out from under his opponent, causing Dusty to crumble to the mat. Even Ric Flair looked confused in the ring, he was obviously as surprised as anyone at what had happened. How could Baby Doll snatch sure victory from her own man's grasp?

With Dusty flailing on the canvas, Flair applied the dreaded Figure Four leg lock, necessity's sharp pinch! Dusty, his fragile leg causing him excruciating pain, was breaking away from Flair's hold when Baby Doll once again gave Flair the leverage he needed to move Dusty back into a position of pain.

Bursting free, Dusty's fury became uncontrollable as he took out his aggressions on Flair, who couldn't bear the savage beating and went down, cowering in the corner. In the confusion, referee Tommy Young was violently bounced from the ring and knocked cold while Dusty roared into Flair with wild abandon.

She had risked it all for Ric Flair and the World Champion now lay in certain defeat. Baby Doll knew that there could be no turning back. The Jezebel from Hell grabbed a metal folding chair, carried it into the ring and began swinging wildly at Dusty. The Charlotte harlot missed her target, but Dusty grabbed the chair and used it on Flair—until Referee Young regained consciousness and called a halt to the fiasco.

Confusion reigned both in and out of the ring. Ric Flair, miraculously recovered, appeared smiling on camera after the match bragging about his victory—and his new trophy. "Diamonds are forever and so is Baby Doll," Flair boasted to announcer Bob Caudle afterward, "It's now the Four Horsemen and one mare!"

EPILOGUE
(by Steve Byrd)

Before Ted Turner bought Jim Crockett's Charlotte company out in the late '80s and turned it into WCW, it was the dominant territorial promotion in the NWA. Crockett's syndicated program was called Worldwide Wrestling, which was renamed WCW Worldwide when Turner took over. As for the NWA, which still has its territorial franchises as well as a few nationally-televised super-franchises, you can find out about them at *nwawrestling.com*

Baby Doll was played by a lady whose name, I believe, was Nickla Roberts. She was, in my opinion, a pioneer female manager (I prefer not to use the term "valet"). I forgot who Baby Doll was managing, but I do remember another female nicknamed Precious (often called "the bodacious Precious"), who was in the corner of Jim Garvin.

World Championship Wrestling was originally the title of TBS's weekly wrestling show starting in 1977, when it was packaged by Georgia Championship Wrestling, Inc., and originally hosted by Gordon Solie, perhaps the best wrestling announcer there ever was (God rest his soul).

When the GCW company shut down in 1985, Vince McMahon's World Wrestling Federation (WWF) had the TBS slot for a short while before Jim Crockett took over later that year, until the Turner purchase.

Two signature Crockett supercards, Great American Bash and Starrcade, were an important part of Turner- (later AOL Time Warner-) owned WCW's pay-per-view roster, while the weekly programs on TBS and its sister channel, TNT, evolved by the mid-1990s into Nitro and Thunder, both of whom gave the WWF a run for its money. But, by 1998, it was the WWF that reinvented itself by making its product more attractive to a new generation of fans, which put WCW out of business by April 2000. Two years later, a copyright dispute with the World Wildlife Fund forced Vince McMahon to "get the 'F' out" and rename his wrestling organization WWE (World Wrestling Entertainment).

"Pray you now, forget and forgive." —Shakespeare

"I've fallen...
and I can't
get up!"

This pretty much sums up the '80s for me . . .

TVparty! CD-ROM

Film edits by Billy Ingram
CD produced by James Counts
Interactive by Jenny Miles

INSTRUCTIONS: This book and companion CD-ROM should give you several non-consecutive moments of pleasure now and in the future if used correctly. Failure to carefully follow these instructions will void the null warranty.

PREPARING FOR USE: BOOK

This book is presented in book format. This requires the manual turning of pages and aggressive user-initiated eye-brain activity. Eyesight recommended, but comprehension not required and can hinder enjoyment.

WARNING: Always wear protective gear to avoid injury when reading books. Plastic gloves at least .10 mil thick should be worn while handling pages for proper protection. Not responsible for blood loss or stainage due to paper cuts.

When burning this book, please do so in a properly ventilated area with fire marshal or clergy supervision. Fumes may cause dizziness as it is printed on 100 percent hemp paper.

CD-ROM INSTRUCTIONS:

Turn computer on (see manufacturers specifications).

Insert CD-ROM into the CD-ROM slot of your computer. If you do not have a CD-ROM slot on your computer, insert CD-ROM into nearest trash bin.

WARNING: Insertion of this or any other consumer product into orifices not intended for reading or viewing could result in embarrassment and deep tissue damage.

The TVparty! CD-ROM is Mac and PC compatible:

(Double-click the icon marked **TVPARTY**)

Once CD-ROM is inserted into computer, point eyes in direction of computer screen. Yell to the kids to shut up, that daddy and/or mommy is busy right now and could mommy and/or daddy please get just a few moments of peace and quiet? If this is ineffective, remind children who pays the rent and the phone bill and the cable. Would they like to see the cable turned off? Would they like to take their lunch in a paper bag tomorrow? Please try these simple ploys before calling tech support and/or 911. Because there isn't any tech support.

If you wish to view the CD-ROM more than once, please buy another copy of the book. Displaying the content of this CD-ROM or showing a page in this book to your friends is a violation of copyright law. If you wish to display CD-ROM content or lend this book to someone, please set up a direct debit account with TVparty by sending your bank account number and a blank check to: *Born Every Minute,* PO Box 666, Greensboro, NC 27401.

ALL STORIES WRITTEN BY BILLY INGRAM EXCEPT WHERE NOTED.

Book layout, graphics, and editorial matter © 2002 TVparty except where noted. TVparty is a trademark. All characters contained within this book are copyright their respective owners. All material copyright their creators unless otherwise noted. All editorial matter copyright by their respective authors.

These magazines and newspapers (and many others) were used as a source: *Saturday Evening Post, Look, Life, Saturday Review, New York Times, Vanity Fair, LA Times, Chicago Tribune, Newsweek, Time, US News & World Report, LA Herald Examiner, Valley News, Confidential, Radio-TV Mirror, Ebony Magazine, Esquire, Playboy, Theater Arts, Film Pictorial, Screenland, New Yorker, Washington Post, Baltimore Sun, LA Weekly, Jet Magazine.*

These books were used as general reference and are highly recommended: *Total Television* by Alex McNeil, *The Complete Directory to Prime Time Network TV Shows* by Tim Brooks and Earle Marsh, *The Encyclopedia of Daytime Television* by Wesley Hyatt, *Unsold Television Pilots* by Lee Goldberg, *TV Guide: The First 25 Years* by Jay S. Harris, and many, many others. If I'd known there would be a test at the end I would have taken notes! In most cases, I had video resources for much of what is covered here as well. Most of the video images we used for screen captures had to be manipulated quite extensively for print.

I am eternally grateful for the input provided by James Counts. This book and CD-ROM is a true collaboration. James and I have worked together on an enormous number of challenging projects over the last eight years; he's truly the most talented and gifted person I've worked with. He's also my best friend.

SPECIAL THANKS TO: Berk Ingram, who saved TVparty from extinction several years ago and who has provided me with a wealth of wisdom, Bill and Mellissa Tankersley for sound business advice, Susan Grant for taking care of business and being such a dear friend, and my sister Rives Cox for being so nice and kind. Thanks also to Rose Owens, Jane King, Mert Johnson, Anne Kersey Keyes, and Bea Vaughn for keeping me fed and Marion Hubbard for the nice getaways. Wheaton and Michael Pike get big ups as well.

GRATEFUL APPRECIATION TO: Jeffrey Stern, Devon Freeny, Alex Boring, Erin Kahl, and the folks at Bonus Books who gave us the opportunity to do this project the way we envisioned.

ALSO THANKS TO: Matthew Coleman for incredible patience and for showing me the best of British television.

WE'RE GRATEFUL TO: Mike Shaver, Brian Karimzad, Justin Kaplowitz, Steve King, Johnnie Putman, Dan Ferreira, James Taylor, Steven S. Butler, Jack Murphy, Hal Lifson, Jim Crotts, Chuck Wild, Kathy Lelli, Mike Ransom, Bob Mosley, Delbert "Dellie Goose" Hutchinson, Hope Fanning Ingram, Randy Cox, and to those who provided comments published here.

JAMES THANX: Billy and Bonus Books for making it all come true. Jennie B. and Howard R. for support, Matt for love, David and Beth for keeping it on the down low. Kacy for flair and common sense. Jen and Nick for bridging the gap. Sharlene my travel ace, Mayaz, Lara my Virginia relative, Ian and Neil across London, Julie anne the musical genius, Kirst, Ricardo, and Marina, Neil the Duke, Emsk in the window, Michael at LCP, Clayton, Andy, and Mo—cooler heads prevail. Cheers to Johnathan, Simon, Sherrie, Byron, Nick, Matt, Paul, Diane, Hampus, Nathan, Richard, Chris, Mike, Craig, Strat, Ian, Steve, Rory, Stephen, Antony, Tony, Simon, Craig, Norman, Joe, Terry, Chris, Wesley, Ian, Jo, Roland, Darren, John and the whole Vauxhall crowd for great times and much-needed inspiration. Waves to Paul, Martin, Abigail, and Toni in Brighton. Always Meredith, Nadia, Leah, Bernie, Jens, Andrea and Joachim for hospitality in Berlin. Passports to Andy in Glasgow, Robie in Milan, and Nate in Paris. Thanks to Anne-Marie, Neil, Georges, and Gareth for team spirit! Kudos to Keith, Stephanie, and the Bindlestiffs in New York, and Jerry, Judy, Kate, and Steve. Kisses to David, Steve, Heather, and Tal in San Francisco. Respect to the Greensboro Crew especially most-loved Chris, Danielle, Michael and Brandi, John, Kirk, Teresa, Ben, Stacey, Lester, Chris and Fred. Swings to Julie, Aaron, and Gabriella in Asheville and Matthew C. in Durham. Props to Betty, Murray, Fran, Angela, John D. and Jim O., Mike B., Wally, Shawn and Ken, Kim, Margie, Jeff, Alan, and all at RC. Thanks to Susan, Sandra, Betty, Tim, and Ann at PHI, Joe and all of the Michels, Jeffrey, Kimberley, Lori, Vicki and all at TEC. Hello to Susan Grant, Ted, John Matthewz, Ricky, Frankleigh, Shawn, Ian at Kinko's, Jeff, Jean, Wendy, Tom, Sharon, and Susan at THP, Arlene at Our State, Michael and Kathy, Chris K., Ed, Kent, and of course our boy Lloyd. I always forget something or spell it wrong, but you're all stars. All hail brave Thai Dave, Jang, and Spooky in Asia!

SHOUT-OUT TO: Elizabeth Bell, my high school art teacher who taught me all I needed to know to be able to achieve my dreams. Good teachers are the real heroes in our society.

ABOUT THE BOOK DESIGNER:

A passion for electronics in the early '80s led James R. Counts to a career in digital media, creating advertising for a wide variety of clients in publishing and business. James has instructed college students in principles of multimedia graphic design, focusing on the significance of art in the digital domain.

James collects vintage drum machines, synthesisers, and personal computers, and has been producing electronic music for many years.

He adjusted his focus to newer media simultaneous to the development of *TVparty.com,* designing the trademarked *TVparty.com* colorbar and test-pattern logos, while developing internationally recognized interactive campaigns on the Internet for radio and entertainment clients.

James art-directed and co-designed *TVparty! Television's Untold Tales,* and produced the accompanying CD-ROM. A native of North Carolina, he is a design consultant in London.

ABOUT YOUR HOST:

As the creator of critically-acclaimed broadcast sensation *TVparty.com,* Billy Ingram became the first to bring the television experience to the internet and now commands an audience of over three hundred thousand visitors a month.

In addition to numerous Clio award–winning print ad and broadcast commercial collaborations, Billy has designed Academy Award™ campaigns for the biggest Hollywood film stars, and created artwork for dozens of major movie posters. He is also a pioneering developer of Internet multimedia content for radio stations, record companies, and other entertainment ventures.

Billy Ingram has appeared in theatrical productions around the country and in several motion pictures. He is currently a sought-after guest on radio and television programs nationally.

Ingram wrote, edited, and co-designed *TVparty! Television's Untold Tales*, and compiled and edited films from the *TVparty!* archives for the CD-ROM.

Living the life of a jet-set superstar playboy, Billy Ingram resides in Greensboro, NC, and London.

For classic TV books, video, or DVD, visit: *http://www.tvparty.com/order*

ON YOUR CD-ROM:

A Very Bette Christmas

"Sit *down*, children!" Bette has a surprise for the kids on Christmas morning . . . no presents! Daddy's at war, so the kids get war bonds instead of bikes. Oh, come on, Bette. You could have afforded bicycles for *both* of those kids if you'd spent a little less on that dress and hairdo! But then, Bette Davis was never known as the perfect mother, was she?

1950s: Flipping Channels

Oh, to go back in time. With that in mind, I spliced together a little edit of 1950s programs. How many can you recognize? *Captain Midnight, Andy's Gang, Super Circus, Lucky Pup,* and *Mr. I. Magination* all fly by as we flip through the channels of our imaginary television set.

Tallulah Bankhead

An example of what Tallulah Bankhead was like on television. Hide the children and small dogs.

Radioactive Models

This may be the most outrageous commercial ever filmed. It's bad enough to find out the government was doing atomic tests on people, now we find out Madison Avenue was doing it too! As the commercial begins, our model is prancing around downtown in a fur coat, completely self-involved, checking her make-up because there are so many shops explore. Later, in order to prove the cleansing power of Dorothy Gray Salon Cold Cream, her face is actually covered in radioactive dirt—verified with a Geiger counter. Busy day, indeed!

Read a Book Lately?

This is a PSA for libraries that ran throughout the '60s. I really like the simple animation and, let's face it, how many books come with a video that explains how reading works? Don't have a computer? Go to your local public library to view the TVparty CD-ROM. That's what you pay taxes for! (Remind your librarians of that if they say they don't have a copy of the book.)

Super 66

In this edit, you can see for yourself the influence that shows like *Batman* had on TV advertising. For example, all you had to do if you were hassled in the '60s (if you believe one of these ads) was buy the right tennis shoes, blow the Keds' Space Whistle that came with every pair, and Colonel Keds would fly in and kick everybody's ass. See, having the right sneakers was just as important then as it is now! Also included: fall previews for superhero and sci-fi shows of the mid-'60s.

Philly Home Movies

Mike Pentz sent us home movies of his fave Philly kid show stars, so we hacked them together for you . . . *you axed for it!* Here's a rare opportunity to see your favorite stars from the past and present! The line-up in order: *Bertie the Bunyip* show opening recorded live off TV in 1963, Happy the Clown live at Doney Park 1960s, *Pixanne* opening, Rex Morgan live at Doney Park 1960s, *Gene London* opening, Sally Starr at Hershey Park 1970, Sally Starr today.

"My mother took me to the *Happy the Clown* show once and I remember getting a ride on the little tractor around the studio and seeing the birthday cake with the candles that would come back on when you blew them out. The guy that played Happy the Clown, unfortunately, was a miserable s.o.b. He was not very nice to us at all, but I still had a good time and I relive that day as if it were yesterday. It's a shame that there are no clips of those shows available so that we can show our kids."—Yvonne Taylor

Quisp vs. Quake

I loved these crazy commercials as a kid. Cool character designs! The cereal wasn't bad either.

1967 Promos I

Every year, the network stars had to film custom promotions for the larger affiliates. These outtakes are from a station in Tidewater, Florida. Instead of running the fall preview special as it came from the network, larger stations could cut in their own customised footage of the celebrities plugging their local shows between the new series' previews.

Local Kid Shows of the '60s and '70s

Here you'll find some examples of the local children's shows covered in the book, including ultra-rare footage of *Clancy and Willie*, *The Old Rebel Show* from North Carolina, Bob McAllister's *Wonderama* when Muhammad Ali was a guest, and mucho mas. This was slapped together with a smattering of crazy commercials that warped a generation!

Kids and Guns

The opening bit is from the *Romper Room* episode referred to in the book (page 100). Remember the little kid who was late to the set and causing problems? He's got a lot to say on the show about guns. Better watch your back, Miss Sally! Followed by toy gun commercials from the mid-'60s.

1967 Promos II

More of the same, featuring Mike Connors (*Mannix*), Irene Ryan (Granny), Bea Benaderet (*Petticoat Junction*) just a year before her death, Pat Paulsen (*Smothers Brothers Comedy Hour*), Jonathan Harris (Dr. Smith), Frank Sutton (Sgt. Carter), and others.

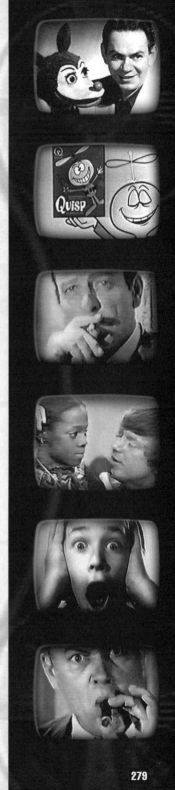

TVafterparty!

WHO KILLED TV'S SUPERMAN

Superman and all related characters, the distinct likenesses thereof, and all related indicia are trademarks of DC Comics. Visit *DCcomics.com* for more Superman-related stuff; there are some great reprint collections available. If you want more information on George Reeves, the best place on the internet is *jimnolt.com*. There you'll find a wealth of info on the TV series *The Adventures of Superman*. *Superman: Serial to Cereal* by Gary Grossman is the best book ever published on the series; it may still be out of print but it's well worth searching for.

A SHORT HISTORY OF THE LAUGH TRACK

Article by and copyright 2002 Ben Glenn, II. Ben is one incredible writer; his work is very popular on *TVparty.com*.

WINKY DINK AND YOU

Illustration of Winky Dink on front page by James Counts. Screen captures from the TVparty collection.

BETTE DAVIS ON TV

In my research I read every damn book ever published on the lady, I suspect, including her two autobiographies. Also: *I'd Love to Kiss You But . . .* by Whitney Stine; *Bette and Joan: The Divine Feud* by Shaun Considine; *Bette* by Charles Higham; *My Mother's Keeper* by BD Hyman; *More Than a Woman* by James Spada; *Mother Goddam* by Whitney Stine; *Bette Davis* by Barbara Leaming; *Past Imperfect* by Joan Collins; *My Story* by Mary Astor; and others. A definitive listing of all of Bette's TV appearances has yet to be compiled. I did my best!

Thanks to Michael Ely for his tremendous help with this.

Thanks also to Dan Wingate who provided needed information and source video. Dan tells me about this entry I missed: "I have a recording of Bette on *Dinah's Place* interviewing Roslyn Carter at the White House! Can it even equal the description?!? Evidently someone else was scheduled to interview the First Lady and got sick. Dinah explains it on the show, but it's just amazing. There's no big climax to it, except that it feels like you're on an acid trip. Can you *imagine* the tension in that room?"

TV'S FIRST SEX SYMBOL: MARY HARTLINE

Illustrations and screen shots from the TVparty collection. Thanks to Becky Carter Kenton Lee for reminding me of how popular Mary was!

MR. ADAMS AND EVE

Much appreciation goes to Jeff Vilencia for the stories and video reference. Jeff is an independent filmmaker and leading video archivist living in Southern California. He was one of the first to submit video to TVparty and I'm very grateful for all of his input, vast knowledge, and generosity over the years. What a guy!

GERTRUDE BERG AS MOLLY

Again, thanks to Jeff V.

JOE DiMAGGIO'S FIRST WIFE

Photos from the collection of Bob French. Article copyright 2002 by Bob French, written for TVparty. This has nothing to do with TV, but I thought it had a lot of heart.

TALLULAH!

I read at least half a dozen books on the actress in preparation for this essay, including *Miss Tallulah Bankhead* by Lee Israel, Bankhead's 1952 autobiography, and many newspaper and magazine articles and interviews. Also the book *Merv* by Merv Griffin. Screen captures from the TVparty collection. I also watched a great number of her TV appearances—thanks to go out to Dan Wingate for video reference and his most valuable input. Thanks go out to Anthony J. Smith for rare photos from his private collection.

LYPSINKA'S TOP TEN

For more on Lypsinka, visit *www.lypsinka.com*. Truly, one of the most exciting and innovative stage performers around. That picture at the bottom is Lucy as "Mad Margo." Photo of Lypsinka by and copyright Russell Maynor, used with permission.

GROUCHO ON TV

Once again, I must have read a half-dozen books on Groucho, and watched hundreds of hours of appearances, and I still have my LP copy of *An Evening with Groucho*. One book I enjoyed very much was *Raising Eyebrows: My Years inside Groucho's House* by Steve Stoliar. Mark Evanier is one of my favorite pop culture writers, and I used his excellent article in *Fanfare* magazine in 1977 and his Web site *POVonline.com* as a source as well. Photo on page 52 from the TVparty collection (photographer unknown). This was an 8x10 Groucho gave out to fans.

PLAYBOY AFTER DARK

Pictured on page 58: 1) Lenny Bruce, Nat King Cole 2) Ella Fitzgerald 3) Marvin Gaye. Pictured on page 59: Hugh Hefner and unknown bunny from the first show. Pictured on page 60: 1) Lenny Bruce, Hugh Hefner 2) Cy Coleman and unknown guest 3) Hefner and Nat King Cole. Pictured on page 61: Top 1) Cy Coleman 2) Ella 3) Barbara McNair. Bottom 1) Pete Seeger 2) Hef + 2 3) Hef and unknown model.

KIDS, TV, AND GUNS

I'm not sure if I did any research for this one—it's a pretty sketchy article! The illustration on the bottom left side of page 64 is from the back of comic books circa 1967. Screen captures and photos from the TVparty collection. Roy Rogers gun set photo courtesy of Marilyn's Antiques in Godfrey, Illinois. Photo at right courtesy of Jerry Meiselman. Thanks to Jeff Vilencia for the video reference.

THE ALFALFA CONSPIRACY

Thanks to Kathy Lelli (aka LAscandals) for the information and detective work on this. It's her story. I'm sure she's uncovering another mystery as we speak. Thanks also to Kevin S. Butler, who you'll be hearing more from in volume two, if we're to be so lucky.

"PLUNK YOUR MAGIC TWANGER, FROGGY"

I get e-mail like this every day, folks!

MILKY THE CLOWN

Ed Golick is the go-to guy for Detroit's great local children's shows. See *www.detroitkidshow.com*, where they say, "This Web site looks best viewed on a Philco Predicta!" Article and photos copyright 2002 by Ed Golick, used with permission.

CAPTAIN KANGAROO

Screen captures from the TVparty collection. Not many episodes of the decades long run of *Captain Kangaroo* even exist, so don't even complain about the fuzzy photos!

THE OLD REBEL SHOW

Photos from the collection of Timm Perry. Thanks to Jim Wiglesworth (far right in picture) former co-host of the show, who also wrote the show's theme song in the '70s. Today Jim is a successful real estate agent and father to Kelly Wiglesworth from the first *Survivor* show. Jim is a true TV pioneer on several fronts: he was the first to bring Winston Cup / NASCAR racing to television. Thanks to John Hitchcock, James Counts, and to James Young for his help in putting on the *Old Rebel Show Reunion* at the Greensboro Public Library in 1999. Young is a published author and a superlative children's book illustrator. Thanks to Lee Marshall (far left) and Martha Perry for participating as well!

CAPTAIN SATELLITE

Thanks to Bob March who can be found on the Web at *www.captainsatellite.com*. Article copyright 2002 Bob March. Written for TVparty, used with permission. Photos from the collection of Bob March.

CARTOONS FROM LOCAL KID SHOWS

Thanks to Chucko the Birthday Clown, aka Charles M. Runyon, who tells us: "As for the whereabouts of Chucko, I am alive and in good health living in Oregon. Upon my departure from television my son took over the title of Chucko from 1971 through 1995. I have a lot of fond memories of the television days and love to converse by e-mail with those who have participated on our TV show from 1954 through 1961. Best regards and thanks—Chucko." Picture of *The Mighty Hercules* slate and screen captures from the TVparty collection. No, I don't just sit around all day watching cartoons—but I could!

SALLY STARR

Thanks to Hank O'Brien for the lovely photos of this Philly legend. See *www.sallystarrshow.com* for the latest on Our Gal Sal. Wasn't Sally Starr the model for the cowgirl character in *Toy Story II?* If not, she should have been! She was in the Three Stooges classic *The Outlaws Is Coming*. Will Hill writes: "One thing about kids TV at that time in the '50s and '60s was that all of these celebrities could co-exist. There seemed to be no ratings war with the three VHF stations. They all did promotions, guest appearances, and

charity work. Once in 1966 all the local kid celebs posed together at some charity event (I think it was Ronald McDonald House) for a group picture. Captain Philadelphia (an astronaut on Ch 48-UHF, sportscaster Stu Neiham), Wee Willie Webber (Ch 6 and 17), Gene London (Ch 10), Pixanne (Ch 10), Chief Halftown (Ch 6), Sally Starr (Ch 6), and Lorenzo (Ch 3) with Ronald McDonald. Does anyone out there still have that giveaway photograph?" (Thanks to Bill Webber Jr. for the picture!)

GIGGLESNORT HOTEL

Article copyright 2002 Rick Goldschmidt, written for TVparty, used with permission. Don't miss Rick's great tribute to animators Rankin Bass at *www.rankinbass.com*. Photos are all copyright 2002 Bill Jackson. All Rights Reserved, used with permission.
Bill Jackson is on the web at *www.dirtydragon.com*.

ROMPER ROOM

Romper Room photo on page 103 supplied by Chris Bischoff. Thanks to V. Scott for the story of her day on *Romper Room*. She wants to remain semi-anonymous because I think she's worried about that evil clown coming after her! I hate to break it to you, but *Romper Room* episodes were erased each day to tape the next day's show. That was typical of almost all local kid shows, so you won't find a copy of the time you were on the program back in 1973!

KID SHOW COMMERCIALS

Illustrations from the TVparty collection.

GAME SHOWS FOR KIDS

Thanks to film collector John Weber. Here's a photo of the *Video Village* home game . . .

WONDERAMA WITH BOB MCALLISTER

I received a very nice e-mail from Bob McAllister in 1998 promising to answer any questions I had about *Wonderama*. I had been getting requests for the show for years and couldn't find anything on it. Bob passed away before we were able to collaborate on a Web site, but he seemed like a really nice person and the outpouring from the industry following his death was astonishing. Equally amazing was the fact that TVparty became a conduit for that outpouring. I collected the best comments I got and created the piece in this book. No, I don't have a storehouse of *Wonderama* videos (no one does) so don't write to me with the date you were on the show and expect me to send you a tape!

SHRIMPENSTEIN

Shrimpenstein video courtesy of Jerry Beck at Cartoon Research, where they promise, "Better Living through Cartoon Research."

JOT

Picture from the TVparty collection. You have no idea how many years it took to find that one!

TWIN CITIES FAREWELLS

Article copyright 2002 Julian West, used with permission. Written for TVparty, this piece is a preview of his comprehensive book on Twin City local children's programs that some publisher should jump on right now!

TVafterparty!

DELL COMICS
Pictures from the collection of Mike Brackett. Characters and likenesses shown are the property of the respective copyright owners.

I WAS A TV CHILD STAR
Article written for TVparty by John Eimen and copyright 2002 by the author. Used with permission.

WHAT WERE THEY THINKING?!?
What was I thinking . . .?

WHY WERE THERE TWO DARRINS ON BEWITCHED?
Text sources: *People* magazine, *TV Guide*, *Radio-TV Mirror*, *Filmfax* April 1992 issue featuring the last Dick York interview by John Douglas.

HONEY WEST
Jeff Vilencia supplied the rare video for my research.

WHO WAS HANK?
Big ups to Dan Wingate! Pictures from the TVparty collection.

MY MOTHER THE CAR / RUN, BUDDY, RUN
Video source courtesy of "Kingpin" Harold Balde.

THE BIG SUPERHERO BUST
The comic book cover is illustrated by Carmine Infantino and Murphy Anderson. Copyright 1965 by DC Comics. *Batman* and all related characters, the distinct likenesses thereof, and all related indicia are trademarks of DC Comics. Photos of *The Green Hornet* TV show copyright 1966 Greenway Productions, from the *TVparty* collection. Information comes from *The Amazing World of Carmine Infantino*

from Vanguard Productions, *The Amazing World of DC Comics*, *Epi-Log Magazine*, *The Official Batman Batbook* by Joel Eisner, *TV Guide* and from an interview with Julie Schwartz by myself in 1988. I also watched the pilot for *Mr. Terrific* (thanks to Dan Wingate) and *Batman* and *Green Hornet* episodes from the vast, ever-reaching *TVparty* collection.

IT'S ABOUT TIME
Screen captures from the TVparty collection.

IRWIN ALLEN'S TIME TUNNEL
Information from *Starlog*, *Filmfax*, *Epi-Log*, *TV Zone* magazines. Also from the books *Lost in Space 25th Anniversary Tribute* by James Van Hise, *The Time Tunnel Companion* by Richard Messmann and James Van Hise, and from watching episodes of every Irwin Allen series as well as the pilot film for *Man from the 25th Century*. I do it all for you!

COMMERCIALS
Screen captures from the *TVparty* collection, thanks to Jeff Vilencia.

NOLO CONTENDO: THE YOUNG LAWYERS / REBELS
Illustration from *The Young Lawyers* comic book #2, April 1971. Artwork by Mike Sekowsky.

PETE DUEL'S UNEXPLAINED SUICIDE
Article copyright 2002 by Sam Hieb. Written for TVparty, used with permission. All characters copyright their respective owners.

THE GOLDDIGGERS

Photos from the collection of Merry Elkins.

THE CAROL BURNETT SHOWS

This article is dedicated to Karen Zabel, who was (is?) a Carol Burnett fan, as I was in the '70s. Here's a sample response to our online Carol Burnett feature: "I just loved your Carol Burnett page! I have been a fan of Carol Burnett's since before I can remember. I recently took the bus from Toronto, Canada, to New York just to see her in *Putting It Together*. She was absolutely wonderful and after the show I got to meet her! It was honestly the greatest moment in my life. She was very warm and kind despite the fact that I could barely speak I was so overcome by emotion."—Shannon M. It's about time CBS recognized that Burnett has ascended to the Queen of Television throne. Screen captures from the TVparty collection. **ORDER CAROL BURNETT VIDEOS:** *www.TVparty.com/order*.

SONNY AND CHER

Thanks to Paul Brownstein. If you're a fan of '70s variety shows, Paul is your savior! He's the guy bringing back that great musical entertainment we remember from years back. Shows like *Sonny and Cher, Mike Douglas, Richard Pryor, Midnite Special,* and so many more. Sonny and Cher videos on the web at *www.tvclassics.com*. Many people don't know this, but the day Sonny Bono died may have been the first time national news reporters turned to the Internet for information on a breaking story. I was bombarded with calls from reporters wanting to know where I got my facts on Sonny's career and if it could be trusted as a source. I was able to pass them along to Paul Brownstein and others; within hours TVparty was all over CNN and CNBC. The reporters I talked to were genuinely amazed that they could turn to the Internet for instant background information.

SUMMER REPLACEMENT SHOWS OF THE '70s

As far as I know, no one has really written about this subject. My research mainly comes from tapes I made off the TV when I was a kid and from back issues of *TV Guide* I picked up at a flea market. You know, *TV Guide* was an excellent periodical in the '50s, '60s, and '70s. In the '80s, the mag was bought up and became absolutely abysmal dreck. *TV Guide* has rebounded into a really fresh package over the last decade, so all's well that ends well, right? I was truly amazed at some of the insightful reporting and wry humorous features I found in those old magazines, back in the day when publications were expected to have a personality.

THE SMOTHERS BROTHERS

Our thanks to Wendy at Knave Productions and to Tom Smothers for taking time from his busy schedule to talk about his career. I've always considered him to be one of the great unsung geniuses of television. See *www.smothersbrothers.com* for more information and concert dates near you.

THE RICHARD PRYOR SHOW

Boy, do people want to see these shows again. You wouldn't believe the requests I get. Someone needs to get Mr. Brownstein on the phone.

TOTIE VS. KISS

The video of this event came courtesy of TVpartyer Whitlock. *Sixteen* and *Tiger Beat* magazines from the overflowing TVparty collection, cover art copyright the respective copyright owners.

WHAT HAPPENED TO PAUL LYNDE?

Screen caps from the TVparty collection, natch.

TVafterparty!

SHAZAM!

Photo of Michael Gray as Billy Batson, from the TVparty collection. *Shazam!* and all related characters, the distinct likenesses thereof, and all related indicia are trademarks of DC Comics. Here's a true American success story: I used to subscribe to a fanzine published by this kid named Paul Levitz. Now the guy is president of DC Comics. Way to go, Paul! DC has been aggressively re-packaging their classic comic book material from the 1940s through the 1980s and doing a great job of it; these are highly recommended products.

GENE RODDENBERRY: WHAT MIGHT HAVE BEEN

Information culled from *Starlog, TV Zone, Filmfax, TV Guide,* and *Epi-Log* magazines, various interviews with Roddenberry and David Gerrold, *The Making of Star Trek* by Gene Roddenberry, and from reading over copies of the twenty-two-page plot outlines and watching the pilots. *Star Trek* images copyright 1974 by Paramount Pictures Corporations. *STAR TREK* is a registered TRADEMARK of Paramount Pictures.

GOOD TIMES (THEY WEREN'T)

Thanks to John Amos, one of America's finest Actors (that's right, with a capital "A") who can be found on the web at *www.halleyscomet.com,* promoting his excellent one-man show currently on tour. Sources include *Ebony* magazine, *Jet,* and *TV Guide. Good Times* is available on video from Columbia House; order online at: *www.TVparty.com/order*

LIFE WITH LUCY

Thanks very much to Michael Stern for sharing his memories of Lucille Ball. Photo from the collection of Billy Ingram. Highly recommended books: *The Lucy Book* by Geoffrey Mark Fidelman; *Lucille: The Life of Lucille Ball* by Kathleen Brady; *Desilu: The Story of Lucille Ball and Desi Arnaz* by Tom Gilbert and Coyne Steven Sanders.

WHAT HAPPENED TO THE SITCOM HOUSES?

This article is one of the best on *TVparty.com,* written by the brilliant Ben Glenn, II. Special appreciation to Gary Gilbin for his photos. Screen captures from the extensive TVparty library of digital crap. Photo to the right of the Brady house at night, circa 1973.

Gary Gilbin tells us: "Here's a picture of the Beverly Hillbillies house in the '80s, just before it was torn down and replaced with a godawful monstrosity. The present house, I believe, retains some of the original structure, but the façade is definitely different."

FABULOUS BRETT SOMERS

Whether the networks are aware of it or not, Brett Somers is a huge star right now. We get more requests for info on this lady than any other celebrity. If I were a TV producer, I would be mounting *The Brett Somers Show* right now! Pictures from the collection of

Match Game Mania and Ryan Dziadosz, on the web at: *www.matchgame.cjb.net.* Thanks also to Justin Kaplowitz, who has been a huge help over the years with *TVparty.com.*

HOLMES AND YO YO

What is this doing in here? I thought I killed that page . . .

TOUGH GUY: ROBERT BLAKE

Info comes from Internet news sites, TV shows and tabloids. I don't watch the news anymore—too depressing. Photos from the TVparty collection, scanned from old newspapers and from ABC affiliate advertising campaigns.

TV POW!

Digital illustration by James Counts. I'll be damned if I can find one shred of evidence that this show really existed, except in people's memories, of course.

REMEMBERING READ ALL ABOUT IT!

Copyright 2002 by Zachary Houle. Written for this book and used with permission. Pictures from the collection of Zachary Houle and Jeremy Pollock. Zach is a Canadian writer who told me *Read All about It!* would make a better story than the *You Can't Do That on Television* article I suggested. I hope you agree!

THE IRONIC DEATH OF REDD FOXX

Sources include *Ebony, Jet,* and *People* magazines, reviewing tapes of the different shows, and my chance encounter with "Iron Jaw" Wilson at the Redd Foxx Building on La Brea near Melrose. *Sanford and Son* videos? Order online at: *www.TVparty.com/order*

THE NIGHT CHICAGO DIED

The background to that page is an actual screen shot of the incident. This video clip was sent by Michael H. Here's another look at the prank in case you think I made the whole thing up . . .

WRETRO-MANIA: DUSTY, NATURE BOY, AND THE LEGEND OF BABY DOLL

I have to thank long time collaborator and friend John Hitchcock for his help on this entire project. John and his pals could always be found with their handmade signs in Front Row Section D, tormenting the Crockett wrestlers all through the '70s and '80s. John and I started drawing and distributing handmade comic books in junior high school and we collaborated on several things after that, including one of my first tries at creating a Web

site (*The Wally Wood Letters*) in 1994. John is represented here with a salute to the southeast's NWA wrestling matches, circa 1986. Looking for vintage comic books or rare original art? Visit Parts Unknown, the Comic Book Store, 906 Spring Garden Street, Greensboro, NC 27403. I wrote this article in a one voice style but the heart of it comes from John because I'd never watched a wrestling match in my life before doing research for this piece. Most quotations taken from *King Lear* by William Shakespeare. The wrestling poster on page 264 comes from John's collection; did you know they sell for over five hundred apiece now!

WORTHWHILE PROJECT:

Bumpity, puppet star of the long-running Oregon show of the same name, comes back for an encore in the retrospective docu-fantasy *Bumpity Returns* (2001, CPR Productions), complete with footage from as early as 1970. Being the only kid's show on during its time slot, *Bumpity* was watched, sometimes reluctantly, by thousands of Oregon kids who tuned in on Sunday mornings.

"We may be gone but we're not forgotten," pipes Bumpity. He and squeaking sidekick Fred Worm were marooned in a suitcase after Oregon's ABC affiliate KATU canceled them in the mid-'80s. Crispin Rosenkranz persuaded puppeteer Bob Griggs to resurrect his puppets and has the film to prove it. VHS videotapes with a 30th anniversary commemorative case are available for $19.95 plus $3.50 shipping at *www.bumpityreturns.com* or by sending a request with payment to Crispin Rosenkranz, 1230 SE Morrison, Portland, OR 97214, USA, or e-mail bumpity01@aol.com.

INDEX

For classic TV merchandise, go to
www.tvparty.com/order